I0299046

Material Devotion in a South Indian Poetic World

Bloomsbury Studies in Material Religion

Bloomsbury Studies in Material Religion is the first book series dedicated exclusively to studies in material religion. Within the field of lived religion, the series is concerned with the material things with which people do religion and how these things—objects, buildings, landscapes—relate to people, their bodies, clothes, food, actions, thoughts, and emotions. The series engages and advances theories in "sensuous" and "experiential" religion, as well as informing museum practices and influencing wider cultural understandings with relation to religious objects and performances. Books in the series are at the cutting edge of debates as well as developments in fields including religious studies, anthropology, museum studies, art history, and material culture studies.

Christianity and the Limits of Materiality, edited by Minna Opas and Anna Haapalainen
Figurations and Sensations of the Unseen in Judaism, Christianity and Islam, edited by Birgit Meyer and Terje Stordalen
Food, Festival and Religion, Francesca Ciancimino Howell

Material Devotion in a South Indian Poetic World

Leah Elizabeth Comeau

BLOOMSBURY ACADEMIC
LONDON • NEW YORK • OXFORD • NEW DELHI • SYDNEY

BLOOMSBURY ACADEMIC
Bloomsbury Publishing Plc
50 Bedford Square, London, WC1B 3DP, UK
1385 Broadway, New York, NY 10018, USA
29 Earlsfort Terrace, Dublin 2, Ireland

BLOOMSBURY, BLOOMSBURY ACADEMIC and the Diana logo are trademarks of Bloomsbury Publishing Plc

First published in Great Britain 2020
This paperback edition published in 2021

For legal purposes the Acknowledgments on p. xi constitute an extension of this copyright page.

Cover image: A row of Shiva Lingams with flowers on top at the Brihadeeshwara Temple (© Ayan82/Getty Images)

A catalogue record for this book is available from the British Library.

A catalog record for this book is available from the Library of Congress.

ISBN: HB: 978-1-3501-2289-5
PB: 978-1-3502-8318-3
ePDF: 978-1-3501-2290-1
eBook: 978-1-3501-2291-8

Series: Bloomsbury Studies in Material Religion

Typeset by Integra Software Services Pvt. Ltd.

To find out more about our authors and books visit www.bloomsbury.com and sign up for our newsletters.

For Erma Elizabeth Knox

Contents

List of Illustrations ix
Acknowledgments xi
Note on Transcription and Other Conventions xiii
Note on Translation xv

Introduction: Material Religion 1
Introduction to the Poem 8
Date of the Poem 8
A Reflection on Sources 15
Forms of the Poet: Story and Sculpture 16
Conclusion 25

1 Materiality in Literary Landscapes 27
Part One: Akam Poetry 29
Grammatical Framework 34
Narrative Sequence 37
Part Two: Development of the Kovai Genre 41
Sighting 47
Doubt 49
Conclusion 55

2 Locality and Movement 59
Distance and Rejection 64
Day and Night Trysting 71
Crushing Waves: Turmoil and Frenzy 73
Love, Loyalty, Slander 82
Conclusion 85

3 On Mountains, Waterways, and Intoxication 87
Medieval Maps 88
Devotion and Elevation 92
Devotion and Place 95
Natural Environments and Inhabitants 99
Birds and Animals 100
Sensuality in Water and Sound 104
Mediated Saints 108
Conclusion 110

4 Bodily Forms of Devotion 113
Two Heroes 114
God-Hero 120
Human-Hero 122
The Heroine 127
The Palm Horse Ordeal 136
Conclusion 138

5 Materiality, Ornaments, and Gifts that Glitter 141
Ornaments in Inscriptions 143
Kovai as Ornament 146
Ornaments for the Heroine 150
Ornaments for Shiva 157
Union of Devotion and Material Aesthetics 164
Conclusion 166

Conclusion 169
Proximity to Desire 170
Lovers, Locality, Audience 171
Transformation 173
Material Religion: A Kingdom of Riches 174

Glossary 177
Notes 180
Bibliography 191
Index 198

Illustrations

Figures

Note: All photos have been taken by the author.

1 Manikkavacakar, Tiruvidaimarudur 2
2 Nataraja temple entrance, Chidambaram 9
3 Mural detail of Shiva and Manikkavacakar meeting, Tiruperunthurai 17
4 Detail of ascetic Manikkavacakar on a stone column, Tiruperunthurai 19
5 Small shrine for *Tirumurai*, Piranmalai 22
6 View of waterfalls, Kutralam 30
7 Bees in flower garlands, Thiruvannamalai 45
8 Goddess Uma at Ekamparanatar temple, Kanchipuram 51
9 Manikkavacakar on an exterior shrine tower, Tiruperunthurai 67
10 View of hilltop temple, Inkoymalai 70
11 Ekamparanatar temple complex, Kanchipuram 79
12 Small pasted poster of the nalvar saints including Manikkavacakar (far right), Tirukkalukkunram 89
13 Temple threshold, Tirukkalukkunram 98
14 South India landscape, field near Bahour 103
15 Stone heroes, Darasuram 116
16 Stone heroine with attendants, Darasuram 128
17 Untiyal at Ekamparanatar temple, Kanchipuram 142
18 Honeycombs on the temple hall ceiling, Piranmalai 148
19 Detail of hair and ornaments in red, white, and black, Pondicherry 154
20 Dancing Shiva woven with red and yellow fabric, Thiruvadavur 175

Map

1 Map of southeast India xix

Tables

1 List of cities and sites xiv
2 *Tirukkovaiyar* love themes and verse distribution 39
3 Sites named in three medieval Shaiva compositions 90

Acknowledgments

I am deeply indebted to the scholars and staff of the École française d'Extrême-Orient in Pondicherry, especially Dr. G. Vijayavenugopal and the late Pandit T. S. Gangadharan. I received institutional support from the Fulbright-Hays Doctoral Dissertation Research Abroad Program and the United States-India Educational Foundation. I also thank my chair, colleagues, and especially my undergraduate research assistants at University of the Sciences for supporting my research in the final stages of this project.

I offer my thanks to the librarians, administrators, and supporting assistants at the following research libraries: Archaeological Survey of India Office at Fort St. George, Bodleian Library at the University of Oxford, École française d'Extrême-Orient Pondicherry Center, Institut Français de Pondichéry, Madras University Libraries, Roja Muthiah Research Library, and University of Pennsylvania Libraries. I am grateful for the generous hospitality of the director and staff at the Epigraphical Branch of the Archaeological Survey of India in Mysore. I thank the Ancient World Mapping Center at the University of North Carolina at Chapel Hill for preparing the map included in this publication.

Heaps of gratitude are due to the following scholars and colleagues who encouraged and enriched this project: Sucharita Adluri, Daud Ali, Kameliya Atanasova, Aditya Behl, S. Bharathy, Sebastian Brock, Anthea Butler, Jean-Luc Chevillard, Michael Collins, Trudy DeLong, Corinne Dempsey, Fanny Dutillieux, Sascha Ebeling, Jamal Elias, Christine Flanagan, Richard Fox, M. S. Gandhimary, Valerie Gillet, Ann Gold, Sally Goldman, Dominic Goodall, Walter Hakala, M. Gail Hamner, Kathryn Hardy, Warren Hope, Steven Hopkins, Nirajan Kafle, P. Soundra Kohila, Elizabeth Lambourn, Sarah Lenzi, David Ludden, Justin McDaniel, Anne Monius, Aroki Nathan, Christian Novetzke, Leslie Orr, Deven Patel, Prerana Patel, Karen Pechilis, Indira Peterson, Brent Plate, Mary Premila, V. S. Rajam, T. Rajeswari, T. N. Ramachandran, N. Ramaswamy, Annette Reed, James Ryan, R. Sathyanarayanan, Charlotte Schmid, Anna Seastrand, Y. Subbarayalu, Eva Wilden, and Glenn Yocum.

I thank the anonymous reviewers of my manuscript, the Material Religion series editors, and editorial staff at Bloomsbury Academic for their thoughtful comments and guidance.

In a study of landscapes and material contexts I must also acknowledge the places that have shaped this book, much of which was written outdoors: Philadelphia, Madurai, Chicago, Pondicherry, Mysore, New Haven, Rattlesnake Island, Oxford, Joppa Flats, Baltimore, and the transient landscape of the commuter's train.

Finally, a love note for my family, for the deep goodness of Aaron and Mary Pearl.

Note on Transcription and Other Conventions

Tamil is usually transcribed in a simplified system without diacritic marks. This will hopefully make the book more welcoming to the nonspecialist reader, while the scholar of Tamil studies should be able to identify the words without difficulty.

The names of most places, people, and deities are given according to a common English form without diacritics. Shiva is used rather than Civan or Aran, and Vishnu rather than Tirumal.

Ancient site names found in *Tirukkovaiyar* are replaced by their corresponding modern cities. Table 1 provides an exhaustive list of these correspondences. The identifications of the ancient cities are based on inscriptions.

Table 1 List of cities and sites.

Current Site Names	GPS Location	Sites as They Appear in the Text
Chidambaram	11° 23' 59 N – 79° 41' 43 E	Tillai
Tiruppalanam	10° 53' 16 N – 79° 07' 52 E	Pal̲an̲am
Madurai	09° 54' 48 N – 78° 06' 51 E	Kūṭal
Kutralam	08° 55' 52 N – 77° 16' 10 E	Kur̲r̲alam
Tirupparankundram	09° 52' 46 N – 78° 04' 16 E	Paraṅkun̲r̲am
Tiruperunthurai	10° 04' 30 N – 79° 02' 34 E	Peruntur̲ai
Tirukkalukkunram	12° 36' 34 N – 80° 03' 32 E	Kal̲ukkun̲r̲am
Inkoymalai	10° 58' 26 N – 78° 24' 10 E	Īṅkōy
Tiruppanaiyur	10° 51' 52 N – 79° 39' 26 E	Tiruppan̲aiyūr
Piranmalai	10° 14' 19 N – 78° 26' 20 E	Koṭuṅkun̲r̲am
Ambal	10° 55' 00 N – 79° 40' 59 E	Ampar
Moovalur	11° 05' 18 N – 79° 36' 34 E	Mūval
Sivapuram	10° 56' 57 N – 79° 24' 54 E	Civanakar
Melakadambur	11° 14' 31 N – 79° 32' 08 E	Kaṭampai
Tiruvidaimarudur	10° 59' 42 N – 79° 27' 11 E	Iṭaimarutūr
Kanchipuram	12° 50' 48 N – 79° 41' 58 E	Ēkampam
Srivanchiyam	10° 52' 16 N – 79° 34' 21 E	Vāñciyam
Thiruvenkadu	11° 10' 31 N – 79° 48' 34 E	Veṇkāṭu
Tiruppuvanam	09° 49' 36 N – 78° 15' 24 E	Pūvaṇam
Tiruchuli	09° 31' 53 N – 78° 11' 56 E	Cul̲iyal
Sirkali	11° 14' 19 N – 79° 44' 45 E	Cīrkāl̲i

Note on Translation

My favorite portrait of Manikkavacakar is a heavy bronze statue that I photographed within the very interior of a temple. The artist gave him such a mischievous smile that I found myself grinning back as I snapped a few pictures for my album. It was as if we shared a secret (or four hundred) about the nerve-splitting task of translation that I had just embarked on.

Translation of a Tamil poem such as *Tirukkovaiyar* takes a number of steps that transform the characters on a palm leaf manuscript into a poem that is not just comprehensible but also attractive to an engaged contemporary audience. There are a number of ways to approach the task of translation with varying allegiances to the language of the original, the target language, idiomatic registers, and textures created by meter, alliteration, spacing, punctuation, and so on. Out of respect for the diversity of methods, as a form of disclosure to Tamil scholars who have their own preferences for translating poetry, and as a peek behind the curtain for students and other readers who have not encountered a Tamil text, I offer these notes on my approach to translating *Tirukkovaiyar*. Translation is trade or a series of trades. Some things are gained and some things are always left behind.

1.3 (A) teḷital
pāyumviṭaiyaraṉṟillaiyaṉṉāḷpaṭaikkaṇṇimaikkun
tōyunilattaṭitūmalarvāṭuntuyarameyti
yāyumaṉaṉēyaṇaṅkallaḷammāmulaicumantu
tēyumaruṅkuṟperumpaṇaittōḷicciṟunutalē

1.3 (A): This version of verse 3 has already traveled from a manuscript to a printed edition in Tamil script, to my rendering here in a style of transliteration consistent with the *Tamil Lexicon*. The pronunciation of the Tamil is immediately obscured by its appearance in Roman script. For example, the second phrase of the first line is pronounced more like vee-dai than viṭai. Tamil palm manuscripts have several significant differences in the writing system compared to how we receive it in printed media. First, manuscripts do not have pulli, points over consonants, to mark hard stops. For example, the word for crow, "kākkā", without the pulli over the second "k" (a mark also lost in the Roman script transliteration) would be transliterated as kākakā. Without the double consonant the pronunciation would change to kaa-ga-gaa, a significant alteration of kākkā. Like the pulli, some vowel lengths are also lost in the writing style of manuscripts along with spaces and punctuation between words and sentences. Nevertheless, trained readers can recognize and edit these neatly written chains of letters using their familiarity with vocabulary, genre, metrical cues, rhyming schemes, and a hearty dose of perseverance. Although I work in script rather than transliteration, these lines reflect the text before parsing and editing begins.

1.3 (B) teḷital
pāyum viṭai aran̲ tillai an̲n̲āḷ paṭai kaṇṇimaikkun
tōyum nilattu aṭi tū malar vāṭun tuyaram eyti
āyum man̲an̲ē aṇaṅku allaḷ am mā mulai cumantu
tēyum maruṅkul perum paṇai tōḷ i-cir̲u nutalē

1.3 (B): This version reflects word breaks and a restoration of characters effected by sandhi. For example, the fourth word of the first line, we find r̲illai, an otherwise unviable initial sound, is restored to reveal the ancient name of Chidambaram, Tillai. The initial "y" in line three, which served as a glide between the "ī" at the end of line two and the "ā" in line three, is dropped to reveal the verb āyum.

1.3 (C) Clarification
Prancing bull aran tillai she-who-is-like weapon eye-blinking
Touching earth feet pure flower withering grief undergoing
Investigating o-mind deity she-who-is-not beautiful great breasts supporting
Fading waist strong bamboo shoulders this small forehead-(emphasis)

1.3 (C): Here I have traded the Tamil words for English words following the word order of 1.3 (B). Although the words are in English, this is not a translation because it does not convey the meaning of the words. This raw form illustrates two things: the way in which phrases and concepts run uninterrupted by line breaks in consecutive strings and the left-branching nature of the Tamil language. Revisiting again the first phrase of the first line we find that the subject of the hero's investigation clearly illustrates the left-branching form; literally, "prancing bull aran tillai like she." Rendered in English word order the hero is talking about "she like tillai aran bull prancing." Again, with a number of small words added to show the relationships between words and capitalization of proper nouns, the subject of the investigation becomes, "she [who is] like Tillai [of] Aran [whose] bull [is] prancing." This phrase also raises two choices for the translator in the words "tillai" and "aran." Tillai is an old name for Chidambaram. I have the option to use this modern moniker or to retain Tillai and indicate the city to which it refers in a note for my audience. For the purposes of this study I have replaced Tillai with Chidambaram and specific locations like ampalam where Shiva dances is consistently translated hall within the translated verses. The second major choice presented by this phrase comes with the word "aran." Aran is a name for Shiva. It is a Tamil rendering of the Sanskrit name Hara. Thus, I could translate aran as Aran, Hara, or Shiva, each with its own references, associations, and even politics associated with the act of translating a Tamilized Sanskrit word found in the Tamil Shaiva text. Finally, in a quick look back at the effect of word order and the addition of conjunctions, articles, and other small words, in order to connect the phrases here, it is helpful to have prior knowledge of Shiva's association with Chidambaram and that his iconography includes a bull as his vehicle.

3
Clarification
She who is like Chidambaram of Shiva with his strutting bull
    her piercing eyes blink
    her feet touch the ground
    her pure blossoms wither.
O grieved and curious mind:
She with small forehead, strong shoulders like bamboo, and a fading waist
                                        supporting big beautiful breasts—
she is not divine.

1.3 (D): There are a number of opportunities in this verse to make distinctions through the nuance of word choice. For example, the bull is strutting rather than prancing to emphasize the strength rather than agility of the animal. I interpret the comparison of the heroine's eyes to weapons to indicate the quality of their sharp looks that pierce, rather than their spear-like shape. The hero's mind questions the status of the heroine, which can also be translated as investigating, searching, or even being confused. I chose to use "curious" to indicate a mix of the seeker and the strangeness of the puzzle presented by the heroine. In addition to these word choices, I also use line breaks to add emphasis and to guide the reader's experience of the English translation. Finally, I'd like to draw attention to the front rhyme scheme used in kovai stanzas. The first words of each line are *pāyum*, *tōyum*, *āyum*, and *tēyum*, or strutting, touching, investigating, and fading. The rhyme scheme matches initial long vowel with short second syllable—um. In some verses, like this one, these four initial words give us signposts for the message of the verse; the hero sees the beauty of the heroine's exceptional slim *fading* waist, *investigates* whether or not she is a goddess, and finds his answer in the fact that her feet *touch* the ground. Finally, the *strutting* bull ties the lovers' story to the main objective of *Tirukkovaiyar* as a whole, the praise of Shiva via the strength of his vehicle.

The four hundred verses of *Tirukkovaiyar* offer an impressive range of diversity in content and form. My greatest challenge as translator is to let go of the Tamil and to accept with optimism new meanings that the English language can bring to the poetry. My greatest successes occur when my reader shares an experience of hopefulness when the monsoon clouds intimate the hero's return or awe at the sight of Shiva's glittering red crown. The thousand-year-old Tamil text is rich. The verses that I offer here in English represent a small sample of Manikkavacakar's ornaments for Shiva.

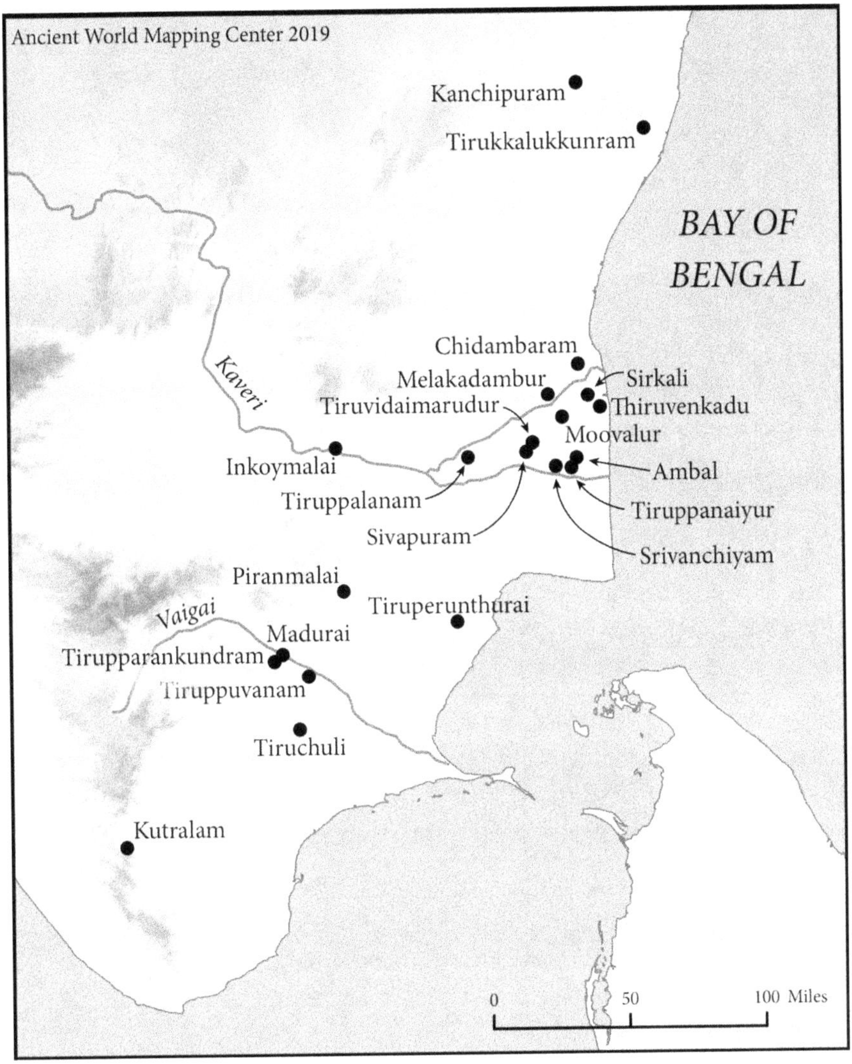

Map 1 Map of southeast India.

Introduction: Material Religion

Tirukkovaiyar 1
Sighting
Admired lotus, famed blue nelumbo, grandly blossoming kumil of the lord's Chidambaram
konku flowers and fresh red glory lily
a garland of these flowers with expanding divine fragrance
  slender like a creeper
  with the gait of the goose
shines like beautiful Kama's victory banner.

On the morning of a temple visit, I rise before the sun and splash cold water on my face. I grab the sack of electronics and snacks that I packed the night before. Just as I hear the car accelerate around the corner of my house, I reach into the refrigerator and pull out a cold wet bag. Inside there is a chilly white coil of jasmine buds that I tuck into my braid as we pull out onto the main road. I've been told, and I start to believe, that these fragrant flowers have a calming effect. I scan the paddy fields from the passenger window and am tickled to find that some of the same plants that crowded my window sills in Philadelphia are reaching out of the Indian soil, fearlessly battling roadside trees to claim territory of their own. Soon, we reach one of the abodes of lord Shiva—one of the places praised by the great poet Manikkavacakar (Figure 1). At the temple I make donations, admire fresh paint, wait patiently for someone to bring a set of keys to unlock an interior gate, chat with interested and curious locals, and pass around a damp Xerox of a stanza that mentions their town by name.

Inside the dark hallways, I find myself pausing to examine stone figures and faces that compel me to swing my camera away from my eye. I lean in to study them more closely. Flanking temple columns, smeared with sandal paste and red powders, or resting in a quiet niche, I can't get a sense of whether the

Figure 1 Manikkavacakar, Tiruvidaimarudur.

sculptor removed the rocks to uncover the deeply buried images or if somehow these androgynous faces floated to the surface of the rock. In either case, I am impressed by the artist who transformed these cold, solid slabs into soft, fleshy cheeks, plumped lips, and tenderly curved ears ornamented with earrings that I can easily imagine cast in gold. These interpretive sculptures and the temples in which they reside embody the union of art and technology embraced by the artists and artisans of medieval South India. This nuanced relationship between skilled craft and creative license also resounds throughout the verbal architecture of early Tamil poetry.

On the temple grounds, I inspect paving stones that formerly bricked the walls, ask permission to photograph a bronze statue of my poet, step into a far corner for a wide-angle view, offer thanks and compliments to the custodians of the temple, and then my body reminds me that it is time to find lunch and shade. As I peel off my backpack I notice that my braid has become matted around my neck and the once tender petals of my jasmine garland are the color of onion skins. They rustle like a tiny pile of scorched autumn leaves. Like the liquid curves of the stone sculptures inside the temple, the flakey remains of the once cool jasmine are a natural illustration of the intense conditions in which beauty can emerge and whither. It is this combination of natural beauty and the sophisticated expressive traditions that flourished in medieval Tamil country that first drew me to the verses of *Tirukkovaiyar*.

This book is about religion and religious sensations as they occur in literary worlds. And it is about utilizing and prioritizing the materiality of such worlds to expand what can be counted as the religious. This study is rooted in my long-term interest in understanding religious experience in the subtle, the common, or in the quiet (sometimes obscure) periphery. We expect to find religion in a temple or in a mosque. We expect to find religion in an ancient liturgical text or in a somber hymn. But can we also find religion in a post office or in a pop song? Can we find it in the ubiquitous friendship bracelets passed between bunks at summer camp? Can we find religion in a sweet honeycomb or in a marriage that has soured?

Borrowing the words of David Chidester, "Religion is an arena of human activity marked by the concerns of the transcendent, the sacred, the ultimate—concerns that enable people to experiment with what it means to be human."[1] This definition marks the three salient aspects of contemporary religious studies: Religion takes place in the human world. Religion concerns the transcendent, the special, the not-of-this-world. And this combination of and contact between human and suprahuman realms spurs an opportunity to experiment with individual human limits, our shared human experience, and the ordinary everyday. Religion can be about confinement and religion can be about the limitless. This combination of boundaries and openness also makes religion an occasion for people to create, to invent, and to test.

In the chapters that follow, the human world is early medieval South India as it is interpreted through a devotional text. The initial explicit not-of-this-world element is the Hindu god Shiva. Over the course of the book and through analysis of the material and sensual cues in the poetry, I demonstrate that the sensuous, fertile environment emerges as another hyper-natural devotional element. This stylized poetic landscape is the context in which literary and devotional figures share space and seek to mingle with divine beings. The study of material religion in literature leads us to an understanding of religion as presence and proximity that is possible and realized not in hearts and minds but rather in heat, blossoms, color, and surging ocean waves.

The physicality and embodied experience of religion in South Asia is a well-developed subtheme in the field, one that intentionally contradicts the exclusivist characterization of religion as a theological or philosophical endeavor cultivated in "the mind" and reliant on texts. The history of South Asian religions, under the influence of Christian debates over icons, has been routinely characterized as one of decline, privileging intellectual, text-based traditions that allegedly deteriorated into "idolatrous" sculptural traditions over time.[2] Performance and ritual studies ushered in critical attention to the importance of practice and physical experience in understanding religious cultures. However, Brent Plate observes the following of embodiment scholarship:

> Some scholarship that at first appears to attend to physical matters uses language about "embodiment," a frequently used critical term. However, in many cases, what is meant is that the theoretical ideas and doctrines are all worked out, and then they find their "expression" in the material world. Even though physical things may be taken seriously, in this framework the ideas are primary and the things are secondary manifestations of the primary thoughts.[3]

Plate's critique applies to the field of Tamil studies, where large portions of the Shaiva and Vaishnava literary canon have been associated with embodied experience, especially eroticism, and physical manifestations of primary concepts of devotion to a supreme god.[4] New material culture studies provide an approach to religion that centers the material world as the primary condition from which people are motivated to act and a method by which the implied dichotomy of mind and material in South Asian religious studies can be dismantled.

In addition to studies of the body and eroticism, much has been made of Tamil religion as it is tied to local geography and the concept of sacred landscapes in the south. This is the first study of its kind to analyze bodies and landscapes together, over time, and in concert with dynamic sensory information using the methodological framework provided by material studies. South Asian scholars such as historian R. Champakalakshmi have indeed initiated efforts to investigate Tamil religions through material evidence. More specifically, she urges scholars of Tamil literature, history, and archaeology to combine their sources when analyzing South Asian religious history.[5] In Finbarr Flood's *Objects in Translation*, he decenters text in order to elevate "materials and materiality even as they relate to textual sources" for fresh insights into South Asian history, primarily in the north.[6] I build on these works using Plate's definition of material religion paired with Inken Prohl's description of the value of aesthetics for the study of religion in order to unite the study of materiality with devotional textual studies:

> Material religion refers to (1) an investigation of the interactions between human bodies and physical objects, both natural and human-made; (2) with much of the interaction taking place through sense perception; (3) in special and specified spaces and times; (4) in order to orient, and sometimes disorient, communities and individuals; (5) toward the formal strictures and structures of religious traditions.[7]

> [The study of aesthetics] … can be understood as theorizing about the sensory experience of the world. The study of the sensuous understanding of the world taking place in religions and cultures has long been neglected in favor of looking at texts, but this does not mean that aesthetics should not examine the ways cognitive recognition is happening. Religions are rather to be seen as venues where the cognitive and sensuous perception flow together, constituting what religious practitioners consider to be the sense of religion.[8]

The careful reader notices that Prohl initially juxtaposes the study of aesthetics with textual studies. However, she concludes, and from within the Tamil religious context I propose instead, that understanding the material aesthetics engineered and communicated by a text yields, in fact, an extremely productive, synthetic result that Prohl calls the sense of religion.

Kathleen Stewart's articulation of worlding, affect, and especially relevant to us, the accumulation of scores, loops, and shimmers, creates even further allowances for interdisciplinary and inter-material inquiry into aesthetics and perception of religion in the South Asian context.

> What is, is a refrain. A scoring over a world's repetitions. A scratching on the surface of rhythms, sensory habits, gathering materialities, intervals, and durations … Refrains are worlding … […] Critique attuned to the worlding of the refrain is a burrowing into the generativity of what takes form, hits the senses, shimmers. Concepts built in this way score the trajectories of a worlding's looping refrains, its potentialities, and attach themselves to the living out of what is singular and proliferative in a scene or moment, to what is accrued, sloughed off, realized, imagined, enjoyed, hated, brought to bear or just born in a compositional present.[9]

In the pages that follow, I combine old poetry, new sculptures, grammatical treatises, hagiographies, inscriptions, modern commentary, medieval stone halls and walls, and contemporary observations as trajectories and threads generated by and around *Tirukkovaiyar*. The combination of these sources, their various attachments to the poetry, and the materiality of religion provides the reader a motley view of *Tirukkovaiyar* as a material object, a literary work, a call to worship, a declaration of localized sectarian identity, the birth of a genre, the words of one of Shiva's most prized devotees, and a sensory super-world inhabited and inspired by both gods and humans. In one sense, *Tirukkovaiyar* is the refrain and I present its trajectories, habits, and intervals. At the same time, this book is designed to invite its own shimmers and new impacts through deep reflection on interactions between land, water, color, sound, bodies, and other sensorial details that give these verses their very pulse. Through this careful gathering of materialities, this study establishes a new category of South Asian religiosity that turns on proximity, vulnerability, and materiality.

My proposal for a new definition of Tamil religion is also offered as a localized response to two interpretive rubrics that initially propelled the study of religion in South India forward but now limit new scholarly growth. The two distinct but deeply intertwined terms used for the study of Tamil religion are the periodization of Tamil literary history and the category of bhakti. These seemingly impermeable terms are further reified by the widespread recognition of South India as the birthplace of bhakti or devotion—a category used in both South Asian studies and religious studies to describe a diverse body of practices, publics, aesthetics, regionalisms, and literary and language distinctions over a substantial span of 1,500 years. Modern historians and religious studies scholars have long ascribed to a periodization of Tamil literature, and by association Tamil culture, that attributes secularism to the earliest classical period (Sangam literature), followed by a middle or medieval period characterized by religious fervor (bhakti literature).[10] Organizing Tamil literature according to these anachronistic and rigid categories has severely limited scholars' abilities to imagine intersections of and life between the two columns.

While scholars work to refine and adjust how the term "bhakti" is applied, its latent mainstays are an expectation of emotional, public acts of devotion conducted in a vernacular language. This definition derived from Tamil sources but applied much more broadly to South Asian devotional practices is frequently framed as "a popular religion of emotional devotion to a personal god."[11] This description is compatible with the current scholarly understanding of the early Tamil *Tevaram* hymns, which are composed in the vernacular and organized according to the tune in which they are sung. The singable qualities of the *Tevaram* hymns and their association with Shaiva pilgrimage routes have long been understood to represent a popular, accessible movement of devoted people.[12] In the Vaishnava corpus, Antal's poetry is composed in the first person and describes her impassioned desire to unite with her immaculate lord, communicating the requisite emotional and personal characteristics of bhakti devotion. While seemingly inclusive in terms of potential variety of experience and person, this definition excludes *Tirukkovaiyar* (in spite of its prominence in the Shaiva canon) in several ways. For example, one implicit ideal of popular devotion is that it is conducted in a vernacular language and thus widely or popularly accessible. Although *Tirukkovaiyar* is written in Tamil and preserved alongside Shaiva hymns, it is composed using highly stylized conventions and technical features likely accessible to a limited scholarly audience. Unlike Antal's poetry, *Tirukkovaiyar* is not told from the point of view of the poet. In fact, Manikkavacakar writes himself into only a handful of the four hundred verses, largely eschewing personal comment on Shiva's excellence. Finally, although there is no shortage of emotion in *Tirukkovaiyar* felt by the heroine, hero, and even the god, most descriptions of Shiva address him with reverence, as royalty, and through reference to puranic legends. Most gushes of passionate desire in this poem are directed toward and shared between the human lovers. These discrepancies between the definition and resultant expectation for bhakti literature and the features of *Tirukkovaiyar*, a panegyric for Shiva, indicate a failure of the category "bhakti" to give a full account of early-medieval Tamil religion. Here, I propose the necessary expansion of "the religious" by prioritizing materiality as it is designed in the poetic world. This study of medieval Tamil literature features holistic inclusion of and slow, close attention to trajectories, refrains, and sources that only when considered together can constitute a sensory corpus of devotion.

Introduction to the Poem

Tirukkovaiyar, alias *Tiruccirrampalakkovai*, is a love story that is rooted in the religious and natural landscapes of South India. The word "kovai" means garland and refers to these verses being strung together into a narrative like flowers are strung into a garland. The love story follows the prescriptions of classical Tamil akam or love poetry featuring the union of the anonymous heroine who drives parrots from her father's millet fields and the hero who wields a flashing spear. Their romance blossoms in the cool mountain groves and is tested when they decide to abscond into the fiery wilderness. *Tirukkovaiyar* is the earliest complete extant example of a style of poetry that we now know as the kovai genre and includes in it the historical names of over twenty towns in South India. In addition to narrating a love story, each verse of *Tirukkovaiyar* must praise a second hero that is figured as the patron of the composition as a whole, the pattutaittalaivan. The patron-hero of this poem is lord Shiva. Thus, each of the four hundred verses was composed as a tribute to Shiva. He shares his body with his beloved, the goddess Uma. Shiva travels across Tamil country to his various abodes—some on the seacoast, others are located on mountaintops. He dances and wears garlands of konrai flowers in his matted hair. He is the object of devotion and the possessor of devotees.

Date of the Poem

As we will see in the following chapters, the poet uses a variety of strategies to incorporate Shiva into the love story, and these include telling the drama of Shiva's heroic deeds with themes that run parallel to the drama of the human lovers and their attendants. One of the distinctions between the patron of the composition and the people figured in the love story is parallel to that of the akam and puram traditions in classical Tamil poetry. Akam poetry addresses the interior love relations between idealized and thus anonymous unnamed lovers.[13] Classical love poetry is complimented by puram-style poetry, which emphasizes the life of the warrior, kingship, and conquest. In puram poems, the poet is free to name historical heroes, kings, regions, and towns. *Tirukkovaiyar* is rendered a hybrid of these two classical styles by the appearance of one akam and one puram hero, thus one unnamed and one named Shiva. The akam hero and Shiva are joined by yet a third heroic figure, Pandya king Varaguna by which the text is assigned its ninth-century date.[14]

Figure 2 Nataraja temple entrance, Chidambaram.

The Pandya king named in *Tirukkovaiyar* does not receive any attention until verse 306 when he is first and briefly introduced to the audience. In this line, Varaguna is mentioned as an extension to the praise intended for Shiva as he is manifested in the famous temple city, Chidambaram (Figure 2). Shiva is the "one of the small hall who is praised by the one of the South, named Varaguna." The rest of the verse speaks to the drama of the heroine who is steadfast in her love for the hero, although he must leave to go to war. Aside from a brief mention of his region using a common moniker of Pandya royalty, tennavan, literally southerner, and his affinity for Shiva in Chidambaram, little more is revealed about Varaguna's attributes or term of rule.

Varaguna appears in a second verse, which highlights his relationship to other historical southern dynasties. In *Tirukkovaiyar* verse 327, he is described as having a big, proud elephant full of rut and having put a carp and a rising big bow into the mountain, the insignia of the Pandya and Chera dynasties respectively. In the first line of 327, as in verse 306, Varaguna praises the small hall of the one who has matted hair full of expanding water; in other words, Varaguna praises Shiva who is depicted with the Ganges River in his matted crown at the hall in Chidambaram.

The appearance of a historical name and explicit reference to two major medieval dynasties are exciting leads for dating the text and possibly its patron. However, the identity of Pandya Varaguna remains obscured by the fact that there were two Pandya kings who ruled in the ninth century called by the name Varaguna: Varaguna I alias Jatila Parantaka Nedunjadaiyan (756–815 CE) and Varaguna II alias Varagunavarman (862–880 CE). We find the story of him carving the carp insignia into the Himalayas in an inscription of praise written about Varaguna I. However, it is Varaguna II who is known for his pronounced devotion to Shiva, as well as his invasion of Chola country. In his foundational history of South India, Nilakanta Sastri writes that Varaguna II likely spent several years in Chola country aiding in the suppression of king Vijayalaya.[15] Varaguna II reportedly became a saint with Manikkavacakar as his companion after he was defeated by Chola Aditya I and left the Pandya kingdom to his brother. Although the story of Varaguna II is an attractive solution to the question of Manikkavacakar's political alliance and location within Tamil country, little historical evidence survives to confirm this chain of events. Fortunately, however, both Varagunas ruled in the ninth century and thereby provide a reasonable approximation for the date of the poem in which the king is mentioned. Despite his royal status and historical import, this Varaguna took a dramatic reduction in literary stature so that the divine hero, Shiva, could receive maximum attention and praise in *Tirukkovaiyar*.

Forms of Text

Beyond this approximate dating, little is known about the original *Tirukkovaiyar* audience or the conditions in which it was composed, circulated, and eventually incorporated into the Shaiva canon. One aspect of *Tirukkovaiyar*'s reception history that we can explore is contemporary models for its preservation and circulation in manuscript form. I present here three manuscripts housed in Oxford, Pondicherry, and Tiruperunthurai, which, when considered together, provide a snapshot of the poem's contemporary custodians and readership. These material forms, the palm leaves, are the carriers of Manikkavacakar's poetic imagination. They are cut from plants, their surfaces scratched, scored, and dyed. They are bundled, tied and untied, bought and sold, handled, treasured, and tucked away. In addition to contributing to the survival of *Tirukkovaiyar* these long slim pages have histories, residencies, and even scents in their own rights.

At the Bodleian Library at the University of Oxford in the UK, a visitor needs a written invitation by a member of the university faculty in order to obtain admission into the library. As the repository of the largest known collection of Sanskrit manuscripts outside of the Indian subcontinent, it comes as no surprise that there are also a number of Tamil manuscripts among them. Downstairs, in the Special Collections room, only paper, pencils, and silent cameras are allowed inside. The catalog of Tamil manuscripts is an oversized, unpublished, handwritten folio. The author of this catalog is none other than the renowned scholar and translator of Tamil literature, Dr. George Uglow Pope (d. 1908). His entry for the *Tirukkovaiyar* manuscript reads as follows.

26
35 leaves, written on both sides.
19th Cent.
Tiru-çittambala-kovai. [tiruccirṟampalakkovai.][16]
By Māṇikka Vāçagar.
See Murdock p. 88. S. C. Chitty's Tam. Plutarch p. 54.
The date is probably the 12th cent. The work is in 400 stanzas, of which
Only 157 are here. Often printed.

Based on this entry, the relative age of the manuscript, approximately 150 years, makes it a candidate for the oldest extant copy of the text.[17] Although only 157 of the 400 verses are present, Pope notes with confidence that this poem is often printed. Toward the end of his life, Pope translated a study by another Tamil literary initiate and French missionary Abbe J. A. Dubois in which Dubois described his observations of "Hindu writing" using palm leaf technologies as follows.

The Hindu method of writing.

They execute it with an iron spike, sometimes six inches long, the upper end of which is commonly formed into a cutting edge to trim the sides of the leaves, so as to make them all straight. In writing with the spike, neither chair nor table is wanted. The leaf is supported on the middle finger of the left hand, and is kept steady by being held between the thumb and the forefinger. The right hand, in writing, does not slide upon the leaf, according to our practice in writing on paper; but, after finishing a word or two, the writer fixes the point of the spike in the last letter, and pushes the leaf from the right hand toward the left, so as to enable him to finish his line. This becomes so habitual and easy, that one often sees a Hindu writing as he walks along.

As this species of penmanship is in fact only a sort of faint engraving, the strokes of which are indistinct and not easily read, especially by weak eyes, sometimes they besmear the leaf with fresh cow-dung, rubbing the surface well, so as to leave nothing behind but the finer parts that adhere to the engraved lines. This they afterwards tinge with black, and thus the writing becomes more visible, and easier to read.[18]

The excerpt provides an account of the writing practices used to engrave and ink palm manuscripts like the one found in the Bodleian collection. Pope's acquisition and description of the Oxford manuscript indicates that *Tirukkovaiyar* was accessible to a foreign scholar in the mid-nineteenth century. His translation of Dubois's description of "Hindu writing" is a testament to the equal portion of precision and curiosity with which these men approached their object of study.

Now, the manuscripts are stored in individual custom-fit boxes, and once they were brought out, I was allowed to take the bundles apart and photograph as I wished. The scribe filled each leaf with six lines of neatly spaced script, and in fact all of the manuscripts that I viewed in India and abroad were written in a legible hand and evenly spaced according to the size of the leaf. The leaves in this manuscript were held together by string that was looped between two evenly spaced holes. The leaves were clean and the creamy color of a manila folder.

The next set of manuscripts that I encountered is also preserved in a European institution, but one that is located in South Asia. The French Institute of Pondicherry located on the southeast coast of India houses an impressive collection of Shaiva manuscripts that has been recognized as a UNESCO "Memory of the World" Collection. Like the catalog in Oxford, the Pondicherry manuscripts are recorded in handwritten journals that visitors must leaf through, page by page, to extract titles and call numbers that are of interest to them. The institute has taken great care to preserve their collection. As part of these measures and in conjunction with their digitization program, photographs are only taken onsite and by authorized institute employees. The manuscripts themselves are darker in color, and since they were collected from a range of institutes, private homes, and donors, some had suffered damage caused by moisture and insects. The Pondicherry collection contains half a dozen copies of *Tirukkovaiyar*, more commonly titled *Tiruccirrampalakkovai* on the bundles themselves. These verses are frequently found alongside their partner in *Tirumurai*, namely the hymns of *Tiruvacakam*. On one Pondicherry manuscript, the copy date is clearly marked April 12, 1940, making it only half the age of the Bodleian example. The collection recently received a cleaning and a protective application of natural chemicals to repel insects. As a result, the distinctive, coffee-stained color of these palm leaves is joined by the smell of citronella, a sensory detail lost in the digital copy that I carry on my thumb drive.

The final manuscript encounter that I present alongside the experiences in Oxford and Pondicherry took place during a site visit in southern Tamil Nadu. The town of Tiruperunthurai is named in verse 104 of *Tirukkovaiyar* and is the place of its poet's legendary conversion. Today, this town is home to the Sri Atmanatacuvami temple complex, most of which was constructed in the fifteenth century.

The entrance to the temple is unassuming with a few newly plastered pillars and a corrugated aluminum roof. Cattle casually wander across the street after grazing on the neighboring field of stubble. Once a visitor steps down into the first pillared hall, however, they enter a world that celebrates and amplifies the fame of Manikkavacakar. The interior of the first structure to the left is painted floor to ceiling in mural panels. It tells the stories of Shiva and the poet in the Pandya court, in the city of Madurai, being locked in jail, building a temple to Shiva, and sitting under a tree with Shiva's foot on his head. In this last image, Shiva sits atop a tiered, jewel-crusted pedestal, wearing garlands and a tiger skin around his waist. This hand-painted scene is replicated in various areas of the complex including statues in stone under a portico and in plaster over a gate.

The temple complex is large and visitors are directed by attendants and enthusiastic locals toward specific samples of the fine stonework on the ceiling, pillars, and walls. The pillars that guide devotees from the temple entrance toward the inner shrine are decorated with the servants of Shiva, the tiger-legged Viyakirapata, and snake-footed Patanjali. Nearby stone women are caged with green fencing to protect them from visitors who might touch their finely sculpted hairstyles. One figure boasts a life-like braid that swings down her back, and all of the maidens have intricate ornaments and headbands carved into their dress.

Upon entering the interior hallway of the main shrine, guests pass a number of small shrines, including one for Manikkavacakar, who is decorated with shining textiles, garlands, and sandal paste. The priest assigned to that shrine on the day of my visit was one of the only priests that I met over the course of my fieldwork who had any knowledge of *Tirukkovaiyar*. He also had a set of keys to one of the locked niches along the corridor. From that niche, the priest removed a cotton bundle and unwrapped a sealed plastic container. Inside that container was a palm leaf manuscript that was short in length but thick with leaves of *Tirukkovaiyar* and *Tiruvacakam*. I was not permitted to hold or photograph this manuscript, but the priest was willing to take the lid off of the container and tip it toward me so that I could see the size and condition of the dry bundle.

It is perhaps least surprising that a manuscript copy is kept in Tiruperunthurai where the poet is said to have met Shiva and composed *Tirukkovaiyar*'s sister text, *Tiruvacakam*. This manuscript is located on "home turf" and it is housed in a religious institution whose business it is to conduct proper worship of Shiva. Temple leaders in Tiruperunthurai identified *Tirukkovaiyar* and its manuscript form as valuable elements of their religious and artistic culture. By housing the manuscript in the inner corridors of the temple in containers also used for ritual icons and their accessories, rather than off site at a monastery or temple administrative office, we also find a text kept in close proximity to the divine life of the temple.

Motivations for preserving *Tirukkovaiyar* manuscripts vary, as does their accessibility. In Oxford, entrance into the institution is exclusive but once inside, there is freedom to touch and manipulate the leaves firsthand and they are considered resources for academic research. While anyone can request digital copies of the manuscripts in Pondicherry, the actual objects are off limits. Finally, the temple manuscript had equally exclusive accessibility. The difference was only in my lack of membership into this community of Shaiva devotees and scholars. The existence of the text was certainly not a secret but it was not to be handled by a casual visitor. Based on the contexts of these encounters, *Tirukkovaiyar* continues to be a significant source for contemporary religious and intellectual pursuits. The manuscripts themselves are also a context in which the significance of the poetry is manifest and through which its transmission is mediated.

To these three palm leaf manuscripts, I add a fourth item. Over the course of my research it was lamented almost universally by my colleagues and interlocutors that the number of people with the training and interest to read, study, or interact with the details of the composition is scarce. However, the small publication that I picked up at a bookstall in Chidambaram tells a different story. A new copy of *Tirukkovaiyar* was printed in 2011 and sold for fifteen rupees (about twenty-five cents) in the shops surrounding the temple of dancing Shiva where pilgrims from all over the world come to visit, worship, and shop. This slim yellow volume is an accessible and high-quality edition that I see as a testament to the enduring interest and value that people, especially Tamil Shaivites, continue to hold for this poetry.

This publication and the manuscripts described here remind us again that *Tirukkovaiyar* is a living, dynamic expression of devotion, and thus my analysis of it is located in the present and is mediated through a variety of pathways and sources. I do not aim, nor do I think it is possible, to access a pure historical mode of ninth-century authorial intent. These publications and manuscripts are my (and many others') gateway through which I access and interpret the poetry and the various fruits that it has born as a literary and religious icon over the last millennium.

I engaged with priests, temple occupants, architectural structures, South Indian landscapes, and evidence left by artists and agriculturalists to inform my interpretation of religious desire in *Tirukkovaiyar*. The palm leaves offer yet another possibility of what the *Tirukkovaiyar* creates as or who it might invite into its sense of religion.

A Reflection on Sources

The Tamil corpus is vast and rich, and even at the end of a research project there are sources and questions that remain unexplored. This is the regular challenge and privilege of working in the relatively young (to the Western academy) field of Tamil studies.

The variety and diversity of sources for the study of devotional literature housed in just one temple complex is astounding. I spent a great deal of time alone, strolling through temples, and perched on stone ledges. In general Indian cities are known to be loud, lively, and congested. In contrast, many of the temples that I visited were massive old stone structures like those in Kanchipuram, where I was the sole visitor, joined only by the priest and the sweeper. Despite their empty halls, a number of these rural temples contain all sorts of bronzes, inscriptions, sculptures, and paintings that, to my knowledge, exist outside the scope of both scholarly knowledge and pilgrimage-based tourism routes that might otherwise bring devotees and revenue to these institutions. Although studies have been made of Shiva's home in Chidambaram, there is no comparable study of temple history and temple life in Tiruperunthurai, for example, where the temple halls, walls, pillars, and shrines are replete with depictions of Manikkavacakar and his adventures with Shiva.

I encountered additional streams of knowledge that were too deep and too wide to include in this study. I acknowledge these areas of study here to further expand the readers' concept of contexts for *Tirukkovaiyar* and to disclose aspects of my research that I did not develop in this book but that nonetheless influenced my approach to the verses. In my search for the poet or poem named in a temple inscription, I limited my sources to inscriptions at the Shaiva temples in the towns named in *Tirukkovaiyar*. Although I didn't find resounding reference to *Tirukkovaiyar* or to Manikkavacakar, there was mention of the nayanmar bhakti saints, hymns, and descriptions of activities surrounding Shiva's localized manifestations. The challenge of working with inscriptions lies primarily with their sheer volume and secondarily with the idiosyncratic collection of records, making systematic or exhaustive study of a single city or of a particular site difficult to verify. Nonetheless, the *South Indian Inscriptions* contain valuable information about the economic support of literati and methods for including poetry and hymns in temple practice, whether during major festivals or smaller-scale daily worship services.

Another resource associated with the preservation and development of Shaiva philosophical traditions into which *Tirukkovaiyar* would naturally fit is the matam or monastery. The monasteries are an important intellectual and historical audience for *Tirukkovaiyar* and other texts like it. Although my brief experience with one such monastery was productive, I determined that being female closed more doors than it opened in this particular setting.

Finally, Manikkavacakar and *Tirukkovaiyar* occupy virtual space in the realm of social media and public life. Devotees host events for competitive recitations and vocal performances of Manikkavacakar's poetry, especially *Tiruvacakam*, some of which are available for viewing on YouTube. Essay contests with cash prizes are held for children and adults for the best description of Manikkavacakar's life and excellence. Local Tamil newspapers run frequent advertisements for lectures on *Tirukkovaiyar*. The saint and his poetry are also alive on Twitter, Facebook, and personal blogs, opening an entirely new domain of digital devotion for devotees and scholars to explore.

Forms of the Poet: Story and Sculpture

Like his poetry, the life and fame of the poet develop in a variety of time frames and forms, resulting in a cumulative, plastic identity for Manikkavacakar. The story of the poet's life is preserved in two hagiographies, *Tiruvatavurar puranam*,[19] composed in the fifteenth century by Katavul mamunivar, and *Tiruvilaiyatal puranam*,[20] composed in the thirteenth century. According to these legends, Manikkavacakar was born to a Brahman family near the Pandya capital of Madurai. He was a bright scholar from a young age and was invited by the king to become a trusted minister in the Pandya court. In one story of Manikkavacakar's courtly adventures, the Pandya king entrusted him with treasure and sent him to a port in the neighboring territory of the Chera king to purchase a number of horses. On his way, Manikkavacakar met Shiva in a grove near a town called Tiruperunthurai, converted into a devotee, and donated all of the treasure intended for the king's horses to the worship of Shiva. When he eventually returned to the king's court empty-handed, Manikkavacakar was

Figure 3 Mural detail of Shiva and Manikkavacakar meeting, Tiruperunthurai.

imprisoned. Shiva took human form and appeared in Madurai to save his new devotee by delivering replacement horses to the king. However, when those horses turned out to be jackals, Manikkavacakar was punished yet again, this time tortured by the hot sun in the dried riverbed of the Vaigai. Shiva made a final dramatic rescue by threatening to release the flood of the Ganges River that rested atop his matted hair onto the earth. Afraid that his city would be destroyed, the king restored Manikkavacakar once more to his elevated status as minister to the Pandya court in Madurai. After some time, Manikkavacakar resigned from his post under the king and returned to the place of his conversion in Tiruperunthurai to worship Shiva. Before Shiva returned to his home on Mount Kailash, he told Manikkavacakar to visit the towns of Uttarakocamankai and Tirukkalukkunram and then to finish his life's work in Chidambaram. Once the poet was settled in Chidambaram, Manikkavacakar faced off with Buddhists from Sri Lanka in a great debate. When he miraculously cured the attending mute princess by making her respond to his philosophical questions, the king accepted defeat and converted.[21] In the final episode of the poet-saint's life, a mendicant from Madurai arrived in Chidambaram and asked Manikkavacakar to recite his verses so that they could be written down. Once the verses were dutifully recorded by the mendicant, he revealed himself to be Shiva in disguise, having traveled north to collect this poetry himself (Figure 3).

Shiva disappeared. In the morning, a copy of the verses was discovered at the entrance of the temple hall. When asked to explain the meaning of these verses, Manikkavacakar pointed to Shiva and said, "Only that One is the meaning," and then he also disappeared into the golden hall in union with his god.

Encounters with the poet's life and works also occur through visual representations of Manikkavacakar. The iconography by which he is most often identified is a short cloth tied around his waist, a palm leaf in his left hand, and his right hand in the raised posture of a teacher. Occasionally, he is seated. In spite of the details of his hagiography, I've never encountered Manikkavacakar represented with the horses or jackals that drive his initial meetings with Shiva. Instead, his statue is most frequently posed alongside the three *Tevaram* poets. In this configuration, Manikkavacakar, Appar, Cuntarar, and Campantar are known as the nalvar or "The Four Masters" of Tamil Shaivism.

There is another series of famous Shaiva bhakti poet-saints known as nayanmar. This collective of sixty-three saints is depicted in sets of small stone or metal figures commonly featured in Tamil Shaiva temples today. The list of sixty-three saints and their hagiographies are recorded in the great epic, *Periyapuranam*, but significantly for our study, Manikkavacakar is not listed among them. Although excluded from the late medieval list of sixty-three saints, contemporary representations of the saints include Manikkavacakar with remarkable frequency. For example, in Srivanchiyam, there is a set of sixty-three nayanmar statues that includes Manikkavacakar. In Sirkali, at the Cattanatar temple, they also have a set of stone nayanmar that includes Manikkavacakar with striking elongated earlobes and dressed with beads and white cloth with red trim. The sixty-three saints include Manikkavacakar but are undecorated behind a gate in Tiruchuli. There are two sets of nayanmar statues in the Sri Margasagayesvara temple in Moovalur. The first set has sixty-three bronze statues including Manikkavacakar. The second set has been expanded to include seventy-three statues; however, Manikkavacakar is absent. These observations indicate that Manikkavacakar's exclusion from the nayanmar proposed by *Periyapuranam* is not consistently applied in contemporary temple practice.

Images of Manikkavacakar are not limited to these various but common assemblages of small statuettes. The best temple to visit for representations of Manikkavacakar is the Sri Atmanatacuvami temple at Tiruperunthurai—the site of Manikkavacakar's conversion, the home of at least one *Tirukkovaiyar* manuscript, and one of Shiva's abodes according to verse 104 of *Tirukkovaiyar*. In this temple, I observed elaborate murals, posters, and sculptures resounding in tribute to the poet and his encounters with Shiva.

Figure 4 Detail of ascetic Manikkavacakar on a stone column, Tiruperunthurai.

Standing against the set of pillars leading to the innermost shrine at Tiruperunthurai are two imposing representations of Manikkavacakar, poised to look inward toward the deity. On one side, Manikkavacakar is dressed for the role of court minister and sports a mustache. His earlobes extend down to his shoulders and are stacked with ornaments. His tall conical crown is embellished with detailed carving. He wears thick necklaces, including one with a huge pendant that appears to be set with gemstones, and his fingers are full of rings. The second statue of Manikkavacakar emphasizes his life as a mendicant after leaving his post in Madurai (Figure 4). His ears are also stretched, but only by a single bead. His hair is exposed, tied in small knots in evenly spaced rows. He wears only a few necklaces made of areca beads. Faint stripes in triplicate represent the ash that he wore in the place of his ministerial ornaments. He stands with arms crossed. Otherwise, the statue has not been dressed or marked by devotees.

There is a similar pillar in the back of an exterior hall where fewer people pass. Manikkavacakar the mendicant stands with heavy, broad shoulders and legs, and yet he appears more relaxed without his arms crossed. He has a small temple carved above his head and he stands on a small slab above a woman dancing with a musical instrument. One hand holds a palm leaf and the other hand holds a string of beads. His earlobes are elongated but without any ornaments. The cobwebs between his arm and fleshy ribs and evidence of rodent inhabitants betray the quiet existence of this figure. Although this Manikkavacakar shows no signs of recent attention from devotees, the natural light that falls over his shoulders is quite striking on the bare stone.

Not far off there is a smaller Manikkavacakar pillar that had caught someone else's attention. He stands in the mendicant dress, recently embellished with a dab of sandal on his chest and forehead. A fresh jasmine blossom is balanced on his head and another rests in the crease of his elbow joint. A fresh yellow flower was balanced on the other forearm. In a separate corridor from the Manikkavacakar dressed for court, there is another stone statue attached to a pillar with his name painted on a sign over his head. This figure has a tall, conical crown, thick rows of necklaces with another diamond-shaped pendant, a smaller star pendant in the middle of his chest, a small smile, and hands facing out. The custodians of the temple dressed the waist of this formidable stone saint with a crisp white piece of fabric wound with an attractive green border. His shoulders were adorned with a heavy garland of yellow and red flowers. A smaller garland of fragrant jasmine was draped around his neck. Cooling sandal paste marks were applied on the palms of his hands, his forehead, his crown, and in the center of his pendant. On the south side of the second hall, yet a third ministerial Manikkavacakar stands at a pillar and in a slightly different style. Both his hair and the fabric of his waistcloth flow outward from his body. The cloth is pleated, embellished with ornate borders. Manikkavacakar is wearing his fair share of jewels around his neck and fashioned in a wide belt.

While the temple in Tiruperunthurai certainly holds the most varied displays of Manikkavacakar's life and works in the examples above, images of the poet appear in nearly all of the towns named in *Tirukkovaiyar* as I observed them during my fieldwork in 2010 and 2011. The age of the Shaiva temples that I visited in these towns varied from some of the oldest cave shrines at Tirupparankundram to new construction; what remained consistent was the presence of Manikkavacakar. Some of the largest temples like those in Tirupparankundram and Madurai maintain costly elephants. The Ekamparanatar temple in Kanchipuram is one of the few temples in Tamil Nadu still able to maintain musicians for daily performance. Temples of this size have made adjustments to their donation procedures to accommodate the wealth of foreign currency deposited in their untiyals. I found some rural temples in disrepair, watched by unpaid itinerant priests, one of whom left the temple keys with a casually employed neighbor charged with keeping the lamps lit. Somewhere between these two extremes, a modest new temple in Manikkavacakar's hometown in Thiruvadavur was built and acquired its first two bronze figures of dancing Shiva and Manikkavacakar, both of which measured under 30 cm in height.

Each sculpture, mural, legend, and smooth palm leaf is a contemporary vector of the Tirukkovaiyar. Each vector is a guideline that reflects the decisions and aesthetics of artists and patrons. These vectors also provide contexts for and echoes of Tamil poetry as well as the particular sense of religion developed by the poet hundreds of years earlier. These observations from South Indian Shaiva temples located in the same towns that Manikkavacakar and other medieval poets wrote into their poetic landscapes are designed to signal and invite the presence of Shiva. The floral and bejeweled ornaments and colorful fabrics adorning figures of Manikkavacakar in contemporary Shaiva spaces find their aesthetic ancestors in the verses of *Tirukkovaiyar*.

In a number of the larger temples, upon entering the innermost shrine to view the linga, visitors turn to view a secondary shrine on the right side containing two significant figures in Tamil Shaivism. The first figure and manifestation of god praised in Manikkavacakar's poetry is Shiva in the form of the Nataraja dancing in a ring of fire. Dancing Shiva is accompanied by a small wooden house with decorative bud-shaped spindles across its peaked roof. Sometimes the house is labeled directly in small letters or on a plaque posted nearby. Either way, peeking through the double glass doors, the interested devotee will find a printed copy of the entire Tamil Shaiva canon *Tirumurai*, of which *Tirukkovaiyar* is a part (Figure 5). What joins this sacred pair, the fiery dancer and the cabinet-sized house of sacred literature, varied from site to site. In one temple, this gated shrine was a safe place to store valuable bronze statues. It was not uncommon to see various lamps, trays, matchboxes, calendars, and sundry items used for daily pujas. In the shrine at Thiruvenkadu, a black and white kitten had crept between the bars of the locked gate to sleep at Shiva's feet. In contrast to the interior placement of the *Tirumurai* canon for some temples, in the Meenakshi temple in Madurai there are two wooden shrines in the exterior corridor surrounding the Golden Lotus Tank, where foreign visitors can see them on display. One shrine labeled *Tirumurai* and the other housed the Vedas.

In addition to Shiva's partnership with printed texts in temple shrines, it should come as no surprise that Manikkavacakar often finds a place for himself at

Figure 5 Small shrine for *Tirumurai*, Piranmalai.

the foot of dancing Shiva. This is the case in Kutralam, where Manikkavacakar's statue had been placed under the raised right foot of a large bronze dancing Shiva. Finally, in the Brahmapurisvara temple located in the rural village of Ampal, Manikkavacakar was also placed under the raised right foot of the dancing god. There, in Ampal, Manikkavacakar was cast in bronze and stood between Shiva and a wooden house containing the sacred canon, *Tirumurai*. He stood tall and his chest was carefully draped with a real string of areca beads. He wore a white waistcloth and a bright orange shawl hung on his shoulders. In a lighter shade of orange, sandal paste marked his chest.

Over and beyond stone and bronze statues, Manikkavacakar also appears in temple texts, in stone texts, an example of which comes from Tirukkalukkunram. This hill has a temple built into the rocks at the top and it is famous for two birds of prey fed daily at its peak. At the base of the hill there is another, much larger temple. According to ARE reports collected in 1932–33, there was an inscription on the south wall of the Manikkavacakar shrine in the base complex of the Bhaktavatsatesvara temple. The contents of this inscription record a contract between merchants for the payment of taxes and for the provision of oil lamps for the lord of Tiruperunthurai (referring to Shiva). In search of this inscription in situ, I entered the temple complex with a copy of the inscription report and headed directly to the south side of the main temple. I found a small shrine but it looked rather new so I sought out the help of a temple officer. He kindly escorted me to the only Manikkavacakar shrine at the temple, which was the very same structure I had passed by. He mentioned while we walked that they had recently celebrated an anniversary festival, during which garlands of jasmine, marigolds, roses, and other varieties of colorful blossoms were strung overhead, across doorways, and around the deities' shoulders. Standing at the Manikkavacakar shrine I asked if he knew about an inscription that should appear on the south wall—pointing to the blank surface. He agreed that there was writing on these areas, but in preparation for the festival, all of these walls have been sandblasted. He spread his arms to show that now the walls were all clean. In preparation for the decorations and processions in honor of Shiva, the temple leaders had taken care to "clean" all of the ancient stones before dressing them with brilliant ornaments made of fragrant flowers, fresh paint, green leaves, newly printed banners, bright lights, and of course gold and silver ornaments for the god. I will never forget his sweeping gesture or my disappointment to have lost the only inscriptional evidence of Manikkavacakar at a site named in *Tirukkovaiyar*. However, this is not the first or last inscription erased for the sake of reviving an old structure for a living god, and when put in these terms, as a scholar of religious studies I find it difficult to criticize the activities of a living practice.

In addition to Manikkavacakar's likeness in stone, bronze, and text that reside within and on temple walls, the poet also travels outside. Saint Manikkavacakar and his poetry are celebrated today in grand temple festivals in Chidambaram and Tiruperunthurai, as well as in smaller processions where he is included alongside other Shaiva saints. For example, in the season known as Markali, Manikkavacakar's figure leads a procession around Chidambaram and a series of his *Tiruvempavai* hymns excerpted from *Tiruvacakam* are recited.[22] In his recent work on South Indian festivals, Paul Younger shares a fascinating account of a Canadian temple that celebrated the festival for dancing Shiva made famous in Chidambaram, during which the traditional male temple singer was replaced by an elderly Sri Lankan woman.[23] According to Younger's account, her emotional performance of Manikkavacakar's verses was appreciated by the attendees, but there was varied agreement on what role the woman ought to play in rituals and offerings made to honor the revered poet.

In addition to the fame of his poetry, Manikkavacakar is often hailed as a mystic and as a foundational figure for the Shaiva Siddhanta school of theology. Although his poetry predates the major texts of this tradition, it is difficult to read Manikkavacakar today without the theological influence ascribed to his life and verses. In total, four commentaries accompany *Tirukkovaiyar* and have certainly had an impact on my own reading of the text. The oldest is known as *Panaiya urai* and influenced the second commentary attributed to Peraciriyar. Little is known about the authors or circumstances from which these first commentaries grew.

Two additional commentaries were composed from within the Shaiva Siddhanta community and are known as *Tirukkovaiyar unmai*, followed by *Tirukkovaiyar unmai vilakkam*. In an attempt to temper erotic themes, this commentary tradition recast the hero and heroine as the soul and Shiva, thereby emphasizing the motif of Shiva constantly longing for and seeking out his devotees. The five landscapes (aintinai) with corresponding phases of erotic love are also assigned corresponding states of contemplation. The five stages move from the mind and eyes to the rites associated with hands and feet. Esoteric interpretation extends beyond the hero and heroine to include the entire anonymous cast of the love drama. In this extended Shaiva Siddhanta allegory, the hero's friend, the heroine's friend, the foster mother, and the mother of the heroine represent self-knowledge, divine grace, creative logos, and the eternal feminine power Shakti. In this particular sect of Shaivism, commentators interpreted *Tirukkovaiyar* through their philosophy of divine love. Numerous theological studies have also been produced by contemporary scholars linking the poet Manikkavacakar, the god dancing Shiva, and Manikkavacakar's poetry, particularly verses from his anthology of hymns *Tiruvacakam*, to theories of divine love, devotion, and transformations of the soul.[24] Manikkavacakar's legacy as it has developed over a millennium gives us a number of ways to access the poet and his poetry.

What remains of historical evidence from the early days of Shaiva poets and of Manikkavacakar's life is a collection of verses, stories, images, fragments, and impressions. Again, this project is not one of isolation or origination. My reading privileges the cumulative, dynamic worlding of the devotional work composed and released by the medieval poet, forms of which now collect dust or flower blossoms in bronze or palm leaf.

Conclusion

This book is designed to generate new considerations of early Tamil religion and of religious studies more broadly through study of the materiality of devotion. I reprioritize the sensory information presented by the ninth-century composition in order to make a larger argument for the critical need for material analysis in the interpretation of literary worlds. By analyzing the material and sensory experiences that are captured by and exist within the literary world as designed by the poet-devotee, I show that this materiality yields the religious. And furthermore, the materiality of the poetic world is an opening by which we as scholars can redefine South Asian studies. Many studies of the surviving medieval Tamil Hindu or bhakti corpus have analyzed theology and eroticism, especially feminine bodies, such as work by Cutler, Hardy, Ramanujan, Prentiss, and others. My aim is to find other types of religious expression, in addition to the erotic whether symbolic or literal, in forms found in the material world and in the sensory experience of the faint jingle and icy plunge.

From here the chapters focus on literary structures of the burgeoning kovai genre, the arc of *Tirukkovaiyar*'s love story as Shiva travels through iconic southern landscapes, the individual characters in the poem, and culminate with the sensory impact of color, scent, and ornamentation that give texture and dimension to our understanding of the god Shiva.

You will be led through technologies of literary expression, sacred cities, rituals of devotion, and flourishing landscapes, all of which are material contexts and contents designed to praise and please lord Shiva. Just as silks, jewelry, flowers, and makeup are used to adorn women, kings, and gods, so too the words themselves take on forms of showmanship and adornment that resonate across the disciplinary boundaries of religion, literature, and material studies. It is with such a world of embellishment and abundance in mind that we embark on this study of *Tirukkovaiyar*.

1

Materiality in Literary Landscapes

50
Reaching the confidante
From now on it will be difficult
to unite with the creeper whose mouth is like ripe fruit.
I will send the confidante with curly hair full of bees as a blessing
I will make her understand that the bright spear-like eyes cause me to suffer
like devotees who are denied the chance to contemplate
the lord who dances
with red matted locks
lit by a lovely slice of the moon.

This verse from *Tirukkovaiyar* conveys a simple heartfelt message from the lover to his beloved: forget me not. The most captivating aspect of *Tirukkovaiyar* is its love story, and even the simplest sentiment is carefully embellished with layers upon layers of sensory details. The soft lips of the heroine are contrasted with her piercing eyes. Like her lips, Shiva's matted hair is red in color and it glistens under the white moon. The suffering of the hero in the absence of his true love is compared to devotees who have been denied their union with dancing Shiva. This hero's message was composed by a poet well versed in a wide range of literatures and expressive techniques, especially the structures and artistry of classical love poetry.

In addition to the voluminous quantity of devotional hymns, by the ninth century, the Tamil literary world had well-developed traditions of love poetry, heroic poetry, epics, and grammatical treatises, as well as documentary corpuses of contracts, panegyrics, and memorials in the form of inscriptions and hero stones. When asked to imagine inspirational sources for a poet writing religious literature, the beauty of nature, sophisticated sculpture and paintings, grand feats of architectural engineering, or even an ecstatic episode might come to mind. In a list of sources for spiritual, philosophical, experiential, or otherwise sensory revelation, technical literary grammars rarely find their way to the top of the pile. Nonetheless, for this study, which aims to locate material religion in the interactions between humans and objects in particular spaces and time, the grammatical framework that influenced the organization and stylization of *Tirukkovaiyar* is an essential component of the sense of religion.[1] The grammatical treatises analyzed here take great pains to enumerate and categorize human dispositions, division of seasons, musical instruments, and many more elements of the ideal lovescape. The material components are then selected and woven together by the poet to create a religious experience. The impact of the composition is at once singular and composite: a unique point on a spectrum of Shaiva devotion and a harmonious chord that only works in relation to the scaffolding of its literary context.

This chapter will focus on the relationship between the established world of akam poetry, the love story in *Tirukkovaiyar*, and proceeding grammatical treatises. I will show that the systems and structures presented in the grammatical works below are the technology by which a poet might cultivate a sense of religion; literary structures are one way to communicate and design the material context in and through which the poet praised lord Shiva.

We begin with an overview of the fundamental characteristics of classical love poetry. I compare classical literary theory with the design of *Tirukkovaiyar* focusing on primary organizing structures and the occurrence of stylized themes in both the poetry and the grammars. As will be shown, the templates for the Tamil love story offered by the grammars include numerous elements of the natural world and the human experience of it.

From plants to birds, waterways to drums, these technical grammars also assign order to the material world, as well as hierarchical value. This is the world into which the poet will write god. The continuity of distinctive motifs between classical anthologies of love poetry and verses taken from *Tirukkovaiyar* demonstrates the poet's conscious understanding of classical styles, his implicit acceptance of the classical literary landscape as an environment ripe for religious experimentation, and his skillful innovations in the materiality of devotional love for the delight of his early medieval contemporaries.

Part Two of this chapter focuses on the development of the genre now known as kovai, which developed from the style of *Tirukkovaiyar* and another partially extant poem *Pantikkovai*, the two earliest examples surviving of kovai poetry. The influence of *Tirukkovaiyar* over the trajectory of what is now a tradition of kovai poems is undeniable and its retroactive status as the ur-kovai is the mode in which *Tirukkovaiyar* is read today. By comparing verses from *Tirukkovaiyar* with more recent kovais, the reader will gain a sense of what is unique or enduring about the ninth-century composition. The comparison also invites consideration of the eligible foci of the kovai-style tribute, the vast majority of which take a religiously signification site or deity as its patron.[2]

Part One: Akam Poetry

Tirukkovaiyar and all poems written in the kovai style utilize stylized themes of love and heroism inherited from classical Tamil literary practice. Tellingly, the full name of the kovai genre, including the poem *Tirukkovaiyar*, is akapporul kovai, (akam meaning love and porul meaning subject matter). Love-themed works known broadly as akam poetry use a variety of methods to associate idealized landscapes extracted from regional natural environments with various aspects of five stages of proper love and two forms of improper love. The following analysis will focus solely on the five stages of proper love because these are the strategies used in *Tirukkovaiyar*. Proper love, as defined by akam poetics, is divided into five forms: union, separation, waiting, sulking, and lamenting. Although the descriptions of these emotions are expressed with great specificity in classical poetry, the people who experience these feelings remain unnamed. That is to say that in the classical love tradition the amorous hero and heroine, though suitably matched in beauty, status, and disposition, do not have names. The hero, the heroine, and their respective entourages are anonymous archetypes that rejoice, weep, languish, and pine with emotion and passions that are pure forms of idealized human love. Of course, the majority of lamenting and pining is conducted by the heroine because, as will be shown, it is the hero who will leave and it is the heroine who is continuously left behind. As a counterpoint to her laments, equal attention is devoted to developing the power and beauty of feminine ideals, which are embodied by the heroine.

The five stages of love present in classical literature are bound to five distinct idealized natural landscapes that correspond with the regions of South India (Figure 6). Taken literally, there are four not five landscapes, because the desert landscape emerges from one of the other landscapes as it deteriorates into a state of ruin. For example, agricultural fields can become like a desert in a season of extreme drought. The volatility of an environment being reduced to desert can be expressed in the poetry by a thirsty elephant, an otherwise common feature of the flourishing mountainous landscape, rendered weak and seeking refuge from an uninhabitable land. The technical term for each emotional state is adopted from the name of a flower or plant that grows in the respective region. The emotional states with corresponding landscape (and flora) are as follows; union in the mountain (kurinji), separation in the desert (palai), waiting in the forest (mullai), sulking in agricultural land (marutam), and lamenting at the seashore (neytal).

Figure 6 View of waterfalls, Kutralam.

These emotional states, regions, and flower names are found in the earliest extant Tamil grammar, *Tolkappiyam*, in the section devoted to akam poetics, and are repeated throughout the myriad Tamil grammars that follow.[3] While these ten terms and five regions remain stable in the grammars, their implementation is considerably more complex, including and perhaps especially as they are interpreted by the poet of *Tirukkovaiyar* long after the classical corpus was composed. For example, if we see a monkey enjoying the scent of a kurinji flower, this is a mountain scenario because kurinji flowers grow in the cool mountain groves of Tamil country and this landscape corresponds with sexual union between the hero and heroine. Even if the entire verse is about flower fragrances with little interaction between the lovers, the audience will understand that a human relationship is being described through environmental discourse.

Examples of this phenomenon are found in an anthology of early love poetry known as *Ainkurunuru*, which contains five hundred poems that are organized according to the landscape regions. Each landscape has one hundred verses that are broken into ten themes with ten verses per theme. In addition to love scenarios like those found in *Tirukkovaiyar* such as bathing, sulking, and addressing a variety of female characters, several themes of *Ainkurunuru* are dedicated to animals such as water buffalo (v. 91–100), boars (v. 261–270), monkeys (v. 271–280), parakeets (v. 281–290), and peacocks (v. 291–300). The following verse is taken from the ten monkey-themed verses of the mountain landscape in *Ainkurunuru*.

> In his land,
> A foolish, strong monkey,
> the young of a black-fingered female,
> disturbs a comb full of sweet honey
> on the treacherous mountain,
> then springs onto a nearby branch,
> long and unsteady.
>
> > That hero doesn't know how
> > to come at night, Friend,
> > and our mother says
> > that someone's coming
> > over and over again.
> > *Ainkurunuru* 272[4]

At first glance this verse is about a monkey making a clumsy attempt to steal a taste of honey, startling himself with the thought of being swarmed with the disturbed bees, and then hastily escaping to an unsteady branch. The failed attempt of this monkey is a description of the hero's attempt at a popular classical love theme called Trysting by night, in which the hero aims to meet the heroine in the yard of her house under the cover of night. This type of meeting is made especially treacherous in *Tirukkovaiyar* by lions and other animals that prowl at night, barking village dogs, prying eyes of neighbors, and the risk of waking the heroine's mother. In the verse above (272), the hero must have disturbed the sweet heroine's home—perhaps the snap of a twig under foot or a squeaking gate—and as a result, had to flee the village or risk the sting of her family. Verse 161 is an example from the night tryst chapter of *Tirukkovaiyar*, which echoes some of the same risks.

161
Determining if mother sleeps
O you like fertile Chidambaram with grand fortified walls
  of the one who rules heaven
  who has a cruel bow that set fire to enemy fortresses
in the garden surrounding our house
  an elephant with small eyes and big white tusks
  pushed aside the nakam tree full of blossoms with petals and nectar
  and destroyed the joints of the swing studded with big brilliant gems.

According to the commentary, this verse is spoken loudly and humorously by the confidante. She reports the fantastical tale of a giant elephant crushing their garden swing. When her dramatic telling of danger and destruction elicits no response from the heroine's mother, the girls know that she must be sound asleep in the house. They are free to unlatch the gate and quietly escape to meet the hero without disturbing their warden. The lumbering elephant takes on a secondary personae like the monkeys, representing the hero's previous or feared future attempts to sneak into the girls' yard with clumsy, conspicuous results.

According to the treatise on love poetry *Akapporul vilakkam*, which will be consulted below, the five landscapes can be indicated by up to twenty-six types of natural elements (flowers, beasts, birds, waterways, etc.). In light of this vast range and network of symbols, modern interpreters of Tamil literature face several challenges in addition to identifying symbols correctly and matching them to the correct emotional landscape. Surviving poetic discourses on akam poetry, which are fragmentary themselves, do not agree on the number or type of elements that indicate the five landscapes. In spite of these and other challenges, use of the five landscapes as a cultural strategy for expressing emotions of love and heroics has become a ubiquitous heuristic for modern scholars of Tamil literature, religion, history, and art, beginning with A. K. Ramanujan's famous articulation of the aintinai, which he calls "Interior Landscapes."[5]

In spite of the deceptive accessibility of an animal or particular plant, many questions about the interpretation of the landscapes remain. For example, rules about mixing elements from more than one landscape and interpretive hierarchies for identifying primary elements and secondary elements vary between commentators, as do interpretations of the content and context of erotic scenarios.[6] Questions remain about the descriptive, prescriptive, or didactic use of these treatises, and certainly more studies are needed.

Three works dominate how akam love poetry developed in the medieval period and continues to be interpreted. The earliest extant grammar is *Tolkappiyam*, attributed to Tolkappiyar.[7] Although foundational to scholarly understanding of classical poetics, the treatment of akam themes found in *Tolkappiyam* is not considered in this chapter, due to its length, date, and organizing principles, which do not correspond with later grammars.[8] A second significant love-themed grammar is *Iraiyanar akapporul* (alias *Kalaviyal enra Iraiyanar akapporul*), which is a short composition that deals exclusively with the akam themes, in contrast to the various topics addressed in *Tolkappiyam*. According to tradition, it was composed by the god Shiva himself. The verses of poetry used to illustrate each grammatical concept are taken from the eighth-century kovai *Pantikkovai*.[9] David Buck's *The Story of Stolen Love* offers a rich study and translation of this synthesized grammar and kovai composition.

The most relevant grammar for this study is *Akapporul vilakkam*. It is a thirteenth-century treatise on love-themed poetry attributed to Narkaviraca Nampi. The author of this work is a Jain scholar whose name is lent to the alternative title for this text, *Nampiyakapporul*. Like *Iraiyanar akapporul*, this treatise is interlaced with examples taken from a kovai poem, in this case the majority are from *Tancaivanankovai*.[10] Like *Iraiyanar akapporul*, this treatise includes characteristics common to all akam poetry, not just the kovai genre. Takanobu Takahashi and others agree that the development of organizing solitary situations as a narrative sequence originated in *Iraiyanar akapporul* and reached its completion in the kovais.[11] *Akapporul vilakkam* is the culmination of formalized akam poetics in grammatical form. Kovai is a literary expression of the content that precedes the grammatical treatise. Worth noting in a study of the devotional value of *Tirukkovaiyar*, each of the kovai poems selected to illustrate grammatical forms is dedicated to a royal rather than divine patron, though elements of the supernatural do appear in select verses.

Takahashi surveyed both of the major grammatical works of the early period, associated commentary, and four of the five early anthologies of Tamil literature (*Kuruntokai*, *Narrinai*, *Akananuru*, and *Ainkurunuru*), to test for occurrences and variants of the thirty-two human behaviors or uri, found in love poetry.[12] Using his model for applying grammatical theory to literary practice, I also tested the uri in *Tirukkovaiyar* against the twenty-five uri described in *Akapporul vilakkam*. *Akapporul vilakkam* and *Tirukkovaiyar* share the opening theme, natural union. *Tirukkovaiyar* then progresses to meeting through a friend and chance meeting at the place. *Akapporul vilakkam* includes these two themes but four additional scenes appear before them, and the actual uri appear in reversed order. In the earlier akam grammar *Iraiyanar akapporul*, the two themes follow the same order as in *Tirukkovaiyar*. Themes thirteen through eighteen of *Tirukkovaiyar* all appear in *Akapporul vilakkam*, but in a different sequence. In addition, the tryst by day and night in *Tirukkovaiyar* is subdivided in *Akapporul vilakkam* into tryst by day, obstacles to the tryst by day, tryst by night, and obstacles to the tryst by night. Finally, *Tirukkovaiyar*'s last six themes describing six occasions for the hero to separate from his wife all appear in the reasons for separation in *Akapporul vilakkam*. The separations also occur in the same sequence, except for separation due to public women. In *Akapporul vilakkam*, this is the first separation-based theme listed in the sequence of six. Separation due to public women is the final section of *Tirukkovaiyar* and with forty-nine verses the second longest theme developed in the poem.

We turn now to the rules of *Akapporul vilakkam* and its definition of the material realm and bounds within which a classical love story occurs.

Grammatical Framework

The grammar *Akapporul vilakkam* is compact and systematically arranged in narrative order. Its description is plain and explicit, and it is viewed as the definitive work on the content of each classical love theme.[13] This grammar is closest in age to *Tirukkovaiyar*, so it is closest in historical proximity to the shape of akam poetics at the time of the poem's composition.

Section two of *Akapporul vilakkam* defines the nature of the landscapes found in love poetry, which includes two types of regional and temporal settings, fourteen environmental elements, and ten human behaviors. The following are the relevant rules taken from the second chapter of *Akapporul vilakkam*.

> The love-theme of rare Tamil that is examined by poets in the expansive world has seven attributes, which are unreciprocated love, five landscapes, and improper love. (1)

> Without erring from the ancient tradition, it is described within two elements, which are the way of the world and the poet's imagination. (2)
> Among the seven, unreciprocated is that which has one-sided desire (kamam). (3)
> The five landscapes are that which have desire with affection (anpu). (4)
> Improper love is that which is called unfitting desire. (5)
> The names that are received for the five landscapes are kurinji, palai, mullai, marutam, and neytal. (6)
> They (the five landscapes) indeed are stated through all three subject matters that are intended in the following order: regional and temporal settings, environmental elements, human behaviors. (7)
> Regional and temporal settings are of two types: land and time. (8)
> Environmental elements are made of fourteen types, namely awesome deity, the high-ranking ones, those who are not, birds, beasts, towns, water, flowers, trees, food, drum, lute, music, and occupation. (19)
> Human behaviors are received in ten types there: union, separation, waiting, sulking, lamenting, and things in response to these. (25)
> *Akapporul vilakkam*

The first two rules of this section name the seven attributes of love-themed poetry. The poet must draw from two resources to describe these modes of love, namely the world in which they live and the poets' own imagination or rhetorical flourish. Although the limits of this sense of imagination are not elaborated upon in this text, it is certainly an indication of a working concept of poetic license that was formally recognized as a part of literary production. In rules three through five, there is a distinction between love associated with a landscape and the two unsuitable loves. The improper loves are based on kamam, which is translated here as desire but can also be conceived of as lust. In contrast, the group of five love themes is motivated by both the carnal attraction of kamam and affection or anpu. Anpu has a broad semantic range that includes physical attraction but can also be described as friendship or devotion, both of which suggest emotional connection that surpasses the limits of kamam.[14] Rules eight, nineteen, and twenty-five articulate the three types of subject matter that indicate the five landscapes. As we encounter these lists of categories, characteristics, or divisions, it is important to remember that these are the poet's building blocks for constructing the heroine's romantic trysts and her sensations of heat and jealousy when she encounters another woman. These categories of classical and medieval love poetry map remarkably well onto Plate's working definition of material religion, addressing components of human experience and emotion, objects in the environment, special places and times, and even encounters with deities. *Akapporul vilakkam* is a guide to the elements of the material world that initially register this poetry—regardless of Shiva's appearance in it—as *love* poetry. Eventually these emotional and environmental frames are selected by the poet to become the appropriate and even preferred sacred settings in which to present Shiva to his devotees.

First, regional and temporal settings are the primary mode for indicating landscapes. The five types of land have been discussed above: forest, agricultural land, seashore, mountains, and desert. Time is presented in two cycles, over the course of a full day and over the course of a year.[15] The year is divided into seasons. The smaller cycle is divided into six periods: midnight, predawn, dawn, midday, afternoon, and night.[16] These two forms of time are representative of a landscape region. For example, the forest region (mullai) is indicated by night or the winter season.[17] These terms have been extracted from *Tolkappiyam* and make up the full cycle of one day, however, in a noteworthy imbalance between theory and practice, all of these divisions of time are not attested in the classical poetry.

According to *Akapporul vilakkam*, there are fourteen elements or environmental objects, which cover the plants and animals of a region, style and instrumentation of music, everyday people, their livelihood, their gods, and their leaders. Some examples of water elements found in *Tirukkovaiyar* are rivers, mountain springs, the ocean, and lakes. Among the occupations included in *Tirukkovaiyar* are bards, bull trainers, honey pickers, merchants, and artisans who make bangles from conch shells.

Themes of human behaviors and emotions or uri include union, separation, waiting, sulking, and lamenting. Initially, these lists are presented in an order that seems to privilege the place and time of the action, followed by the cultural and natural environment that will first speak to the love scenarios of the hero and heroine. However, this order of poetic elements corresponds with the sequence of creation in the opposite order of importance, and should be read like a countdown that culminates with uri as the most critical aspect of the poetry. Thus, the uri or themes of human behavior that are woven into the seaside or the peahen's nest are at the center of the poetry. These same characteristics and items through which a landscape region is portrayed also fluctuate across grammars and their commentaries, alerting us to literary variations both over time and between poets and scholars.[18]

In spite of the invariable diversity of compositions, these rules explicate the permissible and suitable elements of Tamil love poetry. These terms of poetic construction also provide us with the vocabulary for the reception and interpretation of love-themed poetry, such as *Tirukkovaiyar*. As we shift our attention to verses from *Tirukkovaiyar*, the terms outlined above give shape to creative expectations for the basic world into which Shiva is placed and praised. It is within this framework that the poet will build, reference, and respond to new poetic forms, narrative sequence, and images. These lovely, complex landscapes are also the sites for natural sensations and religious experiences to develop.

Narrative Sequence

The narrative sequence is another aspect of the *Tirukkovaiyar*'s structure that is present in the grammatical treatises. Situated between the sequential love scenarios initiated by *Iraiyanar Akapporul* and culminating with *Akapporul vilakkam*, the kovai is designed to tell the progression of a love drama within the parameters of the landscape system. One difference between the love poetry collected in early anthologies and *Tirukkovaiyar* is that, when read as a narrative, *Tirukkovaiyar* maintains the same hero and heroine throughout the course of its four hundred verses. This feature contrasts with the variation of lovers from one situation to another in earlier anthologies of love poetry. While the narrative aspect of *Tirukkovaiyar* is distinctive, a closer look at the sequence of events reveals moments of repetition and brevity suggestive of the poet's preference for specific love scenarios. The opening of *Tirukkovaiyar* is called natural union and begins with the hero's first sighting of the heroine. He is captured by her beauty, and their mutual attraction leads to their first embrace and sexual encounter. In the fourteen themes that follow, the hero plots with his friend and with the heroine's confidante to arrange more opportunities for the secret romance to develop. Meanwhile, the heroine shows physical signs of her own desire to reunite with her lover. The heroine is also repeatedly questioned, and occasionally badgered, by her considerably more vocal confidante about her state of mind. From the moment the heroine and the hero embrace, it is the heroine's desire and the confidante's duty to protect the heroine's modesty and chastity. The confidante's fear is that the hero will abscond with her "flower," that rumors will start, and that the heroine's family will find out about all of it. Ultimately, the cure for all of this impropriety and suffering is marriage, whether it is by elopement or by a proper marriage approved of by their families.

Although we do not have a clear view of the nuptial proceedings, the hero and heroine are indeed married and the nineteenth theme is praising the excellence of marriage and the home life of the couple. In the same way that the five stages of proper love in the grammatical treatises are dominated by the various sufferings of the heroine, so too we find that the happiness of the married heroine in *Tirukkovaiyar* is quite short-lived. The final six themes of the poem cover the six variations on the theme of separation. The six reasons why the hero separates from his wife in *Tirukkovaiyar* are to study, to join the king's security detail, to act against a rival king, to aid the king who is in imminent danger, to pursue wealth, and to rendezvous with public women. The vast majority of the final fifty verses are dedicated to tense negotiations between the heroine, hero, their child, and the hero's public women. *Tirukkovaiyar* does not end happily. Although the heroine married her one true love, in the end she is left with her child to agonize over the public impropriety of her husband. The rough structure of the four hundred verses might be summarized as follows: love at first sight, several secret meetings, arranging and conducting the marriage, the heroine's continuous suffering because her husband continuously leaves her for various reasons. Thus, this kovai speaks to both clandestine, premarital love and known, postmarital love as per the stipulations of the grammars mentioned above. If we consider the Shaiva Siddhanta overlay for the narrative in which the hero and heroine are the soul and Shiva respectively, Shiva delights in his devotees but ultimately suffers from the consequences of his pure, loyal love. It is a story of betrayal by the wandering soul and jealousy stirred by temptations that lure the soul away from receiving Shiva's grace.

The linear narrative of *Tirukkovaiyar* is interrupted in several places by repetitions and variants. For example, in theme four, the hero approaches the paddy field of the heroine and her friend and creates an occasion for conversation with his beloved by inquiring after various things. In verses 52 through 56, the hero inquires about an elephant, a stag, a stag again, the girls' hometown, the girls' names, and in verse 59, the girls' waists. The second example comes from theme twelve. This section opens with the hero offering the heroine a gift of leaves, as a token of his affection. Sadly for the hero, verses 91 through 104 rehearse fourteen ways that the heroine's confidante rejects the leafy gift. Finally, in theme thirteen, in sixteen consecutive verses the heroine's confidante urges marriage with threats issued at the hero (v. 130–145). In the case of all three of these examples, the repetition of themes suggests that they are variants of a popular theme, rather than sequential scenarios. In themes sixteen through eighteen both marriage with family approval and elopement are explored at length. Since the pursuit of one path makes the other obsolete, it is more likely that the various methods for establishing their union are again variations of a scenario rather than a true sequence of events. Finally, in the case of the six separations, taken literally and individually, the hero would have to leave the heroine ninety-three times to fulfill every verse!

Having noted some imbalances in thematic distribution, it is important to give credit to the large clusters of verses that do tell of events strung together in a compelling love story. There is certainly enough continuity to prevent us from entirely dismissing the idea of narrative in *Tirukkovaiyar*.

Table 2 *Tirukkovaiyar* love themes and verse distribution.

Verses per Theme	*Tirukkovaiyar* (Love Theme Sequence)
18	1. Natural union
30	2. Meeting through a friend
1	3. Chance meeting at the place
10	4. Uniting minds
2	5. Coming to understand his arrival when both came to the place
1	6. Coming to understand the earlier relationship
4	7. Coming to understand her distress
5	8. Investigating through a sense of shame
1	9. Investigating through fear
9	10. Palm horse ordeal
8	11. Investigating through bashfulness
26	12. Being at a distance
32	13. Tryst by day
33	14. Tryst at night
13	15. Leaving that place
56	16. Departing together
16	17. Urging marriage
33	18. Separation due to wealth for marriage
9	19. Telling the superiority of union
4	20. Separation due to study
2	21. Separation due to protection
2	22. Separation due to action to reduce enmity [between kings]
16	23. Separation due to a time of eminent danger of the king
20	24. Separation due to wealth
49	25. Separation due to public women

Table 2 lists the titles of the twenty-five themes and verse distribution. The table illustrates that the narrative of the love story, while sequential in the development of the lovers' interactions, is unevenly weighted to favor the themes of Meeting through a friend, Trysting by day and night, and Separation to seek wealth for marriage.[19] Overwhelming attention is paid to two additional themes that constitute more than a quarter of the entire poem. Departing together and the Separation of the hero to pursue public women both speak to the volatility of love. The first of these themes contains some of the most profound expressions of love between the hero and heroine as they face the challenges and dangers of eloping together. The second most developed theme is devoted to the lament of the heroine who witnesses her husband's pandering to the flirtations of younger, more beautiful women, resulting in a portrait of idealized feminine purity and fragility. These two streams of intense emotion, passion, and attraction can be characterized by the two forms of love that push and pull on the hero, heroine, and ultimately Shiva, over the course of the poem, the powerful forces of kamam and anpu. Overall, the most populated themes are driven by particular times of day for clandestine movements and the search for exceptional acquisition in either the idealized heroine, material wealth, or the temptation of other women.

Part One of this chapter surveyed the organizing principles of Tamil love poetry in terms of structures and technical vocabulary. The narrative of *Tirukkovaiyar* and the scenarios experienced by the hero and heroine are deeply rooted in the classical anthologies of love poetry and are also in dialogue with theoretical schemes proposed by grammatical treatises. The connection between the form and content of *Tirukkovaiyar* with the love-themed grammars and classical anthologies suggests a desire to align classical vocabulary with an early medieval Shaiva identity. The poet claims the historical literary past for the god Shiva by praising him in an akam context distinctive to the Tamil south and distinctive from other forms of devotional poetry composed by the poet's contemporaries. The five landscapes that the poet utilizes contain aesthetic boundaries and opportunities for experimentation, including both the emotional and especially the sensational experiences associated with each region. With this unique combination of devotional tribute and classical aesthetics, the poet produces an innovation in love poetry, propels a religious agenda expressing Shaiva devotion, and initiates a genre.

Part Two: Development of the Kovai Genre

Tirukkovaiyar played a foundational role in the development of the kovai genre as it is now known in a collection of genres called the minor literatures (cirrilakkiyam or pirapantam). Definitions of these minor genres are found in a type of grammar known as pattiyal, which functions like encyclopedias or indices of various genres of poetry, with the exact number of genres varying by author.

Composed in the tenth century, *Panniru pattiyal* is the earliest extant treatise on seventy-four of the minor genres.[20] The text includes three verses that specifically address the kovai genre.

> When describing that which is called kovai, it is said that it is composed of four hundred earlier kalitturai verses that adopt the subject matter of akam without altering the five landscapes through statements of that which is appropriately called clandestine love and known love. (341)
>
> Kovai is that which is without deviation and that which states four hundred of established kalitturai verses, having been perfected and without altering the state of landscapes through types of statements in clandestine love and known love. (342)
>
> All four hundred that yield kovai in the state of akam that embraces the five landscapes are indeed kalitturai. (343)
>
> *Panniru pattiyal*

This definition describes verses that are established (muntiya) and it emphasizes adoption of literary forms without deviation or alteration. This vocabulary of establishment and conformity suggests that in the tenth century there was a developed sense of how to successfully execute the five landscapes in love poems. In addition, we find the four hundred verses, specified meter, and the explicit attention to landscapes and love-themed behavior.

The second definition of kovai, taken from *Pirapanta tipam*, provides an expanded definition that reflects the characteristics of *Tirukkovaiyar* and utilizes technical language found in akam poetic treatises. *Pirapanta tipam* was composed in the late nineteenth century and describes ninety-seven minor literatures. Like the early *Panniru pattiyal*, this grammar states that four hundred kattalai kalitturai verses on love-themed subject matter are key elements of a kovai poem. In addition, this definition includes the components of akam subject matter that correspond with the divisions of love poetry listed in *Akapporul vilakkam*.

> When declaring the kovai with the subject matter of akam, one speaks about four hundred verses of kattalai kalitturai that illustrate the nature of clandestine love, known love, and attached love (varaivu)[21] all of which are components of akam songs consisting of two types of regional and temporal settings, fourteen environmental elements, and ten human behaviors.
> *Pirapanta tipam* 1

This verse from *Pirapanta tipam* states that the kovai is four hundred verses written in kattalai kalitturai format. Kattalai kalitturai verses have strict rhythmic and metrical rules for the most skilled poets.[22] I hesitate to call kattalai kalitturai a type of "meter" because, in English poetry, meter is based on the number of feet in a line. Kattalai kalitturai verses are restricted by lines; however, they also require multiple rhyme-stress patterns and end with a long final "ē" sound. The consequence of this format is perhaps best visualized in a printed edition of *Tirukkovaiyar* in which there appear to be four hundred "stanzas" with four lines each, rendering the printed *Tirukkovaiyar* 1600 lines.[23] In addition, there are two more elements that speak to the kovai's intrinsic relationship to and inheritance from classical love poetry. According to this grammar, the love themes are properly attained by using clandestine and known love scenarios within the established framework of the five landscapes.[24]

This brief study on the definition of a genre intersects with the discourse of material religion in several ways. First these definitions affirm the required union between human emotion and natural landscapes. Second, the language of establishment and details regarding characteristic elements of the poetry illustrate the expectations that a poet, audience, and patron might hold for a successful or favorable kovai. Third, the stipulated meter of the verse makes a significant contribution to the aesthetics of the whole composition. Word choice must conform to sound and measure as well as meaning. The required number of verses further dictates individual line length, the time required to recite or perform the text, and the number of palm leaves required to copy and preserve it.

The remaining portion of this chapter will test the relationship between grammatical rules for verses one and two in the kovai genre against several poetic compositions. Following *Tirukkovaiyar*, numerous kovais were composed to honor a variety of subjects. For example, *Tiruvarurkovai* is a kovai poem dedicated to Shiva in his form as Lord of the anthill in the town of Arurar. *Anantarankan kovai* praises an eighteenth-century political figure Ananta Rankan, a dubash to the French East India Company and who conducted most of his career in Pondicherry, South India.[25] Regardless of whether the poem is dedicated to a human or divine patron, Manikkavacakar is typically praised in the introductions to these poems for producing *Tirukkovaiyar*, and his text is referenced as the model for all kovai poems. Through the generative trajectory inspired by *Tirukkovaiyar* the role of the patron-hero developed to include a king, Shaiva and Vaishnava deities, political figures (*Anantarankan kovai*), philanthropists (*Shamcuttacin kovai*), military leaders (*Uttantan kovai*), the sacred city Mecca, and the Prophet Muhammad (*Tiru Makkakkovai*).[26]

The following passages focus on the first two verses of *Tirukkovaiyar* and all subsequent kovais and their marriage to a set of grammatical texts that aim to define them. More specifically, we continue to test the relationship between specific kovai verses and love-themed grammatical treatises and demonstrate the poet's aesthetic attachment and adoption of the inherited landscapes. The two verses under investigation are the initial two verses of *Tirukkovaiyar* known as sighting and doubt and examples of these same tropes in kovais that follow. The two grammars in question are *Maranakapporul* and *Akapporul vilakkam*.[27] Both of these grammars enumerate the human behaviors of proper love poetry and use examples taken from kovai poems to illustrate and complement their proposed theories. The format in which these texts are currently transmitted, alternating between poetic rules, kovai verses, and commentary, is indicative of how these seemingly separate three works have been combined so as to yield the effect of one text rather than three. I do not mean to suggest that every kovai poem has an explicit grammatical treatise as its partner or that there is a "lost treatise" that was the companion to *Tirukkovaiyar*. It is not necessary to identify a customized grammar to apply to *Tirukkovaiyar*, but rather when viewed in the context of *Maranakapporul* and *Akapporul vilakkam* below, the religious poetry's close relationship with so-called nonreligious classical poetics is clear enough. We also gain insight into the organizing principles of the poetry: the opening verses name both the expanse and limits of the realm in which the patron-hero will be praised.

We begin with the first two verses of *Tirukkovaiyar*, followed by these same initial scenarios found in kovai examples embedded in *Maranakapporul* and *Akapporul vilakkam*. There are several advantages to surveying the first two verses of *Tirukkovaiyar* and the other kovais below. Known in all kovais as sighting and doubt or katci and aiyam, these two verses set the stage for the entire love story to unfold and provide the audience with its first glimpse of ideal love. Since they are at the front of all kovais, they receive much of the poets' attention and tend to be more consciously stylized; the poets give these opening moments as much finesse as possible. In the first verses, extra effort is made to create an auspicious beginning, to establish the skill of the poet, and to identify the territory (literary, religious, political, or otherwise) over which the poet and patron lay claim. As the genre develops over the course of its thousand-year life, love scenarios and organizing themes change, but the first few verses remain a consistent focal point for kovai poems. The first sighting established the standard for opening and subsequent kovai poems.

1
Sighting
Admired lotus, famed blue nelumbo, grandly blossoming kumil of the lord's Chidambaram
konku flowers and fresh red glory lily
a garland of these flowers with expanding divine fragrance
  slender like a creeper
  with the gait of the goose
shines like beautiful Kama's victory banner.

The first verse of *Tirukkovaiyar* is the opening scene of the first chapter titled "Natural union." In this stage of love, the reader witnesses the hero finding love at first sight and the union that follows between the perfect pair, hero and heroine. In the first verse, the beauty of the heroine catches the eye of the hero. The lovers' physical beauty is described largely in terms of natural imagery rather than explicit accounts of their physical bodies. Upon discovering the heroine, the hero's actual description is of the most beautiful, swaying garland featuring five flowers. The garland has several qualities familiar to a variety of South Asian literatures that praise the body and movement of women. This garland is slender like a vine, sways its hips when it walks, radiates like the god of love Kama, and smells heavenly.[28]

The most important feature of this verse and the poet's resounding allegiance to the poetic landscapes is the composition of the garland; lotus, blue nelumbo, kumil, konku, and red glory lily flowers. Each of these fives flowers grows in one of the five regional and emotional landscapes developed in the love-themed grammars. Accordingly, lotus indicates sulking in the agricultural land, blue nelumbo indicates pining by the seashore, kumil indicates waiting in the forest, konku indicates separation in the desert, and red glory lily flowers indicate union in the mountains.

By enumerating all five of the flowers in the form of a woven garland in the first verse, the poet immediately acknowledged the poetic context and the vocabulary of the work to follow, namely the love-themed landscapes that

Figure 7 Bees in flower garlands, Thiruvannamalai.

overlay places and emotions with flora, natural material, and other sensory cues. In addition to the literary territory claimed here, the poet also effectively draws a boundary around where the drama will unfold: within the stylized natural topographical environment of Tamil country. The inseparability of the hero's description of the garland and the woman's body and the garland's composition of landscape elements also illustrates the poet's synthesis of human, natural, and literary beauty. Since the landscapes collectively make up the female body, the body of the beloved and the physical landscapes become interconnected vocabularies for polyvalent poetic expression. Finally, the kovai opens with a picture full of inviting, pleasant sensory cues (Figure 7). Freshly blossoming, fragrant flowers of varying color, feelings of grandeur and admiration, and the swaying motion of the tender vine, the gentle goose's gait, and the unfurling flag all contribute to a feeling of easy welcoming pleasure; the poem opens with a sense of invitation.

Returning to the text for the second verse of *Tirukkovaiyar* titled "Doubt," we find a variation in the pairing of the heroine's body and South Indian geography. After the hero is struck by the beauty of the heroine in the first verse, he doubts the origins of this seemingly supernatural garland—seeking her homeland with some concern.

2
Doubt
A flower bud? Or the heavens? Or the waters? Or the world of snakes?
Which is it?
In every way, it is difficult to know which is home to her who stands here.
A messenger sent by Yama? A companion to the bodiless one?
A woman from ancient Chidambaram of the unmatched lord?
Or a gentle peacock?

Through the process of guessing the origin of the heroine, the hero enumerates a new set of wondrous landscapes. This line of questions also draws conceptual and narrative boundaries around *Tirukkovaiyar* and the proceeding religious encounter. Since the hero doubts its origin as well as the divinity of the garland, he proposes the major dwelling places of the Hindu pantheon. The effect of his investigation is an overlay of Shiva's mythological geography over the poetry's love-themed landscape. The world of Hindu goddesses and gods intersects with the human love story. He begins with homes of Lakshmi; Indra; Tirumal, which is another name for Vishnu; and the Nagas in the first line. Lakshmi, the goddess of beauty, dwells in the lotus bud. Indra is the king of heaven. Tirumal is depicted as sleeping on the ocean and is Shiva's rival. The Nagas are powerful snakes that live in an underworld known as Nagaloka. Subsequently, the hero suspects that the heroine is an agent of two equally troublesome figures, Yama the god of death and Kama the god of love, who was without limbs after Shiva burned him to ash with his third eye. The final location suggested by the hero has its foot in two worlds spanning two maps. The ancient city of Tillai, modern-day Chidambaram, is possessed by unmatched Shiva, the patron-hero of *Tirukkovaiyar*. From the perspective of the divine landscape, Chidambaram is elevated to the residence of Shiva, equal or parallel to the better-known residence of Shiva atop Mount Kailash. There is also a second transformation with a telescoping effect that began in the first verse; unmatched Shiva has left his mountaintop abode to take up residence in Chidambaram. The transformation of the sites through proximity to the deity was mutually effective in the human and divine spheres: Chidambaram was elevated to the status of divine residence and Shiva descended to human-inhabited Chidambaram. The significance of these transformative interactions will be taken up in later chapters. For now, it suffices to say that the opening verses establish the integrations of human and divine landscapes, and these sites are where the love story will unfold. We turn now to the theoretical treatment of sighting and doubt to test the content of *Tirukkovaiyar* and similar poems against conceptual frameworks of sighting and doubt.

Sighting

The first example of a kovai embedded in a grammatical treatise is an excerpt from *Akapporul vilakkam*, introduced above. The format of the selection here begins with a rule for literary production. Each rule is followed by an example taken from an actual literary composition. In *Akapporul vilakkam*, the embedded examples are taken from the poem *Tancaivanankovai*, a significant piece of literature in its own right. *Tancaivanankovai* was composed by Poyyamolippulavar in the late thirteenth century. The date has been assigned according to the identity of the patron-hero, Vanan of Tancai,[29] who is identified as Pandya king Maravarman Kulacekara I (1268–1308/9).[30] The first verse presented here is Nampi's definition of sighting.[31]

> The virgin and the bull with a stained spear will see each other, who are generally similar and who depart from equality in the case of union, among the two divisions which are union and separation. They say that even if the one who is lord is superior there is no deficiency.
> *Akapporul vilakkam* 119

In this rule, Nampi explains that the heroine-virgin and hero-bull see each other and when they do, they recognize similar qualities in each other; however, in the poetic situation known as union, occasionally the heroine and hero will not be equal. In the case of inequality, the match is still appropriate if it is the hero who is superior to his partner.

If this rule is applied to the sighting verse in *Tirukkovaiyar*, it is difficult to know whether the heroine and hero were equal in stature since we only have a description of the heroine as the famous five-flower garland. We are led to conclude that with a heroine so beautiful, the hero must match or surpass her with his handsomeness. This is a significant characterization of the hero and heroine because it matches prescriptions and expectations for the skill and the stature of the protagonists in classical love poetry, which we will see in more detail in the next example. The beauty of the lady combined with the expectation of an equal or superior hero serves as a cue to a learned audience that they can expect an entire composition that tells the story of an exceptional couple engaged in ideal love in a remarkably lush environment.

The customized exemplar for this rule provides information about how Nampi prescribed its application to a kovai poem.

Sighting
In the mountains of Tancaivanan
surrounded by wide tanks, red paddy farms, and white swans,
a creeper of fine gold stood next to the Karpakam tree
  blossoming with a lotus
  joined with carp and warring bows
  wearing a crescent moon and carrying a cloud.
Tancaivanankovai 1

In *Tancaivanankovai*, verse 1, the heroine is a creeper keeping with the swaying botanical image of the *Tirukkovaiyar*'s garland; however, the rest of her feminine attributes take up more conventional imagery. Her face is a blossoming lotus with eyes shaped like carp, eyebrows like bows, a bright crescent-shaped forehead, and thick hair as dark as a rain cloud. There are two additional elements to this verse that set the stage for Poyyamolippulavar's kovai. First, the sighting takes place in a mountain, which corresponds with kurinji landscape and sexual union. By making this mountain within Tancaivanan's rule, the patron-hero has been properly mentioned, complimented, and effectively elected to oversee the drama as it unfolds. Second, the Karpakam tree is a wish-fulfilling tree and the creeper's place next to it borrows from a common relational motif in which the hero is the strong, solid tree that supports the wavering and dependent lady-vine. Another example of this motif in a devotional context is found in *Tiruvacakam*, Hymn 6, verse 20, in which the poet laments that without his god he is left hanging "like a creeper without a branch." This Karpakam tree is indeed a perfect illustration for Nampi's grammar because the beauty of this golden creeper is second *only* to the most valuable tree in heaven that can fulfill every heart's desire. Thus, the heroine, if not the couple, is easily mistaken for divinity. Before shifting our attention to the doubting verses, it is worth noting additional sighting verses that replicate more explicitly the *Tirukkovaiyar*'s heroine composed of blossoms plucked from the love landscapes. The first verse presented below is taken from *Tiruvavatuturaikkovai*. The second example is taken from *Ciramalaikkovai*.

One beautiful flowery creeper
  with divine blossoms full of lotus of superior gold, blue nelumbo,
  jasmine in rows that are difficult to pass through, konku flowers, and
                soft red glory lilies,

appeared in the mountain of superior golden Tiyakar
    from the cool banks near wealthy Vavatu.
Tiruvavatuturaikkovai 1

One creeper
    united with the beautiful red glory lily, konku flowers,
    thick kumil, jasmine, blue nelumbo, and beautiful lotus,
appeared to my eyes there in the fresh grove on the slope of Ciramalai
    where lives the one with matted locks full of konrai flowers
        mingled with red cevvanti flowers.
Ciramalaikkovai 1

The creeper of *Tiruvavatuturaikkovai* and its god Tiyakar are embellished with fine gold and reside in a mountain-scape. The blossoming flowers are five in number but vary slightly from the *Tirukkovaiyar*'s bouquet. Long before this kovai was written, the fame of the site Ciramalai was established in the great Tamil epic *Cilappatikaram* when Kannaki sojourned there on her way to Madurai. Like the abstracted kurinji mountain, Ciramalai, also known as the Kailash of the south, is a cool, lush hilly area that is ideal for the opening of a love scene.[32] The poet of *Ciramalaikkovai* added konrai and red flowers and wove them into Shiva's familiar matted locks. These iconic Shaiva flowers signal, yet again, the realm of the gods in a motif naturalized by the classical love landscapes. With such an intense, stylized, and perfected first impression of the heroine, the hero's subsequent feeling of doubt is reasonable.

Doubt

Doubt occurs when the place and the appearance of the shape of the one with the look of a modest deer are excellent.
Akapporul vilakkam 120

In Nampi's rule for doubt, we find the point that is justified by the first verse: the hero's doubt is caused neither by the seductive mountain setting nor by the beautifully composed heroine. Rather, he is struck by the *combination of the two*. The modest heroine exists in a place that surpasses any other. This feeling of a transcendent context found in *Akapporul vilakkam* comes from the word "cirantu" which I have translated here as "excellent". Synonyms found in the *Tamil Lexicon* (TL) include eminent, illustrious, and surpassing. The result is that the poet must suggest a superior or supernatural homeland for the heroine in the example that accompanies the rule. Here we find a nonreligious text, a grammatical treatise, rather than a devotional tribute to a deity, nonetheless mandating that the poet create a world and a woman out of words that, when combined, surpass all expectations. This woman and world are to be so excellent that the audience is drawn into the experience created by the poet and even caused to doubt their human or natural origins—a scenario in which cognitive recognition and sensuous perception intermingle.

According to David Morgan's account of material religion, the sensuous experience elicited by the combination of heroine and place relies on an integrated process that includes senses, memory, and emotions that people have in relation to the physical world.[33] People's embodied expectations and structures of social life are all evidence of "the material conditions under which they seek certain ends," namely, a sense of "self, community, and cosmos."[34]

The language of affect studies further explains the atmosphere that surrounds and creates the experience of a perfect union within the structure of akam poetry. Sara Ahmed, like scholars of material religion, has provided productive ways of valuing the role of objects and emotions in their dynamism and fluidity. In the following passage, she explains how people's feelings are predisposed, change, respond to, and influence the objects around them.

> To experience an object as being affective or sensational is to be directed not only toward an object, but to "whatever" is around that object, which includes what is behind the object, the conditions of its arrival. What is around an object can become happy: for instance, if you receive something delightful in a certain place, then the place itself is invested with happiness, as being "what" good feeling is directed toward.[35]

This approach to affect and aesthetics more broadly enables us to account for literary and emotional influences and transference that are partial and dynamic. The rule for doubt counts on the mingling of sensations elicited by a beautiful environment and the awestruck feeling of love at first sight. The viewer is overcome with hyper-excellence that eventually leads him to question his experience of the heroine's appearance. For classical love poetry, meeting with the heroine is made delightful and even surreal because she is found in a certain place. This is the mingling context or condition of the lovers in which the poet of *Tirukkovaiyar* introduces his vision of Shiva. The directionality of religious sensations oscillates and flows between the land, the lovers, and the

Figure 8 Goddess Uma at Ekamparanatar temple, Kanchipuram.

deity, each of which contributes associations and influences to the overall effect of the verse.

Doubt
Oh heart! Is she who stood here alone the force of the earth?
Is she the force in the lotus who was born from the ocean of sacred milk?
Is she the force who resides in the mountains?
Is she the force of the Vaigai water near south Marai of Tancaivanam
who gives crores[36] of elephants to the renowned poets?
Tancaivanankovai 2

This doubt verse selected by Nampi to illustrate his rule emphasizes the extent to which the heroine is associated with or is a supernatural being in two ways. First, compared to previous doubt samples, the list of places explicitly corresponds with goddesses, rather than the usual mix of masculine rivals. Earth is the place of the earth goddess Bhumi. The lotus is the place of Lakshmi, the goddess of wealth who was born from the milky ocean. Shiva's consort, Uma, is a goddess from the Himalayas (Figure 8). Finally, the Vaigai River is a form of the goddess Ganges that was asked by Shiva to flow into the south.

The second clue to the heroine's potential divinity is the poet's use of the word "ananku," translated above as force. Contemporary Tamil scholars have debated the meaning of this word because its semantic range is vast: it can mean a variety of things including anxiety, destruction, and goddess.[37] Ananku does not have to describe a major god like Shiva or Vishnu—it can also refer to a localized deity tied to earth that might haunt a village or possess a priest. In this particular verse, the poet has used ananku as a nonhuman liminal force to emphasize the hero's doubt about her identity. The overall impression made by the example of doubt is one of union between the superior heroine's beauty and her regional identity.

Maranakapporul, the sixteenth-century grammatical treatise about Tamil love poetry, also uses a full-length kovai to illustrate its literary rules. This composite work is an especially interesting case study for our inquiry into the relationship between kovais and grammatical works because both the kovai and the treatise were composed by the same author. Tirukkurukaipperumal Kavirayar was a scholar and poet from Tirunelveli district.[38] His kovai, *Tiruppatikkovai*, exceeds the length of *Tirukkovaiyar* at 527 verses and praises Tiruppati as its patron-hero. *Tiruppatikkovai* is the first complete extant Vaishnava kovai; however, it is clear from quotations from Jain works *Tirukkural* and *Civakacintamani*, as well as references to lord Murukan[39] that Tirukkurukaipperumal Kavirayar's grasp of Tamil literature reached far beyond the bounds of sectarian lines. The poet also extended the thematic conventions of *Tirukkovaiyar*, adding the wedding theme known as varaiviyal.[40] We turn now to the rule for sighting found in *Maranakapporul*.

> The natural vision, which is seen by the command of the first, most ancient one and which is continuing with the nature of being practiced in this life and in the next as lord and lady,[41] is one in clan, character, wealth, form, and ideology, having become those with status and who are called one of a different region. Impropriety is not there if the hero is superior.
> *Maranakapporul* 135

The basic meaning of this rule is similar to the rule presented in *Akapporul vilakkam* 119. When the hero and heroine, or lord and lady, see each other, they will recognize their similarity in character. If the hero is slightly superior to the heroine, they will still make a suitable pair. This rule has provided a more specific list of shared attributes between the lovers, namely clan, character, wealth, physical stature, way of thinking, social status, and region. In addition, it addresses the enduring nature "in this life and the next" of the ideal love witnessed in this love-themed convention. Furthermore, the union of the perfectly matched couple is overseen by the primordial authority of the alpha god. Contrary to the portrayal of classical love poetry as "secular," it is significant that Tirukkurukaipperumal Kavirayar identifies the union of human lovers as initiated and monitored by the divine creator, a reality not far from the love story of *Tirukkovaiyar*, which is overseen by the god Shiva. We turn now to the rule that elicited two examples for doubting.

> Those with knowledge will say that doubting is upon the shining lord
> among the two who have arrived.
> *Maranakapporul* 136

Compared to the rule for sighting, little guidance is given to the hero and heroine in the doubt situation. Tirukkurukaipperumal Kavirayar simply states that out of the two lovers, it is the hero who will feel doubt.[42] Curiously, this terse ruling is illustrated with the following two examples from *Tiruppatikkovai* in which the heroine appears briefly as a creeper and a bangle.

> *Doubt* (a)
> Is it the place of the flag of Vanavarampan
> who is loved by Arankecan
> who is unreachable to lowly people?
> Is it the place of the flag of he who has the boundary of the Pukar region
> which possesses the Kaveri River?
> Or is it the place of the beautiful golden flag of the Pandyas
> from Korkai in Tamil country?
> Which is the place where the creeper dwells?
> *Tiruppatikkovai* 2

> *Doubt* (b)
> Having taken the clan of the boon-giver
> who is Vishnu, or Brahma, or Indra, or Shiva,
> what is the dwelling place of the fresh bangle who has unfailing chastity

from the great mountain of pure gold of the lord of Kurukai
who became the supreme teacher,
who made an exposition,
who has complete understanding without having studied the four
enduring Vedas?

Tiruppatikkovai 3

The line of questioning in these two doubt verses is the design for two sets of boundaries in two different realms. The first doubt verse lists the places of flags belonging to the three major dynasties of early and medieval Tamil country. Vanavarampan is the title of a Chera king. Pukar was the Chola capital. Korkai is the name of an ancient port town that was the capital city of the Pandya dynasty. These boundaries are based on a political geography of major Tamil dynasties. The second verse asks to which clan the bangle-wearing heroine belongs. The clans listed, however, are not linked to dynastic families or to regional communities identified by specific professions. The clans are headed by the gods Vishnu (father of Ayanar), Brahma, Indra, and Shiva. The poet says that the heroine is from the gold mountain of the lord of Kurukai. This is a particularly meaningful reference for the Vaishnava community because Kurukai is the home of the great bhakti saint Nammalvar. Nammalvar composed a major portion of the Vaishnava canon and is known as a great teacher ranked among other great Vaishnava scholars such as Ramanuja and Yamunacarya.[43] While these two verses feature the kings' and gods' realms, Kurukai, the home of Nammalvar, is a significant site for Vaishnava devotees like Chidambaram or Sirkali is for Shaivites. In addition, we see a consistent characterization of the heroine's chastity and youth indicated by her fresh green ivy-like body, which corresponds with the movement of the unfurling dynastic flags and the flourishing power that expands with each claimed territory. Whether affiliated with kings or clans, the origin of the heroine is unknown but suspected to be of high rank. Although her appearance or character is not described at any length, the audience is assured that her social status is one of excellence—which it must absolutely be in order to stir doubt in the hero's mind. Here the sensational experience of doubt is influenced by the mingling of a woman's form, movement of flags, and marked territory.

Overall, the excerpts from *Akapporul vilakkam* and *Maranakapporul* are instructive in several ways. First, they illustrate the intimate correspondence between sequential grammatical treatises and the practice of poetic composition, in the forms of ordered thematic chapters to the specific flowers tied into the heroine's garland. Second, while in the case of *Akapporul vilakkam* (and *Iraiyanar akapporul*) the patron-hero of the composition was a king, *Maranakapporul* praised a divine patron-hero. This treatise-cum-kovai illustrates that the devotional Vaishnava kovai finds a compatible literary pair in the grammatical treatise. In fact, according to its characterization in *Maranakapporul* 135, the idealized human love theorized in this grammar was indeed created by god himself. Between these texts, some explicitly religious aimed at praising a god and others understood to be scholarly or didactic works but composed by gods, we find clear, open networks across genres and texts, even those attributed to Jains or different sects of Hinduism. This evidence of fluidity and collaboration within the Tamil literary corpus disrupts contemporary expectations for a "religious text" or hard-and-fast sectarian identities of the texts or their authors. The compatibility between kovai and grammar is parallel to the structural harmony between Shaiva *Tirukkovaiyar* and akam treatises, as well as the successful interplay between human love and divine mythological narratives that we will witness in each verse of the kovai poem. Finally, we see that there is diversity in terms of how the patron, hero, heroine, and various landscapes are described, located, and made to interact with one another. The diversity of expression and creative repurposing of classical motifs are strategies used by the poet to praise a form of Shiva that corresponds with and is local to the unique landscape designed for *Tirukkovaiyar*.

Conclusion

The kovai genre and *Tirukkovaiyar* in particular exist and interact within a kaleidoscope of influences. This chapter emphasized the life of the poem *as a model* in relation to the commentary of grammatical treatises. By highlighting the structural and organizing principles of *Tirukkovaiyar*, we gain a better understanding of where the poet placed emphasis, pulled back, or innovated a new poetic form for the specific task of praising Shiva. The comparative portion of this chapter yields a both-and perspective of the religious identity of the poetry's audience. On the one hand, there are clear cases of fluidity between religions captured in kovai poems. The diversity of suitable kovai patrons, human, divine, Shaiva, and so on, and intertextual references within the poetry demonstrate that literati composed in conversation with texts across what we now perceive as religious boarders. On the other hand, by adapting and adopting the classical structures and styles of early love poetry, the poet intentionally wove *Tirukkovaiyar* into Tamil literary history. *Tirukkovaiyar* can be read as an explicit claim for Shiva and Shaivites over the shared literary territory of classical love poetry.

Over the course of *Tirukkovaiyar*, alias *Tiruccirrampalakkovai*, Shiva lays claim to the akam realm *as well as* to the city of Chidambaram. By dedicating a kovai to a city such as Kurukai or Tiruvavatuturai the poem draws from both the legacy of early classical poets and the fame and history of the celebrated city. By naming a famous place as well as the beloved patron, the poet encourages the mingling of influences and sensations and potentially doubles the cultural capital of the composition. Like the poets of the later kovai poems dedicated to South Indian temple towns, *Tirukkovaiyar* also accomplished this productive fusion of three significant threads for South Indian Shaivism: classical love poetics, the god Shiva, and the site of his sacred dance in Chidambaram.

While we acknowledge the potential cultural prestige associated with composing in the vocabulary of the classical style, what is the religious purpose or even advantage of praising Shiva from within the akam realm? We know that *Tirukkovaiyar* is saturated with classical love-themed elements but we do not have a surviving explanation by its author of why his panegyric took this particular form. There is not a single answer to this question. I conclude with a review of several elements gained by the poet's enthusiastic adoption of classical forms.

The primary anchor of the akam world is the set of five landscapes and the temporal, environmental, and behavioral cues through which the emotional landscapes are expressed. By adhering to these aesthetic forms, the poet inherits drums, trees, early mornings, bodies, birds, and beasts. The very nature of the akam world relies on categories and varieties of things. If we return to the premise that religion is propelled by human activity and engagement with the material world, then the poet will *need* smells, colors, rattles, jingles, thunder, and the things that possess or produce these effects to communicate a religious message—and even more, to cultivate a religious experience in his audience. The selection of the landscape-specific emotions for the emotions of religious devotion is a significant one. In the context of *Tirukkovaiyar*, the landscapes offer a double effect because, in addition to the sensory delight of the akam "things," each object, timeframe, craftsperson, or region is also part of a register of symbols that indicate intense, idealized, human emotions felt between lovers. The poet of *Tirukkovaiyar* cultivated an association between the deep and determined emotions of the lovers with the feelings of the devotee seeking Shiva's grace, a point that will be illustrated in a number of excerpted verses over the next chapters.

These deep roots and accumulated creatures and realms are adapted for a devotional agenda but the verses for Shiva simultaneously gesture back through organizational strategies of love-themed poetics. These inherited tropes and structures are the methods by which love for Shiva is displayed. The saturated environments largely designed to overwhelm the audience with beauty and opulence remain legible because they are anchored by the framework of the love-themed anthologies. Over time, this design of *Tirukkovaiyar* became a template for new kovais to repeat and riff on to praise new figures and sites. These patterns, rich with emotion, are the akam legacy and help to identify feelings and attitudes that are vitally important for understanding the ways in which the divine landscapes are integrated with the human. Through *Tirukkovaiyar*, the poet established a place for Shiva in classical literary history and created a style of devotional expression that is a fusion of the deity, poetics, and southern landscapes, which, borrowing from *Akapporul vilakkam*, draw from "the way of the world and the poet's imagination."[44] Moving forward, when akam themes and structures are invoked in this study I refer not to classical, so-called secular, early Tamil anthologies of love poetry, but rather to trajectories of literature, networks, and varieties of things, inhabitants, sensorial responses, powerful emotions—an entire flourishing realm into which the medieval poet placed everything from a single buzzing bee to the soaring Mount Kailash. With this knowledge in detailed terms of what makes a love poem, a scene that portrays lovers' union, or an ideal if not surreal heroine, we can incorporate and appreciate the literary structure of *Tirukkovaiyar* as part of the material context. Such interactions and encounters are both foundational for and invitations to join the poet's sacred garland of verses assembled for Shiva.

In the next chapter, we plunge deep into the waters of *Tirukkovaiyar*. The more steeped we become in the landscapes and as we witness praise for Shiva being woven into this world of human lovers, the more a religion of sensations emerges, one that is free to move about a beautiful, natural, sacred domain.

2

Locality and Movement

Transformation, frenzy, rejection, abundance, travel, and turmoil—these are the stuff of Tamil religion in the early medieval poem *Tirukkovaiyar*. This chapter explores intersections between locality, sensation, and devotional experience that are expressed in the narrative of the poem. This is accomplished by analyzing shared encounters between the god and the human lovers in twenty-one historical South Indian temple towns, each treated as elements of the sense of religion. The *Tirukkovaiyar* verses are presented in sequential order, clustered by Tamil literary themes established in classical love poetry and found in contemporary editions of *Tirukkovaiyar* as assigned by earlier commentaries. The verses in this chapter are all of the scenes that name the twenty-one historical towns in ninth-century Tamil country. These towns are variously used to indicate Shiva's territory, his homes, and sites of the lovers' activities. As the narrative of the four hundred verses unfolds in individual scenes, the reader will be led deeper into the complexities of the love story and will also experience the constant and compounding deluge of praise heaped upon the deity Shiva. The poet transports us through the cosmos, landscapes, sensations, and across emotional spectrums, and although presented in linear order, intertextual and intratextual references radiate from each verse.

Drawing from the works of two scholars of religious literature, one corpus Buddhist, the other Vaishnava, I will present a tour of Shiva's homes that treat *Tirukkovaiyar* as a guide or vehicle for sensory experience. In Jinah Kim's analysis of eleventh- and twelfth-century Buddhist manuscripts, she shows that the practitioner is led to recognize simultaneous three-dimensional space that connects the text, the manuscript, and the iconographic program, and that understanding will result in an emergent "mental picture" of iconographic structure.[1] In the Buddhist context, these textual iconographic programs are made comparable to actual sites and stupa structures, transforming the practitioner's experience from a physical journey into a "mental journey" or "imagined pilgrimage."[2] In *Tirukkovaiyar*, we can also understand the specific places named as cues for forming "mental pictures" of Shiva's homes in the south. Kim argues that through the illustrated text, "a Buddhist practitioner could roam freely beyond the spatial boundaries and physical limits and absorb all the cultic power that these sites embodied."[3] This model suggests that religious texts that emphasize space and movement, such as we will see in the *Tirukkovaiyar* verses, create an opportunity for the devotee to travel throughout the poetic world. Little to no evidence survives of how manuscripts of *Tirukkovaiyar* were treated or utilized in the medieval period; however, the place names do provide local anchors that the devotee might recognize.

Furthermore, the named towns collectively embody a map through which the devotee could roam and savor. Much like the "mental journeys" inspired by Kim's Buddhist manuscripts, sixteenth-century South Indian poet Appayya Dikshita guided his audiences to and through a visual experience. His poetry employs a telescoping effect beginning with a view of the city, then gradually focusing on the temple, into the temple interior. Finally, the verses scan from feet to crown up the body of the deity in the central shrine in an "extended meditation" on the image of Vishnu.[4] Appayya Dikshita's description of Vishnu's limbs and ornaments was then outfitted with pedagogical commentary on verbal ornaments.[5] According to Yigal Bronner, "the speaker repeatedly reports to Varadaraja, his addressee, the wonderful experience of his visual tour, and constantly interprets and amplifies his impressions through a series of tropes and fancies (utprekṣās) typical of Sanskrit poetry."[6] The text is a journey of guided visualization and a cultivated experience of ornamentation and appreciation. Kim and Bronner demonstrate that verses and text can be harbingers of travel. On the one hand such a literary map encourages its audience to participate in a mental journey. In addition or alternatively, a devotee might undertake an embodied journey if the map is local to its audience, a point we will return to in Chapter 3. The notions that texts can move, instigate movement, ornament, and inspire ornamentation all resonate deeply with the composition of *Tirukkovaiyar* and help to blur the distinction between textual and material experience.

In addition to plotting the *Tirukkovaiyar* map, I will analyze clusters of the narrative to show how the poet designed and executed an aesthetic program devoted to natural and divine beauty. My interpretations of the Tamil verses incorporate commentary that accompanies most printed editions of the *Tirukkovaiyar* available today. I do not seek to uncover a single original text, the intent of the attributed author, or a direct line to the ninth century (if indeed that is the date of composition). Instead, I embrace the form, cumulative context, and contact point through which I access these verses in the twenty-first century. Thus, although presented individually, each verse must be conceived of in concert with one another and each offering radiating trajectories of harmonies and influence. It is often the case that special moments steal the spotlight only when placed in stark contrast to situations of calm or frenzy, in the darkest depths of earth or the highest heavens. This chapter, like *Tirukkovaiyar*, highlights the physical sensations, sounds, and smells of movement through arduous journeys and crashing waves. With each city and each experience, between lovers or devotees, the poetry accumulates stories, histories, and fame for the composition—a gift to Shiva.

Tirukkovaiyar names twenty-one towns to mark the bounds of the human love story and to construct a vast playground or kingdom for Shiva. Aside from Chidambaram (alias Tillai or Puliyur), which figures in the majority of verses, most sites are mentioned only once. The sites that do warrant multiple verses are noticeably all located south of Chidambaram and in fact seem to radiate from the Pandya stronghold, Madurai. Beginning with territorial boundaries woven into a flower garland in verse 1, and over the course of building these characteristically southern landscapes, the realms of humanity and divinity frequently intersect. An example of this phenomenon is available early on in the *Tirukkovaiyar* and is also the first verse containing one of the unique sites, Tiruppalanam. Our journey begins.

4
Affection
These are spreading loins. Those are breasts.
My heart, why talk such nonsense?
She has a waist!
She who has many bangles is like Tiruppalanam
  of the one who destroyed strong enemies' cities taking the mountain as his bow
  the lord of Chidambaram
  our lord
  the one who smashed his rival Pakal's jagged teeth.

In many types of poetry, comparing a beautiful woman to a city is a common trope.[7] In Tamil poetry, cities are centers of commerce, arts, and scholarship. They are full of mansions, protected by fortified walls, and sparkle with gold. These cities are also fought over by, and are home to, powerful kings and gods. When a woman is compared to a city it emphasizes that she flourishes, wants for nothing, and has never been taken by a foreign king. In this verse, the site is embellished with an additional divine layer. The heroine is like the land in which Shiva appears. Subsequently, the most frequent strategy for incorporating specific sites into a verse in Tirukkovaiyar relies on the relationship between woman and place. More literally, the poet makes comment on "the heroine who resembles (site)" to both connect and transition between the love story and a significant locality. Eight of the unique sites are incorporated using this formula. Here the heroine is like Tiruppalanam.

The relationship between the heroine and a town creates a conceptual bridge between the activity of the lovers and the presence of Shiva. Shiva does not enter the love narrative by symbolically standing in for the human hero. Rather, Shiva is more frequently and effectively included by using parallel imagery taken from his mythology and cosmology that runs alongside the distinctive love story and corresponding landscapes. The parallelism achieved in well-balanced verses relies on the individual strength of both the lovers' and the god's tales.

In this verse, the hero points out to his heart there are her breasts and there are her swelling, aroused genitals. His description of visible anatomy implies that her waist is nearly invisible because of her body's perfect, exaggerated hourglass shape. The perfected sensuality of the heroine is balanced by the second half of the verse, which is dedicated to the names of Shiva. He destroyed cities, defeated the sun god Pakal, holds a bow as his weapon, and has claim on Chidambaram and on his devotees. Here, Shiva has the qualities of a victorious king or warrior. Shiva's heroism is praised in a naming exercise that resembles that of the names sung in a stotra, a type of Sanskrit praise hymn referenced in Bronner's work. Similar to the distribution of praise and perfection, the two sites named in this verse, Chidambaram and Tiruppalanam, are split between Shiva and the heroine; both sites are possessed by Shiva but only Tiruppalanam is associated with the heroine.

After opening with an encounter between the hero and heroine in a mountain grove followed by him questioning her seemingly divine origin, the hero is already deeply muddled in his feelings for the heroine. Verse 20 is a conversation between the hero and his best friend after the initial meeting and union of the hero and heroine. The overall focus of this theme in *Tirukkovaiyar* is the effort of the hero's friend to arrange or initiate another secret meeting for the lovers. The friend is motivated by his concern for the suffering health of the lovesick hero.

20

The friend inquiring

O supreme one! What happened to your vast hill-like shoulders?
Do you long for the orbit of seven-tones or did you penetrate
the discipline of sweet Tamil studied in Madurai with great walls

of the one who is excellent
who is in my mind
who is at the small hall in Chidambaram where the river has strong banks.

The friend looks at the slump of the hero's shoulders and asks the hero what has caused his declining virility. It is within the concerned inquiry of the friend that the poet frames his praise for the city Madurai, called Kutal in the text. Madurai is the most famous cultural center in Tamil country. Here, the eminent city is possessed by Shiva, the excellent one. Home of classical Tamil arts and literature, Madurai was also the political capital of the medieval Pandya kings. Thus, the inquiry of the friend into whether the hero has been absorbed in the scales of classical music or the scansion of Tamil literature is a historically specific description of Madurai. Madurai is also named in both the early classical and heroic anthologies under the moniker Kutal often in a comparative position with a woman. For example, in *Purananuru* a woman is compared to Madurai, which is ruled by the hero of the verse: "She is like the city of Kūṭal surrounded by deep waters, ruled by Akutai who is courageous in war."[8]

In his article on the geographical planes of *Tirukkovaiyar*, Norman Cutler delineated four realms: akam landscapes, places of Shiva's residence, cosmological and mythological places from Sanskrit and Tamil sources, and the interior of Shaiva devotees' hearts and minds.[9] Cutler concluded that the real artistry of *Tirukkovaiyar* is in the blending of worlds and that the resultant union of human and divine spaces reflects Manikkavacakar's vision that "humanity is like divinity" and that "humanity and divinity cohabit a common universe."[10]

In verse 20, in contrast to the role of Madurai in the human action of the verse, the small hall and Chidambaram are not in a position that is relational to Madurai but rather are used in a list of Shiva's attributes. The compiling of the human story and unique site and Shiva's praise with Chidambaram is a reoccurring structure over the course of the poem. Shiva takes a humble third place of residence compared to his prominent seats in Madurai and Chidambaram. Although it is generally uncommon for the poet to reveal himself in the poetry of *Tirukkovaiyar*, here Shiva is in the ultimate interior in the poet's mind.

The divine patron is praised by presenting him with three unique and highly valued sites. These references fit into the schematic realms set out in Cutler's study: the interior of the devotee's mind, the abode of Shiva in Madurai and Chidambaram, and a place of study for the human hero. Dividing these sites across categories of human and divine, however, does not yield the same mental journeys proposed by Kim. Rather than look for blended divine-human spaces, Kim's model allows the audience to engage not only with the deity in the space but with the city or place on its own right. The devotee-audience is guided by the poetry to encounter a special cite. The site is simultaneously special enough to attract Shiva's presence as well as made special by Shiva's presence. The city of Madurai appears in one more verse near the end of *Tirukkovaiyar*, but this type of engagement with space and place reoccurs along with additional localizing strategies throughout the text.

Distance and Rejection

Almost eighty verses lapse before we encounter the next three sites, clustered in the twelfth theme. In the ten themes that have passed between verses 20 and 100, the hero and heroine have been interviewed, teased, and chided by their respective companions for their not-so-secretive sulking and pining. The heroine's confidante has managed to extract the intentions of both the heroine and the hero and has warned both with her doubts about the propriety of the match. The overwhelming source of both of the women's anxiety is that the heroine surrendered her modesty and her chastity to a stranger in the forest. By uniting with the hero, the heroine placed herself at the hero's mercy: he may choose to protect her chastity and reputation through marriage or not. Although *Tirukkovaiyar* is characterized as an idealized love story, it is also laced with a precautionary tale about the risks of making a spontaneous, secret union. Over the course of the lovers' trials and reunions, the two equally powerful forms of love found in the literary grammars, kamam and anpu, also dance in tension with one another. At this early stage in the narrative, if the hero does not marry the heroine or if their relationship is revealed before he has made a proper proposal to her family, she will be the disgrace of her family and relatives. Thus, the confidante is assigned with the difficult job of either permanently running off the hero or pressuring him to marry the heroine, all the while managing the fragile nerves of the heroine who waits in the wings.

It is in this context that the twelfth theme, Being at a distance, presents the reader with a fresh lovers' dilemma. The hero has presented the heroine with a gift of tied-up leaves. This single fist of foliage sends the woman into a flurry of postures and rejection. The confidante discourages the hero's gesture with a list of excuses.

94

Rejecting by false pretext

The tender vine is amorous too but there's a little catch.
These flowery leaves are only found in the grove of fine pinti trees
on the vast hillside of Kutralam
    of the one who shares his side with a woman whose voice is sweet like a flute
    who is the flame dancing in the hall
    who glitters
    the light of fire.

100

Refusing, stating the family's status

My little girl whose words are honey
is from a small town
    where lions roam and hill-like beasts tremble in Tirupparankundram
    of the one in the hall whose side is filled with Uma.
You belong to a cool, lustrous land
    where ripe coconuts fall
    crushing bunches of areca palms
    destroying plantain trees in beautiful pollen-filled paddy fields.

104

Refusing, saying she is young

No man's embrace has crushed her breasts[11]
her hair grows more fragrant like honey but cannot be knotted
she is a child of Tiruperunthurai of the one who stands
    as ever-expanding light
    in the hall and in the ever-melting heart.
Aiya! What will you say to her with just a few lisping words?

In verse 94, the confidante tells the hero that the leaves that he offered to the heroine only grow on the slopes of Kutralam. Since this is not where the heroine lives, if she returns to the village with these leaves, it will be obvious that she has had contact with someone from the outside. The confidante does give the hero a small consolation by telling him that the heroine also wishes to reconnect. It is only from the commentary that we learn that the confidante is being devious in her claims about the leaves. We nonetheless assume that she is acting in the best interest of the heroine.

The portrait of the patron-hero in this verse has four elements. First, Shiva is bright as fire and dances in the hall, appearing as a flickering flame. He has his consort, the goddess Uma, on half of his body. The last attribute is his possession of the vast hillside of Kutralam. Like in verse 4, the hall and Kutralam do not share function or placement in the verse. Kutralam is the bridge between the action of the lovers in the idealized human realm and the description of Shiva. There is a sense of a slight jab aimed at the hero spoken by the poet through the words of the confidante. The hero is in a state of desire, attempting to deliver gifts and flattery to his beloved. Not only is the origin of these plants an impediment to his plan, but the prime resident of Kutralam serves as a stinging reminder of the hero's failure to unite with the heroine. Out of all of the names and qualities of Shiva given in the verses of *Tirukkovaiyar*—a dancer, creator, conqueror—it should not escape our attention that in this verse, he is united with his female companion whose perfected femininity is heard in the melody of her sweet voice. In the contest of winning his bride, Shiva has surpassed the hero by leaps and bounds. Verse 100 repeats a similar motif to the theme of verse 94, namely, the confidante tells the hero that the heroine is from a different place.

The contrast emphasized in verse 100 is between the hometowns of the lovers. The heroine is from a small place in the wilderness where lions hunt elephants. The hero is from an agricultural region that is bursting with fertility, prosperity, and wealth, as indicated by the abundance and variety of ripe produce. Like in verse 94, the hall and Tirupparankundram are not directly connected to one another and it is Tirupparankundram that connects the human world to the divine patron-hero. Shiva is possessor of the hill Tirupparankundram and is described with Uma at the hall. There is a slight echo carrying over from the goddess in verse 94 to the girl in verse 100. Despite her rustic origins in the wilderness, the heroine has inherited the honey-sweet voice of the goddess Uma. The description of Shiva in both verses includes the goddess who coexists in his body and his place in the hall. In this verse and in verse 104, the god of the hall in Chidambaram possesses a town that is home to the young heroine.

Verse 104 is a portrait of innocence. By declaring the purity of the girl's youth, the confidante aims to deflect the advances of the hero and perhaps even shame him into silence. She infantilized several aspects of the heroine. The heroine has lisping speech because she has not yet learned to speak clearly. Her virgin breasts have never been touched by a man. She is called a child of Tiruperunthurai, the link between human and divine. She has the soft, wispy hair of a child that is not long or heavy enough to put in the thick dark braid or bun that is so intensely praised as feminine attribute in other verses. The petite, not yet formed quality

Figure 9 Manikkavacakar on an exterior shrine tower, Tiruperunthurai.

of the heroine is in stark contrast to the growth of the hero's desire, and even to the expanding light of Shiva, suggestive of the erotic tension characteristic of classical love poetry. In this verse, the heroine is portrayed as fragile and new, in contrast to the developed, voluptuous hourglass figured version of her that was praised earlier in the poem. This softened femininity is a counterpoint, in this case, rather than an equal match to the powerful and expanding desire of the hero. In this verse, the poet has dared to compare the lusty kamam of the hero with the gracious anpu that Shiva offers as light to his devotees. Furthermore, the praise of Shiva's expanding light is made more compelling by placing it alongside the sexual passion of the hero. The combination of types of affection demonstrates that kamam and anpu are equally persuasive and far-reaching forms of desire.

According to Manikkavacakar's hagiography, Tiruperunthurai is where Shiva first appeared to the poet and inspired him to build a temple (Figure 9). Verse 104 is the only verse that names this special place in *Tirukkovaiyar*.[12] In addition to Tiruperunthurai, Shiva is given another human abode in the melting heart, a common motif found in bhakti hymns including verse 20, used to indicate the intimacy and physicality of one's devotion. Notably, verse 104 does not specify that it is Manikkavacakar's heart, but rather the heart belongs to the anonymous devotee. In light of the poet's dedication of the heroine to this town and the melting heart as an abode for Shiva, the poet's absence is a puzzle. Verse 104 seems like a lost opportunity in which Manikkavacakar could have celebrated the place of his conversion and committed heart with more explicit enthusiasm.

Finally, this trio of verses, all set into motion by one bunch of leaves, is saturated with sites for religion, sites for devotion. In three brief scenes, shaded groves, pollen-powdered fields, small towns, the heroine's soft skin, fragrant trees, lions, elephants, a fist full of leaves, and the goddess Uma inhabit these landscapes and bodyscapes. The combination of these material contexts is the occasion for this theme. The overall mood or intention of this theme is rejection. In the akam grammars, the hero's attraction to the heroine occurs at the intermingling of the young woman's beauty with the beauty of the environment around her. In theme twelve, the confidante and poet acknowledge the idyllic context of the akam narrative but are compelled nonetheless to deliver a heartbreaking message. The environmental cues and a few well-placed objects are the triggers for emotional shifts. If the contents of this text were love, beauty, love, and more beauty, the text would lose its ability to pull and sway its audience. Thus the conflicts in theme twelve provide an environment of urgency in which a devotee might pursue god. The sensations of rejection become the sense of religion in this theme and the arch of devotion through which the poetry guides a devotee. The confidante continues to antagonize, play coy, and feign confusion over which girl the hero loves.

107
Inquiring about intentions, as if having failed to understand
Oh king! With whom is your grace
  from among the countless girls playing ball
in the sandal wood garden
  spreading cool fragrant pollen at Tirukkalukkunram
of the lord in the hall at Chidambaram,
  who surpasses the gaze of the two excellent gods
  called he who cut open the earth and he who crossed the sky?

The fragrant garden where the heroine and all of her girlfriends play is located on the cool pollen-covered slopes of Tirukkalukkunram. This mountain top site has both a legendary and literary history of its own. Histories of this mountain are told in *Tirukkalukkunra puranam*, attributed to the poet Kavivira Rakava Mutaliyar. According to tradition (Tiruk-)kalukkunram got its name, kite mountain, from two devotees who did penance on the peak and were reborn in the form of these mighty birds. Until recently, the priests at the summit temple were responsible for feeding the twin kites that returned for meals every day.

This famous mountaintop also received its own kovai poem, *Tirukkalukkunrak kovai* composed by Iramanatapuram Comacuntarak Kavirayar. The 455-verse kovai poem opens with a fertile flowery sighting reminiscent of *Tirukkovaiyar*.

Sighting
What is this one green creeper
flourishing with kantal, elevated tender coconuts,
full of joyful honey suitable for a beautiful canpakam tree,
lustrous blue nelumbo, water lilies, and lotus crowded with beautiful bees,
standing inside this forest in Tirukkalukkunram of the one with a black neck?
Tirukkalukkunrak kovai 1[13]

This sighting verse from *Tirukkalukkunrak kovai* reminds us of the continuity achieved not only within the genre but also surrounding the significance of Tirukkalukkunram hill for Tamil Shaivism.[14] The stunning heroine stands—and blossoms—in the forest possessed by Shiva, described here in his salvific blue-throated role as Nilakanta in Tirukkalukkunram. The forest of Tirukkalukkunram has a similar fragrant, floral quality to those in *Tirukkovaiyar*.

The cool mountain grove where the heroine plays with her friends in verse 107 is a pleasant locale for Shiva; however, it is only the platform from which our attention is diverted by Shiva's most divine devotees. In hopes of finding the limit or feet of Shiva, Vishnu turned into a boar and tunneled into the earth. Brahma turned into a bird and flew beyond the heavens in search of the crest of Shiva's head. The resultant imagery of this story leaves the audience with head tilted back, peering beyond the slope of Kutralam, and into the soaring path of Brahma. This sense of height and Shiva's ascension takes another form in the next verse (v. 113).

113
Saying and analyzing[15]
Oh beautiful ornament! If you accept the leaves shame will ride us.
Otherwise, if you do not accept he will mount the palm-horse.
What can we do for the one who destroyed the mountain
who raised up and scorched our dark millet field at Inkoymalai
where resides Shiva who raised the bull flag then ascended the hall.

In verse 113, the confidante consults with the heroine about their impending public shame whether she accepts the gift of leaves or agitates the hero with her rejection to the point of mounting a palm horse. The ordeal of the palm horse consists of the hero building a horse made of thorny leaves of the palmyra palm,

Figure 10 View of hilltop temple, Inkoymalai.

painfully riding it through the heroine's village, while holding a portrait of his lover overhead, and proclaiming his intentions for her.

While perhaps a romantic gesture to some, for the heroine the hero's public declaration will bring social shame to the heroine's entire family. In verse 113, the hero's performance of the palmyra ride threatens to create the same amount of shame as the gossip that would follow the acceptance of a gift from an outsider in another plant-based form of courtship. In spite of the low-hanging head of the heroine, the directionality of devotion follows the imagery associated with the patron Shiva flying high as a flagstaff. The heroine's family's millet field is located at the fourth hill attributed to Shiva, Inkoymalai. Inkoymalai is described as a residence of Shiva, while Shiva is described as the one at the hall and whose emblem is a bull, referring to his mount Nandi. The name of the hill is attributed to the Tamil sage and legendary father of Tamil literature, Agastya, who took the form of a fly so that he could soar past the crowds of devotees to the top of Shiva's peak (Figure 10). Thus, the story of Inkoymalai connects Shiva to the human lovers as well as to the secondary but eminent literary hero Agastya. The chapter of distance and rejection concludes with the feeling that the magnetism of love for Shiva and for the beloved is subject to opposition and pushback. This is a model of religious experience proposed by the *Tirukkovaiyar*.

Day and Night Trysting

In theme thirteen, Tryst by day, the confidante changes her negotiation tactics and begins to urge the hero to marry the heroine. The distance between objects and subjects of desire closes for a moment in favor of union. Meanwhile, the heroine plays with her girlfriends but continues to fret over her chances of meeting with the hero in secret.

135
Inquiring about marriage, telling about the meeting and accepting
You possess her bamboo-like shoulders.
It was witnessed by all at Kutralam of our dancer
    who is praised in the hall by throngs of celestials.
Just like me, mother will rejoice immediately.
Our father will come and stand by your words too.
The others have had their say. Why make so many excuses?

137
Urging marriage, saying others are speaking
After I stood before the man of the hills
and told him that she will be adorned with gold tomorrow
    she who resembles Tiruppanaiyur
    where celestials stand after going to the hall to worship the alpha
    whose fiery form burned the mighty cities
    who peeled the hill-like elephant with a trunk shaped like a palmyra palm
what else can I a sinner say?

In verse 135, the confidante tells the hero to stop making excuses to delay his decision and assures him that the heroine's parents and relatives will support him when he takes the heroine with beautiful shoulders into his care. The possession of shoulders is a euphemism for the lovers' relationship that is borrowed from classical love poetry. For example, in a verse from *Ainkurunuru*, the heroine asks, "Mother … if he has abandoned our shoulders, then whose shoulders could he possibly want now, I wonder?" (v. 108).[16] Verse 137 is an example of pressuring the hero to make a proposal by telling him that other men will come with the required gifts of gold.[17] The confidante's threats to convince the hero to marry the heroine will continue to haunt him in the fourteenth theme, Trysting by night.

According to verse 135, Kutralam is the site of the lovers' union. This is the southern-most site in *Tirukkovaiyar* and already appeared once in verse 94. In the description of Shiva attached to the first mention of Kutralam, he is portrayed with Uma on his side, resembling light and dancing like a flame at the great hall. The description of the lord of Kutralam found here does not include as many attributes. Nonetheless, the poet has isolated a powerful and complete image of Shiva as lord of Kutralam and a union of movement through space with the deity's iconography: "Our dancer praised by throngs of celestials at the hall." This verse provides us with the most concise expression of the relationship between the hall or ampalam at Chidambaram and the other sites mentioned as Shiva's abodes. The specific manifestation of Shiva that is visiting the waterfalls at Kutralam is the dancing lord from Chidambaram. Subsequently, Tiruppanaiyur is the place where celestials stand *after* they have visited Shiva at the hall. Celestials connect Shiva to the town and to the lovers' world. One might even view the celestials in verse 137 as the same throng of celestials from verse 135 that were praising Shiva's dance at the hall, thereby linking the narrative between verses. In addition to Shiva's human devotees in *Tirukkovaiyar*, he has attracted the attentive devotion of Brahma and Vishnu, as well as the divine celestials.[18]

Like the theme on Trysting by day, this theme, Trysting by night, is assigned to over thirty verses and is a continuation of distress over an entirely new set of obstacles and restrictions that prevent the lovers from meeting. The threats range from roaming wild animals to the danger of waking the heroine's mother, all keeping with the wilderness motif through which Shiva travels. In the first two verses of the theme that precede verse 150, the hero speaks to the confidante to propose a meeting for the lovers. The confidante, in true form, rejects the idea on account of the dangerous mountainous path that leads to the ladies' hometown. Verse 150 continues to direct our attention upward to the mountain peak of Kotunkunram, modern-day Piranmalai.

150
Standing with a broken heart
Oh heart, languishing
like a lame man who desires honey from the highest mountain peak of Piranmalai
    of the dancer from cool Chidambaram
    who is wild honey
    who crushed the timely one who came saying, "I will not change"
        and made him cry for help
I cannot endure because of your love for that rare woman.

178

Speaking having seen the situation

If any other thought is considered other than paying homage and praising you
strewing thick, fertile, grand flowers when you enter and stand like the son of Shiva
who wears snakes that come from anthills
who resides at Tirupparankundram
the supreme god at Chidambaram
who is attached to those who are without even one attachment
is the lady capable of living?

Here the poet orchestrates an encounter between Shiva and Yama, the god of death. Yama, like time and death, marches forward and cannot be waylaid. Yet Shiva crushed him and made death cry out. The endurance first shown by Yama and ultimately championed by Shiva mirrors the enduring love of the hero's heart.[19] It is equally impossible for the heroine to attend to any thought or thing other than the hero. The significance of her dedication is strengthened through a parallelism between the hero and another famous hero of the south, the son of Shiva, Lord Murukan. We have a picture of the heroine performing a ritual, scattering flowers in worship of her lover. The poet makes obvious the devotional imagery of the heroine's action by comparing the hero to the son of Shiva. In addition, though we do not mistake one hero for the other, in this exceptional verse the two heroes are kin. In his role as Shiva's son, the hero of the love narrative is elevated to a (nearly?) divine status, creating a seamless integration of the human world and Shiva's world into one reality. Although certainly not the norm, the in-between-ness of the hero's status and simply the occurrence of such ambiguity acknowledge the possibility and potential range of human-divine interaction. It remains unknown if this meeting place is intended as literary fantasy or a religious encounter the poet hoped would materialize in his lifetime.

Crushing Waves: Turmoil and Frenzy

Theme fifteen, Leaving that place, is thirteen verses long and demonstrates how *Tirukkovaiyar* both tells a story and gives variations for the course of the narrative. This theme is an intimate portrayal of the heroine's lamenting, primarily drawing from the classical neytal landscape to express the distress caused by separation. The emotional terrain of the heroine's suffering intersects with the presence of the god through the rich life of water. At the opening of the theme the confidante tells the heroine that she needs to separate herself from the hero in order to suppress the gossip that has begun to develop around the lovers. Left to suffer alone, the heroine's state of mind deteriorates so she reaches out to natural elements for sympathy, seeing her own suffering paralleled or contradicted by the creatures around her. The audience of *Tirukkovaiyar* is led to check the natural environment and its inhabitants for dramatic cues. The first body that the heroine turns to is not that of her sister-like confidante, but rather a body of water, the roaring sea.

182
Asking the sea about the arrival
O relentlessly roaring bounded sea
    that dashes and surrounds supreme Ampal
    of the pure one at Chidambaram
he left
    the man from the bright shore that glimmers
    like the supreme sky spread with stars and clouds
    while the sea churns with waves spread with pearls.
Did he mention the nature of his return?

Verse 182 is ruled by the characteristics of the ocean and the separation of neytal scenarios. In this verse, the water has the qualities of both the sea and the sky with sparkling *mīṉ*, a word for both fish and stars. The water is roaring, dashing, and churning in a turmoil that mirrors the violent anguish of the heroine. The pearls spread across the waters also parallel the streams of pearl-like tears of the heroine, a common literary motif in *Tirukkovaiyar* and beyond. The heroine asks the ocean, which she assumes witnessed the hero's departure, if the hero mentioned any details about his return. The fact that the first act of the heroine following the confidante's demand for isolation from the hero is to inquire after his return speaks to the intensity of her attachment to him and leads into her obsessive desire to reunite with her lover.

At first glance, the role of Shiva in this verse is relatively minimal. The verse requires of its audience, including devotees, that we accept the sensations of splash and gush as religious sensations and sounds. The sensation of an encounter with the divine *is* the glimmer of a fish flashing across the water. And, the same ocean that has flooded all other aspects and imagery of this verse also splashes up around the site, Ambal. The water that surrounds Ambal ties together the anguish of the heroine, the origin of the hero (who is from the seacoast), and

Shiva's site. Different from the effect of comparing the heroine to a flourishing town, in this verse the same waves are splashing at the feet of Ambal and at the feet of the heroine. She is not compared directly to a town but rather is included alongside it, sharing the waterfront imagery.

In the following brief excerpts from the early anthologies of love- and heroic-themed verses, we learn that the poet of *Tirukkovaiyar* was not the first to capitalize on the presumably well-known waterworks surrounding the town of Ambal. Speaking first of a heroine, an early poet writes, "I won't let go completely of the broadly sprouting tresses of her who [is] like the clear water of the Aricil river that surrounded Ampar, with high flags for a fresh decoration" (*Narrinai* 141).[20] In a blessing for a great warrior, another poet praises, "the overlord of Ampar where the fields grow their paddy and the water of the Kāviri River laps into the low-lying land of the gardens" (*Purananuru* 387).[21]

The waterworks in *Tirukkovaiyar* verse 182 continue in the next verse, in which the heroine commands the ocean, "Open your mouth!" She asks the ocean for information about the nature of the hero, and when the sea does not satisfy the heroine's investigation, she turns her attention to the goose in verse 184. She complains to the bird that the punnai tree will not tell her whether or not the hero will ever pass by her riverbanks again. In the next two verses, the heroine finds herself on the sandy beach with her attention returning to the sea. In verse 185, the heroine begs the ocean not to wash away the tracks left by the hero's departing chariot. In verse 186, she draws circles spiraling across the wet sand and tries to calculate her hero's return.[22]

These verses combined, again, in step with the classical neytal landscape, represent another modality for Tamil religion—that of lonely searching, distress in separation, and taking counsel in one's natural context. The following excerpts from themes fifteen and sixteen highlight the consolation that humans seek from animals, birds, trees, and bodies of water. The pressure and anxiety caused by their union are interrupted by moments of reprieve and bursts of vitality for both the heroine and the hero. And, like much of the story of the human lovers, the images of growth and liveliness are transferred onto the lush greenery of the natural environment through which the lovers travel. Parallel growth between nature and lovers is another relevant element of these verses as we consider the role of the *Tirukkovaiyar*'s environment as a landscape through which the audience may take a mental journey. In the next series of verses from the theme titled Departing together, the heroine finds honor in her persistent preoccupation with the hero.

204
Telling the virtue of chastity
O soft shoulders that surpass lovely bamboo!
O forehead like a crescent moon who excels in supreme knowledge
    spoken by our dancing lord
    who dances at the small hall and who is excellent in Inkoymalai
for women, humility is excellent like her mother's
but humility is not more excellent than steadfast fidelity.

209
Informing about the decision
O desired one
to the small flower-like feet that quiver if they tread on red-cotton
    of her with eyes that shoot long red streaks, scaring arrows back into their quivers
even the rocky wilderness is like wide tender leaves
    in Sivapuram of the desired one of Chidambaram
    who blackened the furious trembling body of Calantaran.

220
Sporting along the way
Our eyes are rich
    having seen the beautiful woman just now
Come so that I can drink deeply the even melody of your soft words
until the cruel forest cools like the tank in cool Melakadambur of our king
who has the soft-natured one as his side in Chidambaram
lord of the celestials.

With fifty-six verses, theme sixteen, called Departing together, is the longest series of verses in the same theme and focuses on the elopement of the lovers. In addition to the primary content of the love theme, this chapter also offers lessons in vitality and transformation. In the verse above (204), the poet is explicating the hierarchy of a woman's character. Through the words of the confidante, which are directed at the heroine, the audience is taught that bashfulness is a superior quality. Bashfulness is the same quality that the confidante exploits in an attempt to extract a confession from the heroine in theme eight of *Tirukkovaiyar*, Investigating through evoking bashfulness. More superior than bashfulness, however, is steadfast fidelity or chastity. It is for the sake of protecting or maintaining the heroine's chastity that the confidante encourages marriage. In addition to her modesty, the heroine's idealized femininity is incomplete without two other qualities, one perhaps more surprising than the other. The salutations directed at the heroine identify her by her physical beauty—a perfectly arched forehead and soft shoulders. The final quality praised in this verse is the heroine's mastery of the superior knowledge given by Shiva. Her education, which is administered by Shiva and not by formal study like the hero, is an important aspect of the heroine's spiritual knowledge and overall competence as a good woman.

Verse 209 tests the well-matched pair and the heroine's willingness to faithfully follow her hero into the wilderness. Both the hero and the confidante question the heroine's ability to endure the hardships of elopement, including the difficult terrain over which they must travel. In verse 209, the heroine is a threateningly beautiful woman. The blood vessels in her eyes spray out streaks that intimidate the arrows of a warrior. Normally, her feet are so delicate that even walking on cotton is difficult. When the poet says that the rocky wilderness is like walking on fresh green leaves, the audience discovers that the heroine's love for the hero has a transformative power. Not only is she able to set out into the wilderness on her own, but the very landscape that she crosses softens for her ease.

In verse 209 the poet situates that cool transformed environment in a town that belongs to Shiva. This town appears once in *Tirukkovaiyar* as Civanakar. Nakar is a general term for a town or city. It can also mean a house, shrine, or place. I've translated it as a proper name of a place because it only occurs once and tentatively identified Sivapuram as its contemporary name, but Civanakar could also be a general reference to a town for Shiva. The legend associated with Shiva in this verse is the story of Calantaran. Calantaran was a demon born from Shiva's angry third eye that grew into a powerful menace. Shiva's patience was finally exhausted when Calantaran dared to express his attraction to Shiva's consort and found himself decapitated as a result.

Parallel imagery occurs between the trembling feet of the heroine, trembling arrows, and trembling Calantaran and between the heroine's fierce eyes and the fiery anger of Shiva eliciting sensations of vibration and heat. The point of comparison for the volatility that reverberates throughout the verse is the wide tender leaves in Sivapuram. Without knowledge of the legends or location of Sivapuram it is difficult to further analyze the significance of the counterexample beyond the cooling nature of thick green vegetation. However, this verse does emphasize a sense of vitality through a complicated combination of ferocity and vulnerability shared by the young lady and the great god, a point to which I will return in Chapter 5.

We find a similar environmental transformation of the cruel forest in verse 220. The cruelty of this forest is derived from its fiery heat. The lovers hope that the conditions will temper to the more tolerable and even pleasant climate in Melakadambur. The stark contrast of the fiery jungle with the cool tank is complemented by and runs parallel to the image of virile Shiva who shares half of his body with the soft, sweet-voiced goddess. We meet this Shiva repeatedly throughout the poem. He is virile, alive, active, burning, dancing. In a much softer but simultaneous moment, we can't help but hear the wistful fantasy of the hero to be similarly united with his sweet and gentle companion however short-lived their union might be in proceeding verses.

Theme eighteen inaugurates the final phases of *Tirukkovaiyar*, separation. For the remaining third of the poem, the lovers will continuously struggle to unite, the hero will continuously be called away, and the heroine will pine and immerse herself in the art of lament. Part of her suffering includes the trials spurred by her family's suspicion that her unrest is caused by possession, introducing a type of frenzied love to the devotional vocabulary of *Tirukkovaiyar*.

268
Saying I will speak about separation for marriage-wealth
After I deliver the gold and wealth demanded by your family
and pass through the hills and valleys
I will join you with a waist like lightning.
O you with sweet words go there now and describe the unfading waist of the golden lady[23]
who resembles Tiruvidaimarudur, Kanchipuram, and Srivanchiyam
where the king who reaches the hall resides.

286
Summoning the priest
Let the priest enter, dance, and cut the white goat
because of the boy who arrived and made us stand like this
the boy who resembles Thiruvenkadu where he was
who entered and stood in me
who is the one above all
who stands in beautiful Chidambaram
where the anklet was placed on Kalan and burned him when he arrived.[24]

Figure 11 Ekamparanatar temple complex, Kanchipuram.

292
Preventing the frenzy
Let those with good fortune[25] drink in the frenzy.
We won't stop them.
Let stand the shining shoulders
of the one whose fate it was to be in the rushing waters
that flow from Tirupparankundram of the one whose home is the hall.
O god, if you think differently
is there anyone in the world today with knowledge like yours?

The hero's plan to collect gold for the heroine's family and then to return to his beloved is described in verse 268, in the sections dedicated to variations on that theme. Here, Shiva is simply praised as the king of three towns, Tiruvidaimarudur, Kanchipuram, and Srivanchiyam (Figure 11). This trio of sites is a singular one in *Tirukkovaiyar*. Despite my best efforts to connect these three sites in historical materials, the relationship that binds these towns together is yet to be discovered. Geographically, Kanchipuram is the northern-most site in *Tirukkovaiyar*. The other two sites are located between Madurai and Chidambaram and are not known to be major political centers like Kanchipuram.

These three towns do appear clustered together in *Tiruvacakam*; however, this context offers no more information about why they are connected to each other.[26] Unfortunately, all that can be said at this point is that the triple cities follow the most common pattern for introducing a site via its similarity to the heroine.

Verse 286 contains three important elements: the priest, a unique method for integrating one of Shiva's sites into the poetry, and a complex boy character. When the heroine displays erratic behavior at home a spear-wielding priest is called by the heroine's family to perform an exorcism. According to this verse, his ritual of exorcism includes frenzied dancing, possession by the deity traditionally understood to be Murukan, and the slaughter of a white goat. The priest and the ritual described in *Tirukkovaiyar* draw from a robust tradition of possession tropes in akam literature. The following excerpts are two of many appearances made by the frenzied priest in the earliest classical anthologies.

What if I told it, friend,
  [with the words] "this [is it]"
    to the man from the land inside the forests ...
  ... because Murukaṉ, in whom mother resorts,
    after she realized [something is] different, the crookedness
    of the plague-knowing Molucca beans having been shown,
    [and] she had a lamb['s throat] cut, with a mind that realized
      "the Veṟi dance [is the remedy]",
  did not contribute to your gold-like pallor?
  Narrinai 47[27]

[In response to this] pain is fitting, friend,
upon the event of [their] saying: "she is possessed by a spirit!",
  cutting a kid's throat [and] preparing millet offerings
  [and] praising with many [songs] different great gods,
without [that] being a remedy for the pain apart from appearance,
  while many instruments are sounding on the crossing
    of moving rivers.
That this [should] happen to us who haven't wronged
  the man from a land, where rain is playing on the great mountain!
Kuruntokai 263[28]

In both of these examples, family members detect the suffering of the heroine and summon the priest to cure her. In both verses, it is also the case that the true root of her deteriorating condition is her love-sickness in the absence of the foreign hero. In the verse from *Tirukkovaiyar* above, not only is the hero the cause of the ritual, he is also the linking figure that connects the human love-themed drama to Shiva's town. In fact this is the only verse in which the hero is used to play the role of "resembling a site," which is usually occupied by the heroine.

In fact, the boy proves to be a very complex character in this verse, somewhat similar to the son in verse 178. On one level, the boy can be read as the hero of the love story. Merely standing in the presence of this intoxicating young man causes the heroine to behave like a girl possessed by a demon. The boy of verse 286 also resembles the town of Thiruvenkadu, literally "the white forest," which is possessed by Shiva. The boy can also be read as a son. One might imagine that this is the son of Shiva, Murukan, who also wields a spear and is known for possessing young women. With the final reference to Shiva's destruction of Kalan, another name for the god of death, the boy in this verse also becomes associated with the young boy saved by Shiva, Markandeya. The complex identity of this boy reminds the reader of the poet's skilled combinations of local akam, mythic, and practiced ritual traditions. The frenzy created by the boy continues in verse 292.

In the final excerpt from theme eighteen, the intoxicated frenzy of the priest is brought on, yet again, by the handsome hero who resembles Murukan. The mention of rushing waters refers to an earlier incident in which the heroine nearly drowned in a whirlpool. Luckily, the hero was there at the right time and right place to dive in and save the young woman from near death. According to verse 292, the source of rough water was flowing out of Shiva's Tirupparankundram. Just south of Madurai, Tirupparankundram, literally the "supreme hill," is one of Murukan's primary residences in Tamil country, along with Palani Mountain. In addition to being a hill-home to both Murukan and Shiva, Tirupparankundram is also recognized as a symbolic substitution for Mount Kailash. In keeping with excerpts from previous verses, here we find tension, conflict—even suspicion and possession—that drive the expression and plot of idealized classical love. Significantly, these expressions of devotion to the beloved, whether human or divine, continuously rely on and interact with the emotions *and* materiality of the human world. Lovely bamboo, a quiver of arrows, and a white goat elicit the emotions of a desirous lover, a frenzied priest, or the devoted heroine. The imagery and sensations associate with each of these scenes are also the realm of Shiva as he inhabits these southern towns, draws devotees to him, and destroys death itself.

Love, Loyalty, Slander

Tirukkovaiyar does not conclude with a happy ending. In verse 306, and throughout theme nineteen, marriage is presented as a celebration of loyalty. The hero and heroine are united in body, mind, and character—like honey is bound to its sweetness. However, the hero's fidelity is a fleeting notion. All subsequent verses are sequences of and commentary on the hero's departure and betrayal.

306
Speaking about union
Although he goes to the battlefield of the king's enemies like a great lion
his chariot won't stay outside.
She who is like Moovalur
    of the one from the small hall who is first over all other gods
    who is praised by the southern one, Varaguna
she won't think of any other god.

338
Speaking about separation
O golden woman who resembles Tiruppuvanam
    surrounded by gardens with grand, gold, glittering walls
    of the lord who dances with fire
        keeping his anklet on my splendid head inside the small hall at Chidambaram
        removing the stain of the great southern region.
Today our king left with a strong elephant.

The stories of three distinct figures, the hero of the love story, lord Shiva, and the Pandya king are joined in verse 306. The heroine's hero is a courageous warrior but he and his chariot never stay outside in a foreign land for a moment longer than the king's service requires. The supremacy of Shiva is parallel to the lion-like hero and is amplified by the loyalty of the great king Varaguna. The royal stature of Shiva's devotee is a testament to Shiva's preeminent status above other gods. Just as the Pandya king will not waiver in his praise of Shiva, so too the heroine thinks of none other than her beloved.

A glimpse into theme twenty-four, one of the variations on separation, betrays the southern-centric view of this poetic world—and more importantly, of Shiva's world. The heroine's beauty is comparable to the town of Tiruppuvanam, located south of Madurai and glittering with wealth. Both the poet and Shiva are located in the hall in Chidambaram. The story referred to in the last two lines of this verse about Shiva tilting the world adds literal and figurative weight to his home in the south. For his wedding, Shiva and all of his guests travelled north to Mount Kailash. The great shift in population caused the Himalaya Mountains to fall down and Tamil country to rise up high. To repair the upheaval, Shiva had to return south to balance the world again. Based on its golden, glittering cities—its material appeal—the Tamil south certainly appears to be an appropriate place for a divine figure to reside.

In the final and longest theme of *Tirukkovaiyar*, the hero leaves his marital home to enjoy the company of public women—a theme discussed at length in Chapter 4. In this next verse, the confidante criticizes the hero as one who is generous with outsiders, a subtle reference to public women, while ignoring the needs of his wife. The heroine is compared to the great southern city Madurai and wears a smile that matches the color of Shiva's ruby-hued matted hair. Nearly at the end of the composition, the poet is careful to describe Shiva's iconography specific to his role as dancing Shiva: the crane's feather in his hair and imposing physique. Finally, Shiva and the hero radiate their charisma in a shared direction—outward. Through this poetic phrasing the audience is guided south to a sensation that drives us outward, as well as toward an encounter with the dancing god. In the case of the hero, his generosity to others has a destructive effect on the heroine. In contrast, the electricity that shines from Shiva is beneficial for all who it reaches, and in this verse, Shiva's grace reaches from Chidambaram to Madurai.

376
Confidante slanders (the hero's) nature
Our sole patron who stood with a red spear
proved himself unsuitable today
because he gives in the direction of outsiders while this woman suffers
  she with a ruby smile resembles Madurai in the south
  of the one who stands and dances
  who wore the feather of that crane at the small hall
  in Chidambaram of the lord with strong shoulders shining in all directions.

377
Neighbors slander (the hero's) nature
While she with a heart full of affection became distressed in Tiruchuli
  of the one who stands and dances with ambrosia
  that seeped between the bones of devotees at the hall
the man from a town with a field is without limits
  where a goose sleeps with the tough mate of a rare right-circling conch
  while his companion fades, his reputation destroyed.

379
Saying after thinking and wondering
Whenever I think of her with the nature of entering my mind
  like a flood enters a pit
I think she will enter the heart once and never leave
  she who resembles Sirkali
  where resides the lord unseen by those with hearts where deception enters
  he of the small hall
  he with matted hair where the clear beautiful flood of the Ganges abides.

Verse 377 is the gossip of neighbors and it takes place in a coastal town called Tiruchuli. According to a fifteenth-century story, Shiva sent a spear into a water column and stirred the water into a whirlpool, giving the town its name, which is derived from the verbal noun for swirling. The final verse with a unique site in *Tirukkovaiyar* also takes up the imagery of churning water. The neighbors tell the story of an unfaithful goose who leaves his mate in their nest while he trysts by night with another female creature. Of course, the concern of the neighbors lies not with a wandering goose but with the recent scandalous behavior of the hero who left his wife to rendezvous with a new love interest. The suffering of the heroine corresponds with the profusion of affection she feels for the hero. The amount of suffering and affection of the heroine also corresponds with the amount of ambrosia that oozes from the devotees' bones in the presence of dancing Shiva. The heroine, Shiva, and his devotees seethe with passion while the hero misbehaves. The turmoil of the characters' emotions and the churning water carry the audience into the next verse containing the last unique site named in *Tirukkovaiyar*.

Two verses after Tiruchuli, and about twenty verses from the end of the poem, we encounter the last of Shiva's unique sites: Sirkali. Coastal town Sirkali is famous for being the home of *Tevaram* saint, Campantar. In this verse, flood imagery associated with the passion of a devotee, the gushing tears of the heroine, and the various water sources of the classical landscapes culminates in the overwhelmed mind of the hero and the cleansing waters of the goddess Ganges. The waterfalls and floods call to mind the visual image and crashing sound of powerful surges. The first movement is the experience of the beloved entering the hero's heart and mind. The second movement is in the desire of devotees to have Shiva reside in their hearts—hearts that must be without deception. In his expectation that the heroine will never leave the hero's heart, the poet implies that it is equally difficult to separate oneself from deception once it has taken root. Binding union is a reoccurring theme between hero and heroine, between heroine and confidante, and between Shiva and his servants, including the poet. Binding union is not only expressed between people but also communicated in the intentional naming of Tamil towns for a devotional purpose. Shiva is bound to the poet's map of Tamil country, and by extension he is also bound to the people who inhabit those places.

Conclusion

The excerpted verses in this chapter illustrate the major love themes developed by the poet: an instant, dazzling union, tension, rejection, and negotiation between lovers and companions, and a great deal of passion that resembles possession, frenzy, and the free fall of rushing waters. Moving through the sequence of verses and shifting from one theme to the next, we found a range of emotions including desperation, affection, and anger. Many of these exchanges and flaring tempers trade on the appearance or disappearance of material things. The heroine's body—her slim, wavering waist, her breasts, and baby soft hair—drives the highs and lows of the hero's health and pursuit of his beloved. The hero draws near and then withdraws with a gift of leaves, a spiny palm horse with rippling flag, or the gold of suitors. The feather of a crane, Shiva's thundering anklet, and the sweet honey at Piranmalai are objects that the audience can feel and see, hear, or taste and that devotees can savor as gifts of the iconography of their god. Shiva's divine presence is accompanied by other gods who fly, tunnel, and claim the dead. The action of the verses is propelled by frantic ritual possession and praised by royalty, while the dancing god and human are connected through the materiality of subtle items: the soft feather and honey. The feather connects *Tirukkovaiyar*, the audience, and the devotee to the more widely circulated legends and iconography of Shiva, while the honey, on the other hand, connects the text, the devotee, and the god to the local work of the bees in a modest town in the Tamil south.

To this world of human love and divine affections and the objects that tie these experiences to one another, the poet adds animals and natural environments that further embellish their shared world: elephants, lions, Shiva's bull, snakes, and the goose populate sandalwood gardens, lush fields, coconut groves, cool forests, gushing rivers, and mountain peaks. Furthermore, there is a second geographical-devotional overlay in the form of the towns named in verses. Initially, the list of sites might tempt the reader to shift her attention to political or pilgrimage routes woven into *Tirukkovaiyar*—and this is a possibility that is explored in Chapter 3. Instead, I propose that these sites invite all on an "imagined journey" through the fiery wilderness or toward Shiva's dancing hall.

The themes of *Tirukkovaiyar* where the most sites appear are (12) Being at a distance, (13) Tryst by day, (14) Tryst by night, (15) Leaving that place, (16) Departing together, (18) Separation due to wealth for marriage, and (25) Separation due to public women. The drama of these themes is provoked by movement, separation, travel, and distance between the lovers. In other ways, this relationship between space, locality, and movement can be understood in terms of uprooting from one's home and traveling through or toward foreign lands. Focusing on themes of departure and foreign travel, we can read *Tirukkovaiyar* as the story of Shiva's departure from his home in Chidambaram (formalized by the architectural cues like the hall) and his travels through the wilderness of these other twenty towns. Shiva does not aim to inhabit other established temples; rather he tours the country side, or wilderness, in which he is actually quite at home in his ascetic persona. The orientation of *Tirukkovaiyar* is not static, nor is Shiva focused on one point. Instead, when the material is prioritized, this poetry proposes a type of devotion that travels. In one sense, the religious is locked in union with the local landscape. Yet, Shiva's wilderness also suggests an expanse where a devotee or group of young girls might encounter unfamiliar animals or dangerous rapids.

Reified by the suspicion felt by the girls from the plains about the hero from the seashore, the outsider is another concept that relies on our perception of limits and boundaries and can be applied to anyone outside the threshold of the home including a god. The spatial dichotomy suggested by Shiva's movements and the heroine's social circles are parallel to akam and puram aesthetics, which distinguish between interior and exterior—or framed differently, home and the wilderness, a wilderness full of lions, honey, and sandalwood gardens. For humans, the wilderness is a test of desire, commitment, and perhaps penance. Shiva's movement from Chidambaram out into the landscape engineered by the poet is a physical lesson and tour of the material wilderness for the devotee who follows god. The landscape in either cultivated or wild form is simultaneously presented as a special place in its own right as well as transformed into one that is flourishing, wonderfully fragrant, and sweet for the deity to enjoy.

3

On Mountains, Waterways, and Intoxication

The devotional voice of *Tirukkovaiyar* emerged after the earliest saints had composed their sizable corpus of hymns, but before the saints' hagiographies had been collected. South India has long been hailed as the origin of the bhakti movement, a style of predominantly Hindu devotion that privileges intimate relationships between god and devotee. These exchanges are often modeled after human relationships such as parent-child, lover-beloved, or master-servant bonds and use styles of language that reflect the close connection even evoking familiarity between the pair. The earliest vernacular bhakti hymns are attributed to saints beginning in the sixth century. However earlier classical Tamil texts also express characteristic personal relations with and praises for local deities. For example, *Paripatal* and fifth-century *Tirumurukarruppatai* are both traditionally classified as classical literature but explicitly address gods rather than kings or warriors.[1]

Karaikkal Ammaiyar, hailed as the earliest of the Shaiva saints, composed hymns characterized by her fascination with gruesome scenes of Shiva in cremation grounds and her depiction of sacrificial love for her lord.[2] The *Tevaram* hymns are attributed to three seventh-century poet-saints and among them name hundreds of villages and towns in the Tamil south.[3] Vaishnava devotees developed their own corpus of hymns and cult of saints, among them a poet named Antal. Known for her unbounded devotion to Vishnu that resulted in the god taking her as his wife, Antal is also believed to be a contemporary of Manikkavacakar.[4] Famed poet Nammalvar (eighth or ninth century) also composed a love poem to Vishnu that, like *Tirukkovaiyar*, utilized classical love themes to praise god.[5] These devoted poets had deep knowledge of the Tamil literary tradition and drew from a variety of mythological, theological, and literary sources in order to express connections felt between early medieval devotees and their gods.

This chapter frames *Tirukkovaiyar* as a relational expression of devotion rather than as an insulated, closed corpus of four hundred verses. Comparisons between a variety of hymns to Shiva and Vishnu illustrate how they were influenced by akam poetry and which principles were adopted, adapted, or left behind. The excerpted expressions of devotion that preceded *Tirukkovaiyar* provide us with the literary context from which the poem emerged and to which our poet may have responded. Through comparison, we discover which sensations, physical and emotional, are favored by poets conveying messages about Hindu deities. We also learn which material elements of the human experience are selected as fitting contexts for the worship of god. This selection of verses also reflects the poets' studied commitment to intertextual dialogue. To these verses we pose the question, what is the image, feel, and sound of devotion in early medieval poetry? The answer to this question includes a look into lively descriptions of the human experience, towns, animals, landscapes, and lovers, beginning with a renewed analysis of the sites named by the Shaiva bhakti canon.

Medieval Maps

The Tamil Shaiva canon as we know it today comes bound in twelve volumes of poetry, philosophy, and hagiography collectively known as *Tirumurai*.[6] Among the most influential components of *Tirumurai* is the anthology of hymns known as *Tevaram*.[7] The staggering number of sites that appear in the *Tevaram* hymns, the majority of which are located on the north and south banks of the Kaveri River, indicates that naming sacred territory was a poetic practice employed by the earliest Tamil saints. *Tevaram* is a collection of about eight hundred hymns dated from the late sixth to early eighth centuries, which are anthologized in the first seven volumes of *Tirumurai*. The hymns are attributed to three poet-saints known collectively as muvar: volumes one, two, and three are attributed to Campantar;[8] volumes four, five, and six are attributed to Appar; and the last volume of *Tevaram* is attributed to Cuntarar (Figure 12).[9]

As the term "hymn" suggests, this type of poetry was and continues to be sung by devotees, often within temple walls, to praise Shiva.[10] These verses are also known by a more general term, "patikam," which can refer to Shaiva or Vaishnava poems of praise, generally consisting of ten verses. In this case, each group of ten verses praises qualities of Shiva, often by including details from well-known puranic episodes in which Shiva is the hero and by referring to a specific manifestation of Shiva manifested at a particular temple town in South India. In total, the muvar named 274 places thought to constitute pilgrimage sites, a point to which we will return.[11]

In addition to the sites named by *Tevaram* poets, I also include for comparison the sites named in *Tiruvacakam*, in another collection of poetry attributed to

Figure 12 Small pasted poster of the nalvar saints including Manikkavacakar (far right), Tirukkalukkunram.

the same poet of *Tirukkovaiyar*. Manikkavacakar's works, *Tirukkovaiyar* and *Tiruvacakam*, together constitute volume eight of the Shaiva canon. *Tiruvacakam* is composed of fifty-one hymns in fourteen different meters that range from interrogating a chattering green parrot about Shiva to the lamentations of a longing soul.[12] Like *Tevaram*, the hymns of *Tiruvacakam* are popularly known and have been incorporated into daily worship and special festival occasions in contemporary Shaiva temple life.[13] T. N. Ramachandran, the most recent translator of *Tiruvacakam* and champion of his local Shaiva Siddhanta Society, describes *Tiruvacakam* as the spiritual biography of Manikkavacakar that draws in its reader to experience the immersion of the saint's bliss, his trials, and his ultimate victory.[14]

Table 3 is divided into three columns. The first column shows all of the places named for Shiva in individual *Tirukkovaiyar* verses. The next column shows where Manikkavacakar's map aligned with *Tevaram* sites. The third column shows correspondence with Manikkavacakar's second devotional landscape contained in the verses of *Tiruvacakam*.

Tiruvacakam emphasizes four sites in particular, three of which also appear in *Tirukkovaiyar*: Tirukkalukkunram, Tiruperunthurai, and Chidambaram.[15] These three sites play significant roles in Tamil Shaivism. Tirukkalukkunram is a hilltop site with a kovai of its own, Tiruperunthurai is the site of Manikkavacakar's

Table 3 Sites named in three medieval Shaiva compositions.

	Tirukkovaiyar (verse number)	Appears in *Tevaram*	Appears in *Tiruvacakam*
Pal̲an̲am	4 (1.4)	✓	✓
Kūṭal	20 (2.2); 376 (25.25)	✓	✓
Kur̲r̲alam	94 (12.5); 135 (13.20)		✓
Paraṅkun̲r̲am	100 (12.11); 144 (13.29); 178 (14.31); 292 (18.27)		
Peruntur̲ai	104 (12.15)		✓
Kal̲ukkun̲r̲am	107 (12.18)		✓
Īṅkōy	113 (12.24); 204 (16.11)		✓
Tiruppan̲aiyūr	137 (13.22)		✓
Koṭuṅkun̲r̲am	150 (14.3)		
Ampar	182 (15.2)		
Mūval	191 (15.11); 306 (19.8)		
Civanakar	209 (16.16)		
Kaṭampai	220 (16.27)		✓
Iṭaimarutūr	268 (18.3)	✓	✓
Ēkampam	268 (18.3)	✓	✓
Vāñciyam	268 (18.3)		✓
Veṇkāṭu	286 (18.21)	✓	✓
Pūvaṇam	305 (19.7); 338 (24.7)		✓
Cul̲iyal	377 (25.26)		
Cīrkāl̲i	379 (25.28)	✓	✓
Tillai	More than can be listed	✓	✓

legendary conversion, and Chidambaram is the iconic home of dancing Shiva. The fourth popular site named in *Tiruvacakam* is Uttarakocamankai. Although absent from the *Tirukkovaiyar*'s literary landscape, according to his hagiography, Uttarakocamankai is where Shiva told Manikkavacakar to stop on his way to Chidambaram.

The hymns of the *Tevaram* anthology share a number of sites in common with the *Tirukkovaiyar* map.[16] Four common sites were located in Chola territory, in relative proximity to Chidambaram and the Kaveri River delta area: Tiruppalanam, Tiruvidaimarudur, Thiruvenkadu, and Sirkali. The town Sirkali, legendary birthplace of poet-saint Campantar, is mentioned with greatest frequency. *Tirukkovaiyar* and *Tevaram* have two other major sites in common. The first place is the artistic and political center of the southern Pandya territory, Madurai.[17] The second place is Kanchipuram, the center of the Pallava dynasty, located north of Chidambaram. Today, Kanchipuram remains a famous temple town containing a number of ornate stone temples significant to both Vaishnava and Shaiva devotees. In *Tevaram*, there are seventeen verses that refer to various sites within Kanchipuram; however, only twelve specifically name Ekampam. In *Tirukkovaiyar*, only Ekampam is mentioned.

Much has been made of the appearance of these specific places in the *Tevaram* anthology and the medieval Tamil corpus more broadly. Originally thought to be pilgrimage routes or claims for dynastic territory, a recent study by Leslie Orr shows that the places named in early hymns and later hagiographic texts like *Periyapuranam* do not represent a neatly organized "network" or connected routes between temple towns.[18] In spite of the seeming obsession with the specificity of place, in the case of the *Tevaram* verses in Orr's study, sites named in temple inscriptions on the ground do not correspond with emphasis or authorship claimed in the poetry. Orr concludes that despite the prevalence of town names in *Tevaram* verses, the temple remains the "most centrally concerned with place"[19] because temple inscriptions provide many more details about a particular city, its relationship to governing bodies, property boundaries, and the local form of Shiva indicated by his name, lord of place-name. In contrast, the poetry typically engages with Shiva through his mythology, by placing Shiva in the human world, by localizing his activities, and ultimately by associating a Tamil shrine with each miracle or major victory of their deity.[20]

Orr's revision of the role of sites in poetry and its *lack of* correlation with pilgrimage practices jives with the style of naming practiced in *Tirukkovaiyar*. Although a common trope in studies of religion and place or religion and geography, the logic of the order and location of the sites presented in *Tirukkovaiyar* does not speak to a strong pilgrimage motif. If you follow the order of places as they appear consecutively over four hundred verses the pilgrimage would be very haphazard and redundant in route. Instead, the value of place relies on at least three strategies for locating Shiva and devotional expression in the human world. First, religion is in the south. In the case of *Tirukkovaiyar*, the map covers a wide expanse of Tamil territory that is especially weighted toward the far south, in contrast to the *Tevaram* sites clustered around the Kaveri Delta.

Second, nearly every single verse of Tirukkovaiyar includes Chidambaram or the hall (ampalam) as the dwelling place of Shiva. Indeed, Chidambaram is the site after which the poem is named. In this poem, Chidambaram is called

Tillai and Puliyur. *Tiruvacakam* and *Tevaram*, like *Tirukkovaiyar*, emphasize Shiva's association with the hall in Tillai. According to tradition, the temple in Chidambaram is the primary site of Shiva's cosmic dance—an identity that is associated with his Sanskrit name Nataraja. In spite of this long-standing association of dancing Shiva with Chidambaram, the dance of Shiva is not one of the favored ways by which the poet of *Tirukkovaiyar* identifies the god. Rather, Shiva is more often identified with the ampalam. Ampalam is a common noun that means court or public hall. In the context of Tamil Shaivism, ampalam has come to stand for the Golden Hall in which Shiva performs his legendary dance, in the same way the word "temple" has come to mean the Nataraja Temple in Chidambaram, indicating its supremacy as the sole destination for Shaiva devotees. Chidambaram and the hall function in two ways in *Tirukkovaiyar*: as integrated parts of epithets naming Shiva or as sites to which he traveled or in which he resided. *Tiruvacakam* includes additional aliases such as golden hall for the hall in Chidambaram. The omission of the adjective "golden" and the use of the term "ampalam" throughout *Tirukkovaiyar* suggest that this association with the Golden Hall was not fully developed or perhaps not widely used at the time of *Tirukkovaiyar*'s composition. Even though the sites named in the *Tirukkovaiyar* draw the map much further south than Chidambaram, the poet maintains the supremacy of dancing Shiva in verses that include additional sites by incorporating the hall or Chidambaram into an epithet for Shiva. For example, Madurai is possessed by the one who resides in Chidambaram.

The third characteristic of the *Tirukkovaiyar*'s material context and its roots in the far south communicated by the poet is that of great height. Although Shiva's primary home is on the silvery peak of Mount Kailash within the Himalaya Mountains, *Tirukkovaiyar* speaks of many other hills and peaks. With height, the poetry elevates the love story and the lauded deity to an air of excellence and supremacy.

Devotion and Elevation

Five of *Tirukkovaiyar*'s named sites are in mountainous landscapes: Tirupparankundram, Tirukkalukkunram, Inkoymalai, Piranmalai, and the waterfalls at Kutralam.

In addition to the five mountaintop sites, *Tirukkovaiyar* also makes reference to the Potiyil hills, the southern-most peaks of the Western Ghats, continuing the southern tradition of identifying the Potiyil hills (alias Potiyam hills) as the "Kailash of the South." These hills are a common feature in Pandya panegyrics and are referred to in major earlier works in Tamil literature such as the Buddhist epic *Manimekalai* (v. xvii. 24), the Jain epic *Civakacintamani* (v. 1371, 1267), and the *Tevaram* hymns. Potiyil is also the mythic home of Agastya, sage and champion of the Tamil language—the same Agastya who flew as a fly in the legends of Inkoymalai. In the following excerpt from a classical Tamil heroic anthology the Potiyil and the Himalaya ranges are side by side and equally endowed with unwavering strength. In this case, Potiyil is not the junior substitute but rather a local peak legitimated by kings, with legends and associations equal to its northern counterpart.

> Even if milk becomes something sour, or the sun goes dark,
> or the Four Vedas swerve from the truth,
> may you shine on, with no loss, on and on with your unswerving
> ministers!
> May you never be shaken, like Mount Potiyam, like Himalaya
> with its golden peaks where long-eyed does sleep
> on slopes in the faint dawn near fawns with tiny heads
> under the glow of the three fires
> in which the Brahmins offer ghee according to their difficult rites.
> *Purananuru* 2[21]

The bard extols the king's enduring reign by comparing him to natural and supernatural rites, such as the rising of the sun and the prestigious rites of Brahmins. By including Potiyil among these enduring aspects of an elite human experience, we understand the mountain holds the status of a known geographical feature of the local landscape as well as a symbol of social and political prestige.

Potiyil is mentioned thirteen times in *Tirukkovaiyar*, six times by name and seven times under the alias Malayam.[22] The mountain consistently appears in the "beautiful south." In verse 394, "Potiyil [is] in the beautiful south of the man of the small hall." In verse 392, the heroine and her girlfriend humbly confess that their "house is a house of small people in beautiful southern Potiyil of the one of the small hall who wears anklets." The hero and heroine also had a secret tryst "having avoided their friends on the stone strewn slopes of the hills of Potiyil" in verse 8. Potiyil hills represent a distinctive southern geography, one that is aesthetically pleasing, familiar, and has captivated audiences since the earliest Tamil epics.

The mountains that are equal to Himalayas and home to Agastya are also an anchor for a larger political and cultural maps of the Tamil South. In verses 338 and 376, Shiva straddles two major political and cultural centers of medieval

South India, Madurai and Chidambaram. In the south, the poem names a Pandya king but does not emphasize Madurai with any exaggeration. In the north, Shiva is repeatedly housed in Chidambaram (in Chola country), but the rest of the sites are not clustered in that area, especially the Potiyil hills. The southern sprawl corroborates the geography of the poet's hagiography, which locates his childhood and years of service to the king in and around Madurai. By creating a map that stretches to the far south and takes special account of hills and heights *Tirukkovaiyar* accomplished two geographic goals: Shiva is placed in the wilderness and among the sensory experience associated with this particular landscape.

Whether weighted toward the far south or toward Chidambaram in the action of the verses, Shiva's association with Chidambaram and the hall remains consistent throughout *Tirukkovaiyar*. His reach from Kutralam to Kanchipuram shows a discernible preference for the south. The breadth of territory claimed by this poet suggests that the Shaiva community was securely fastened to Tamil land but not limited by the contemporary political boundaries of their kings; Shiva's movement across lands also resembles that of a king surveying his territory. The regal god and divine king are figures that saturate the literary, liturgical, and political cultures of early South India. Reading Shiva of *Tirukkovaiyar* as a royal god or divine king is consistent with his role as primary patron and explains the prominent role played by the Potiyil hills, especially since the role was somewhat abdicated by the great Pandya Varaguna. Despite being tempted by the list of sites mentioned in *Tirukkovaiyar* and the Shaiva temples that now stand in these towns, we should not assume an institutional motive for this mapping project. Significantly and unlike verses found in *Tiruvacakam*, *Tirukkovaiyar* names sites but does not speak of visiting or entering temple gates or courtyards and largely lacks architectural cues. More than a cosmetic absence, the poet has thus highlighted Shiva's preference for dwelling along mountain slopes and wild places, as opposed to fine courts or other formal settings. The sites named in *Tirukkovaiyar* are an opportunity for Shiva to roam through and enjoy the natural wonders of the southern hills. When the poet composed this map, he both invited Shiva into the landscape and gifted him the territory of the Tamil south to take and travel through as his own.

In addition to the mythic and sociopolitical impact of mountaintops, those elevated landscapes contribute to the immersive material experience of the hero, heroine, and the imaginative audience. The emotional and physical vocabulary of intense devotion is translated into the sensory and sensual experience of scaling a mountain peak, pulling in a deep breath of cool air, and looking down through the mountain mist at the variegated greens of the paddy fields below. The slopes of Potiyil and the other southern peaks are simultaneously examples of the mountainous literary region, kurinji. Environmental characteristics of the observable natural world in the regions where Shiva's sites are located inform and color the audiences' vision of where Shiva dwells and where devotion takes place. The sociopolitical history of medieval South India while relevant to the general study of *Tirukkovaiyar* is not what drives the lovers to abscond into the fiery wilderness and does not implement the *sustained* placement of Shiva in exceedingly beautiful and opulent environments.

Instead, this map is foundational to the devotional and narrative design of *Tirukkovaiyar* and must subsequently be populated by the poet—by devotees, erotic bodies, elements borrowed from classical landscapes, waterways, and any other elements commensurate with medieval religious aesthetics.

Devotion and Place

We turn now to an initial example of how Shiva was praised within the territory claimed by the verses of early bhakti poetry. Excerpted from the fourth volume of *Tevaram*, the following verse combines four common elements of devotional Tamil literature that occur in *Tirukkovaiyar* and its predecessors: sacred sites, eroticism, natural landscapes, and their inhabitants. Chapter 1 laid out the conceptual space of akam poetics. This section explores the *place* of Tamil religion in poetry.

> The one of Virattan on the Ketilam River
>   full of clear water that bubbles with kentai fish
>   where striped carp become ill after devouring sweet honey made by bees
> has as his other half her with bangles
>   a flower garland rising on her coiled hair
>   expansive hips
>   a waist like a tuti drum
>   a red mouth pouting on a creeper.
>
> *Tevaram* 4. 24. 10[23]

In this verse attributed to Appar (4. 24. 10), the town Virattan is named a sacred site, the river Ketilam indicates the natural environment, the kentai are the fish that inhabit this nature-scape, and the description of Shiva's consort captures her divine sensuality. This verse shows the adoption of classical Tamil imagery in several ways. First, the description of the river has vivid natural features that emphasize the abundance or wealth of the water. It is so full of life that the fish are nearly out of space to swim, bubbling up over the surface. Some of the fish are further indulging in the sweet nectar of busy bees, which is another common motif for fertility and amorous intoxication in classical Tamil literature. The second aspect of this verse that corresponds with classical themes is the description of the goddess. In classical Tamil love poetry, the lovers are not named but rather take the generic title of hero and heroine, talaivan and talaivi. Her red mouth, garlanded hair, wide hips, and bangles are all common ways to describe the heroine and also her confidante. The matured beauty of the goddess's figure is further emphasized by her likeness to the physical qualities of the creeper-vine, which is flexible, slim, and swaying, and by her waist being likened to the curves of a tuti drum, an instrument shaped like an hourglass. The combination of the environmental cues presented by the river and the buzzing bees with the overlay of the goddess's body creates an overall impression of boundless fertility. Ultimately, the image of the goddess enhanced by environmental elements serves as an embellishment of the divine icon specifically manifest in the town of Virattan. The union between devotion or bhakti and eroticism in early medieval poetry is well established, especially in the work of Friedhelm Hardy who identified three components of what he called Krishna emotionalism as it arose in South India. Hardy's divisions, aesthetic, erotic, and ecstatic are easily spotted in verses presented here from the Shaiva tradition as well.[24] Daud Ali also addressed the eroticism of medieval devotional poetry by proposing that the pleasure derived from the feminine lover not be rejected but rather its fruit redirected for the pleasure of the god in a period of transition from classicism to bhakti.[25] In this chapter and in the book, my claim is that the scholarly reading of medieval religious literature must certainly acknowledge the use of eroticism, but so too we must reprioritize the material details of land, water, and bodies presented in the texts for equally physical, aesthetic, and religious effect. The material world, while the site and certainly supplementing the sensual qualities of human love, must be recognized as a host and producer of sensory information and devotional effects in its own right.

As the engaged audience, we see the red lips, smell the flowers in her hair, taste the sweet honey, hear the bubbling water, and imagine the slippery touch of the kentai fish. Appar's use of classical vocabularies to express the goddess's beauty and body in material terms demonstrates that the *Tevaram* poets were conscious of and influenced by their poetic predecessors. They also produced examples of dense descriptions that are similar to the explicitly erotic themes found in *Tirukkovaiyar*. The next two verses are excerpted from the first volume of *Tevaram*, attributed to the poet Campantar.

Those who seek Sirkali surrounded on the sides with the sea
    possessed by the lord with a flag where resides the murderous bull
    who lives with her whose curly hair is full of palmyra palms
are the ones of the pure path.
Tevaram 1. 34. 1

Always sprinkle rows of flowers in worship at Sirkali
    surrounded by gushing water with banks
    possessed by the fortunate one
        who wears gushing waters full of waves
        who rejoiced with the daughter of the lord of the mountain.
Tevaram 1. 34. 2

In verse 1.34.1, Shiva has three qualities. He has a consort with curly hair, he is the lord of Sirkali, and his insignia is the fierce bull. These qualities correspond with and guide the devotee to make associations between Shiva and his feminine counterpart, local Tamil towns, and recognizable iconography. If we remove the description of Shiva, what remains is a directive for action that lauds those who visit Sirkali as true devotees. This directive is made yet more significant by the relationship between the poet and the place; Sirkali is traditionally known as the birthplace of Campantar, and by elevating his own hometown to the hometown of Shiva, the poet solidified his own connection to Shiva.

Although hidden by this translation, the rhyme scheme of this verse in Tamil also contributes to the emphasis of the hymn's message. The first syllable units rhyme in sound and vowel length, leaving the listener with four key concepts: the murderous bull (atal eru), the palmyra palm (matal), the sea (katal), and those who follow (totaravar). Again, the Lord's iconography, consort, coastal location, and his devotees are the main components of Campantar's composition. Those who sing this hymn can easily grasp Campantar's image of Shiva in Sirkali and imagine themselves as initiates along the pure path.

In verse 1.34.2, Campantar addresses the devotee with more directions for worship. In this case, he directs, "Always sprinkle rows of flowers at Sirkali." Here again, Campantar has specified an act of service that includes the arrangement of flowers for the enjoyment and beautification of the god, and tells the devotee exactly *where* to perform this worship at Sirkali. Shiva has four qualities. He is fortunate and he is the lord of Sirkali. He also has two feminine partners. The first is the "gushing waters full of waves" that he wears on his crown, which refers to the story in which Shiva takes the Ganges river, here personified as his goddess-consort, into his matted hair. The second, rival lover is his usual consort Uma, whose father is the lord of the Himalaya Mountains. The verse itself contains ten metrical units in each line, which is considerably shorter than the sixteen and seventeen metrical units in each line scheme of *Tirukkovaiyar*. The brevity of this format is by no means a defect of the poetry but shapes the methods used by the poets to convey their message. Here too, the poet took advantage of the initial words in each phrase to pack extra punch into very few words: the waves (tirai) of the Ganges, the hill (varai) of Uma's origin, the riverbanks (karai) of Sirkali, and the rows (nirai) of flowers to be set out for Shiva's pleasure. The overall message of these songs is to offer acts of worship to Shiva, acts which include the recognition and praise of his attributes in specific places at the crest of a wave, bank, hill, or row of flowers (Figure 13). Furthermore, in order to answer Campantar's call to worship, the devotee must move, engage with waterways, touch feather-light flower petals, and recognize the joyful union of Shiva with his exemplary consorts.

Figure 13 Temple threshold, Tirukkalukkunram.

Natural Environments and Inhabitants

The verses analyzed above in terms of sites and eroticism all contain "natural identities" demonstrating a way to indicate place, locality, and here-ness through regions not delineated by political territory but rather through the regional environment and its inhabitants. Rather than read a garden or riverbank as the background of the verse-scene, these details identify and highlight the natural location of the devotee's worship and the deity's manifestation in the human world. When brought to the fore, insects, fish, and wispy vines are characters that contribute to the overall action, religious message, mood, or each verse like (and sometimes more than) their human counterparts. The next set of verses takes us deeper into the aesthetics of the natural environment and inhabitants of the Tamil south. Beginning with the twentieth and last verse of *Tiruvempavai*, the most often sung and most often inscribed verses by poet Manikkavacakar excerpted from *Tiruvacakam*, we find plant life at the center of this declaration of Shiva's excellence.[26]

> Praises! Grant your flower like feet that are the beginning.
> Praises! Grant your red tender sprouts that are the end.
> Praises to the golden feet that are the origin of all life.
> Praises to the flowery anklets that are the joy of all life.
> Praises to the pair of feet that are the end of all life.
> Praises to the lotus that is not seen by the one with four faces nor by Vishnu.
> Praises to the golden flowers that graciously took us and ruled us
> so that we can escape.
> Praises! We bathe in water in Markali.
> Our little doll.
> *Tiruvempavai* 20[27]

Shiva takes center stage to be hailed with the refrain translated above as "Praises!" Flowers and sprouts are used to describe and decorate the theology of Shiva, emphasizing his roles as the beginning, the creator, the savior from rebirth, and the end of all things. The devotional attitude of submission is also amplified by floral and botanical imagery. It is a common gesture of humility to praise the feet of a deity as a portion of the god that literally stands in for the whole divine being. Here, Shiva's feet are compared to plant life frequently used to describe the beauty and tenderness of women's feet. His flowery anklets conjure an image of the thundering metal anklets worn by warriors, which are also extensions of Shiva's feet and being. The application of jewelry fashioned from both precious metals and natural elements like flowers is included among significant acts of worship. The repetitive praise of the divine feet draws the audiences' attention to a series of colors, flowers, and by extension the places and seasons where such plants are known to grow. The poet also references the mythic when he praises the one who is so great that even the two gods, Brahma whose five faces have been reduced to four and Vishnu, cannot reach him. Additionally, there is an element of religious practice embedded in this portion of *Tiruvacakam*. The month of Markali is the time of year when this series of verses is explicitly designated for women and girls to sing at festival time. Not only does Manikkavacakar receive annual accolades for his divinely inspired poetry during this season, but temple images are also taken to rivers and oceans to be ritually bathed as the girls are in these hymns—a combination of a specific town with a specific natural environment. To the land formations, dynamic bodies of water, and lush plant life, we add creatures to the cast of akam and early devotional poems. The slow study of birds' desires and elephant quarters will illustrate some of the specific ways in which religious devotion can be expressed through nonhuman subjects. The emotions stirred here are critical contributions to feeling desire for and of Shiva.

Birds and Animals

191
Being disheartened with the goose
This four-fold world sleeps
 having embraced the jaumoon-plum tree and the three-fold ocean
 of the one who is first
 the wealthy one of Chidambaram who embraces Moovalur with his grace.
The joyful, gracious goose sleeps
 having embraced its delightful, desirable mate.
It won't tell my protector
I suffer without sleep.

In verse 191, the bitter heroine describes the pleasant, guilt-free sleep of the goose after it refused to aid her inquiry into the hero's location. In the context of South Asian love poetry, the expectation of the heroine that the goose might carry a message to her lover is not an unreasonable one, as we find many examples of the goose, bee, and cloud utilized as messenger between lovers.[28] The peaceful slumber of the goose has also swept over the classical landscapes in the fourfold world, namely the hills, forest, seashore, and agricultural tracts. Even the ocean sleeps. In the last line, the entire universe at rest is abruptly confronted with the heroine's sleepless nights and restless heart. The voice of a heroine asking after her absent hero is heard by birds in flight over the following Vaishnava hymn.

She Said:
O geese, O herons, flying above
I entreat you
Whoever arrives first
don't forget

if you see my heart with Kaṇṇaṉ
lord of Vaikuṇṭha
Tell him about me
Ask him why he hasn't returned
Inquire if *this* is his name.
Tiruviruttam 30[29]

Tiruviruttam by Vaishnava poet-mystic Nammalvar is composed of one hundred verses that like *Tirukkovaiyar* embrace the aesthetic vocabulary of both classical and devotional literary traditions.[30] Nammalvar sends the geese and herons to find out when (or if!) the divine hero intends to return. However, the audience suspects that the birds are not as affected by the hero's absence as is the young woman. There is a certain amount of frustration present in the tone of these verses, while the birds sleep, while they travel, and next—while they play.

189
Speaking with distress to the birds
The ibis are seeking food, cheerful during the day on the black backwaters.
They do not yet understand my mental agony.
Oh, I have sinned!—
like those who do not reach Chidambaram
of the one with matted hair that is bright as gold
glitters like rubies and flashes like coral.

The heroine turns to the ibis to express her lonely suffering. This time she addresses the cheerful birds feeding on the backwaters, but the heroine herself barely appears in the text. Instead, this verse is a rare example in *Tirukkovaiyar* of the heroine speaking explicitly about Shiva and the practices of his devotees. There is of course some play here in ambiguity that allows the audience to hear the confession of the poet as well. The heroine's sadness fades into the dark hinterland, while Shiva's famous locks, worn in the style of ascetics and home to the Ganges River, steal the message and the imagery of this verse—bright, glittering, and flashing in the most precious red-hued material, namely gold, rubies, and coral. Here the girl and god are paired together, but their partnership is used to play up the stark contrast between the suffering of one and the effulgence of the other. The ibis is a representation of how oblivious the heroine feels that the world and perhaps her kin are to her darkened state of mind. The parrots in the next verse take up an entirely different facet of the lover's behavior.

144
Urging marriage, saying separation is difficult
Even though the mountain paddy is harvested in the low fields
created by streams from Tirupparankundram of the one who lives in the hall
who rules and creates love
young parakeets stay in the stubbles of grain stalks today
as if to remind us that, "Once joined
separation is difficult, even from demons."

The confidante tells the hero that breaking away from a relationship is always difficult, even if that relationship is with the devil. How much more difficult will it be for him to give up his true love? It seems that the hero will end up like the foolish parakeets that are still earnestly picking through a field of stubble for any hints of grain on the ground, even though the field has already been harvested. He will be searching for the tiniest trace of the heroine once she is gone.

In verse 144, the poet's reference to the parrots is part of a well-developed theme of the parakeet searching an empty field found in both akam and puram anthologies. For example, the following lines, extracted from a puram anthology *Purananuru* verse 138, use the image of parrots lingering in a millet field to describe the devoted lover waiting for his beloved's return (Figure 14).

Like tall ears of millet in a broad field where on trees
the parrots sit and wait is that husband of women
with lush dark hair and adorned with costly ornaments!
Purananuru 138[31]

The attraction of parrots to their familiar fields is a motif that is also found in early love poetry, as in the following example.

They're to be pitied,
those red-beaked green parrots!
Even though they see long stretches

Figure 14 South India landscape, field near Bahour.

of green-stemmed millet stubble
cut down by hill men,
they don't want to leave
out of their fondness for the fields.
Ainkurunuru 284[32]

Like the human and animal behavior in *Ainkurunuru* analyzed by Martha Ann Selby, the animals in *Tirukkovaiyar* are utilized in a zoomorphic rather than anthropomorphic manner.[33] The animals in classical love-themed landscapes do not typically have conversational, emotional, or logical processes. Rather than ascribing human qualities to the animals, the natural behavior of the individual creatures is applied to explain the behaviors of humans. In this particular verse, the hero's inability to leave a relationship with the devil is explained using the parrots' attraction to a familiar field even when it is barren. In this comparison, humans share the animalistic instinct of the parrots to remain with what is known. The desperate search is simultaneously made to resonate with the devotee seeking Shiva at the hall. In this verse, Shiva is characterized as creating love or devotion. In fact, Shiva attracts the devotees to him and instigates their devotion to him. Once this desire for the god has been ignited, the devotee will also find it difficult to separate from the blissful relationship. Clearly, birds were used to portray strong devotional and affectionate ties between humans and gods. I close with just one more example of other creatures and celestial bodies enmeshed in the drama of *Tirukkovaiyar*'s love story.

305
Saying that which is produced by fidelity
The golden woman who resembles Tiruppuvanam
  of him with matted locks like rows of gold at the small hall
  in Chidambaram with thick walls that shine with sculptures
even surpasses the fidelity of twilight's North star.
The cool elephant
  except for the doorway of the stable
  not even crossing the step
he won't leave that place.

Verse 305 captures a poignant moment between the lovers and between the devotees of Shiva and their god. The theme of this portion of *Tirukkovaiyar* is The excellence of marriage. The fidelity of the hero is established by comparing the occupation of his marital home to that of an elephant unwilling to leave his pen. However, despite the physical and symbolic girth of the hero's commitment, the star of verse 305 is the golden heroine. The faithfulness of the heroine to her husband surpasses the exemplary model of the pure wife, Aruntati, indicated by the North Star. The comparison of a woman to the exemplar Aruntati is a well-established method of praise for a faithful wife. For example, in *Ainkurunuru* verse 442, a warrior's mother is praised, "her chastity like that of Aruntati, appearing in the celestial world that arcs above the sky." In *Purananuru* verse 122, no place is more pleasurable, "other than the arms of your woman who speaks so softly, who is as faithful as Arundhatī."[34]

Recalling the grammatical rule for symmetry between the character of the hero and heroine, when the heroine is praised for her loyalty, the excellence of the hero is implied. In the scenario described above, the devoted elephant and the faithful North Star are a perfectly captivating pair.

Sensuality in Water and Sound

Evidence of sensuality expressed and enhanced by the natural world abounds throughout this entire book. It is cultivated in botanical and animal realms. Felicity and fertility are also indicated and enhanced by the musicality of the poetic environment. This section focuses on two related elements; water and the sounds that it makes, and their simultaneous contribution to sensations of devotion and eroticism in bhakti verses. The first example is from *Tiruvempavai*. It is a verse sung by women standing outside of a girl's house who call for her to wake up and to join them in worship of their god Shiva. Here we find another effective union of classical erotic and theological concepts to sing the praise of Shiva and entice the audience with the pleasant sounds of splashing, jingling, tinkling, buzzing, and murmuring.

> He is from the sacred water where we play and shout
>   so that the sorrow of our binding births are destroyed.
> While the dancer who dances with fire at the small hall in good Chidambaram
>   plays by hiding, creating, and protecting all of us and the world and the sky
> while words are spoken
> while bangles jingle
> while tied ornaments tinkle
> while bees buzz on beautiful bustling curls of hair
>   having praised the golden feet of the master
>   having plunged into the pond where flowers shine
> bathe in the water of the vast mountain spring!
> Our little doll.
> *Tiruvempavai* 12

Verse 12 contains several theological aspects of Shiva's power that are praised throughout *Tiruvacakam*. He is capable of destroying human rebirth, and he is the creator and protector of the entire world and its inhabitants. Shiva is also a trickster who plays hide-and-seek with his devotees as part of his divine play celebrated in the *Tevaram* hymns. In this verse, Shiva takes on a specific manifestation in a specific Tamil city, namely the dancer in Chidambaram. A significant city for many poet-saints, Chidambaram is also the legendary city in which Manikkavacakar is said to have composed *Tirukkovaiyar*. Since Chidambaram is not located in a mountainous region, the audience understands the girls' play area in the mountains as a reference to the kurinji landscape, the classical theme that indicates sexual union. The description of beautiful singing girls whose ornaments lightly jingle while they jump and play in the fresh mountain waters leaves no doubt that erotic imagery is a viable vehicle for devotion to Shiva. The water imagery and the girls' plunging and bathing are excellent examples of bhakti poems that engineer double meanings from well-known classical themes. Rather than read the girls' play solely as a metaphor for spiritual life, I pause here to instead acknowledge the sensory and physical joviality as the religious. Shiva's dance in this verse is not a corrective or intervention or macrocosm of the girls' play. The music and the splash are the transcendent sacred place of Shiva and his power. In fact, he is from that very mountain spring. Themes of immersion and compelling water play have been made most famous by Ramanujan's translations of hymns by Vaishnava bhakti poets known as alvar, the immersed ones, aptly titled *Hymns for the Drowning*.[35]

A ship drowning,
calling out for help
in the lashing sea,

I tossed in this ocean of births
when the lord
  in his splendor,
  bearing wheel and conch,
called out to me: "O, O, you there!"

showed me his grace,
and became one with me.
Tiruvaymoli 5. 1. 9[36]

In this example from the Vaishnava canon, the water motif is utilized to compare the devotee's soul to a ship in peril on the sea. In their seminal article "From Classicism to Bhakti," A. K. Ramanujan and Norman Cutler demonstrated that poets infused symbols and themes inherited from the classical tradition with new *religious* meaning.[37] According to their study, and as has been shown here, numerous elements of classical love poetry were re-signified in order to indicate different types of loving relationships. For example, the theme in which the heroine longs for her absent hero after he has left for battle is abstracted and reapplied to the devotee-poet speaking from the feminine perspective and longing for his absent god, a model exemplified in Nammalvar's *Tiruviruttam* but not practiced in *Tirukkovaiyar*.[38] In the Vaishnava verses above, the poet-as-heroine addresses and praises Vishnu in his role as the akam hero. At the end of this verse, the turmoil is resolved when the devotee is ultimately united by immersion with his lord. Here, the roles of the hero and heroine are reimagined to suit the devotional narrative of the devotee-poet seeking and achieving union with his beloved, lord Vishnu; although transformed for the purpose of a devotional relationship, the erotic undertone of their union remains intact and undeniable. The emotional outcry of the drowning ship is that of one who is separated from his or her beloved. Like the verses seen above, this example from the Vaishnava poets asserts the power of Vishnu to rescue the devotee from rebirths as well as provides the audience with the recognizable iconography of Vishnu in the form of his wheel and conch. Returning to *Tiruvempavai* in the next example, we will find that the watery emotions of the devotee also spill into the Shaiva context.

She who came into the world once
  with dewy eyes with unending long streams like canals
  having reached ecstasy in her mind
will not stop her mouth from telling the fame
  of sometimes our lord and other times of everyone's lord.
She will not worship the celestials.
As if becoming a madman for the great king, who is this person?
O you with ornamented breasts shaped by straps
  having sung until our mouths are satisfied with the feet of the talented one
      who takes and rules us in this way,
  having plunged into the beautifully shaped flower-filled water, bathe!
Our little doll.
Tiruvempavai 15

The image of a devotee or bhakta pouring out emotional cries to god is expressed through the imagery of gushing streams of tears and the unceasing praise pouring out of her mouth, like the ranting of a madman.[39] She is paired with an especially fierce manifestation of Shiva who is sung about by the devotee and takes the devotee as his slave. The word "yittakar," which I have translated as "the talented one," refers to Shiva, but more specifically to a manifestation of Shiva known as Bhairava. Bhairava is the name of the form of Shiva that is the fierce destroyer who cut off Brahma's fifth head, also significant to verse 20. The intensity of the destroyer Bhairava is matched by the intensity of emotion expressed by the weeping, insanity, and enslavement of the devotee. The ecstatic and bodily passion of the devotional mood parallels the unceasing longing and desire expressed by the heroine of Tamil love poetry. The suffering of the devotee does not convey an eroticism that is immediately desired or pleasurable. However, the palpable physicality of her ecstasy evokes strong visceral passion that is equal to the suffering felt in absence of sexual union. The following verse from *Tirukkovaiyar* illustrates this absence of the erotic, addressing the hero's heart and enumerating the fine qualities of the heroine that have caused it to ache.

198
Being disheartened, having heard about her rareness
O good heart
growing faint from trembling
    having thought about sweet joys of musical words[40]
    moisture from sharp teeth
    a waist like a snake from the anthills
    and breasts of her like Chidambaram
now you sob and sob unheeded with eyes full of tears
like a child crying for the moon in the sky.

The heroine has a voice that is sweet like the melody of a flute. The sharp teeth in the heroine's wet mouth indicate that she is very young, and in fact the heroine's confidante often cites these sharp teeth in her defense of the naive heroine. Although she is young in age, the attention of the hero's heart is drawn to the heroine's figure, which is developed with breasts and a slim waist that moves like a snake when she walks. It is no wonder that the hero's heart trembles at the thought of this young, erotic body that sways and ripples to the soft music of the heroine's voice. The poet, however, does not entirely grant the heart its arousing fantasy, but rather he ribs the heart and hero for exaggerating their childish desperation for this woman. The lighthearted dig references a popular motif found in a genre of children's poetry known as pillaittamil, in which the child notices the moon and cries out for it. The mother then requests that the moon be a playmate for the child.[41] This familiar child's plea and the sharp teeth of the heroine convey endearing childlike qualities of both the hero and the heroine. As a result, this verse captures the innocent love between the beautiful young woman with ideal qualities and the impatient desire of the hero through the watery tears of the latter.

The erotic imagery in these verses also connects the literary composition to the stuff of human bodies. Bodies drive audience encounters with the materiality of teeth, saliva, hair, waist, sweat, and the smell of the beloved's skin. In Chapter 5, we will witness more manipulation of these attractive bodies through the application of perfumes, ashes, and more ornament-objects like breast straps and jingling bangles.

Mediated Saints

I pause here with one last comment on the relationship between place, poet, and deity, one that is raised, for example, by the connection between Campantar and Shiva in Sirkali and by the theological characteristics of Shiva in verse 20 of *Tiruvempavai*. Contemporary audiences encounter this poetry not only through mythological and landscape cues, but also through the personae of the Tamil poet-saints. My nomenclature "poet-saint" alone indicates the combined literary and religious authority credited to the prolific hymnists. The lives of the poet-saints are preserved in the final book of the Shaiva canon and famed hagiography, *Periyapuranam*. The saints described in *Periyapuranam* number sixty-three and are recognized as an indivisible set of Shiva's devotees known as nayanmar. The hagiographies of three authors of *Tevaram* are included, but Manikkavacakar is entirely absent from *Periyapuranam*. *Periyapuranam* is attributed to Cekkilar, minister to the Chola king Kulottunka II (1133–1150 CE). According to tradition, a list of sixty-two saints was originally revealed to *Tevaram* poet Cuntarar in the Tiruvarur temple in the eighth century. This list, titled *Tiruttontattokai* (*Assembly of Holy Slaves*), was organized by criteria known only to Cuntarar. Two centuries later, Nampiyantar Nampi compiled the hymns of the saints into eleven volumes and wrote a longer poem called *Tiruttontar tiruvantati* that listed the sixty-two saints found in *Tiruttontattokai* and included Cuntarar as the sixty-third. Cekkilar used the same list of saints as Nampi and Cuntarar to organize *Periyapuranam* and framed the work with the story of Cuntarar's exceptional life.[42]

Contemporary audiences' reading, recitation, community performances, and other interpretative practices that engage these hymns and the Shaiva canon as a whole are shaped not only by the content of the verses and literary commentaries but also by stories of the poets' lives and inspirations.[43] In the case of Manikkavacakar, he is excluded from the list of sixty-three saints that drives the narrative of *Periyapuranam* and yet is sometimes included in the sculptural representations of the sixty-three saints found in contemporary Shaiva temples. His late medieval hagiography still plays into modern readings of *Tiruvacakam* as manifested Shaiva mysticism. Though it is not terribly surprising that contemporary reading and religious cultures shape literary reception, it is worth acknowledging that the narratives of these saints' miraculous encounters with Shiva shape subsequent expectations for Shaiva devotional literature.

Periyapuranam contributes to devotional Shaivism by placing saints in specific towns, developing their biographies, and developing the saints' individual iconography. *Periyapuranam* also marked the advent of a mainstream devotional tradition that propagated a particular "brand" of Shiva and his community of devotees.[44] Anne Monius's study of *Periyapuranam* and *Tevaram* hymns shows that a number of Shiva's attributes celebrated by the *Tevaram* poets were excluded from the medieval hagiography, especially his role as playful lover, charming mendicant, and devoted spouse.[45] Out of the eight feats of Shiva described by the muvar's hymns, only four survived in the details of the hagiography. Shiva of *Periyapuranam* emerged as a heroic father and warrior-lord praised for his burning the triple cities, skinning the elephant, burning Kama, and slaying Yama.[46] With the author's deliberate fatherly turn, there is scarce mention of women, wives, or active participation by Shiva's consort Uma (as seen in *Tevaram* 1.34.2 and 4.24.10 above), thus eliminating potentially erotic or romantic scenarios from *Periyapuranam*. The criteria by which attributes of Shiva were selected and edited in *Periyapuranam* illuminates one interpretation of medieval Tamil Shiva and calls our attention to the diversity and malleability of Shiva-s that occur in Tamil literature as the god is characterized by different poets and over the course of time. This provides a welcome invitation for the discovery of more Shiva-s in Tamil Shaivism, including the identity of the Shiva of *Tirukkovaiyar*, a poem that is generous in its sensuality and feminine forms. Taking this claim further, we must anticipate that Shiva of *Tirukkovaiyar* is distinct from Shiva in *Tiruvempavai* or *Tiruvacakam* as a whole, although all attributed to the same author. In the same way that literary styles change over time, so too, devotional forms for and descriptions of deities are contingent on historical and cultural contexts. In the environment designed in *Tirukkovaiyar*, the god dwells in and possesses a landscape of natural wonders and sensuality. In the context of this poetic world, we expect a deity who is beautiful, satisfied, and takes pleasure in his curated and shared landscapes.

Conclusion

I've intentionally selected akam-heavy verses in this chapter to show that there is an established precedent for the strong classical love-themed composition carried out in *Tirukkovaiyar*. Shiva and Vishnu both enter the text with heroic and erotic characteristics. Shiva's superior nature is illustrated through conflicts with his rivals Brahma and Vishnu, his intimate connection to his consort Uma, and his cosmic power as creator, protector, and destroyer of all things. These examples show that when *Tirukkovaiyar* was composed the integration of akam poetics with devotional iconography was an advanced literary practice. Poets developed various ways to integrate messages of devotion and direction for worship into existing styles of Tamil poetry, especially themes of playful and sensual eroticism experienced in the natural environment. Rather than suggest a clean break and transition from stories about idealized love and heroism to hymns sung by devoted pilgrims, we find instead verses dedicated to gods that are very much influenced by and indebted to the classical tropes. The poets of the Shaiva and Vaishnava bhakti corpus demonstrate deep intertextual roots with their classical predecessors, but they inherited much more than just the eroticism of the love story.

In this chapter we have encountered elevated maps, gushing waterways, floral feet, bathing women, and a loyal elephant. In one sense, these bhakti verses place Shiva in the stylized classical landscapes. But, based on the first portion of this chapter, the medieval poets also modified those idealized regional environments by planting names of towns and cities of the southeast. While the site names *feel* more concrete and historical to a scholar of religious history, Orr's work on the *Tevaram* sites shows that the site named in the devotional hymns are not as localizing as the language used in temple inscriptions. In my own work on the sites named in *Tirukkovaiyar*, I've found the sites do not suggest a sequential pilgrimage route, nor are they centered around the most frequently named city Chidambaram. Instead the sites skew south, clustered around Madurai, and quite a few highlight elevated hilltops. The combination of these factors, along with the poet's attention to water bodies, water imagery, and plant life, has convinced me that we have other (maybe more) information and attitudes to learn about religion from both social and geographical landscapes, including stars, jackfruit, and backwaters teaming with fish. I am not convinced that these two ways of expressing place or space by town name or botanical feature require resolution as to which is more pervasive or prestigious in expressions of Tamil religion.

There is a great deal of variety between anthologies, deities, and geographical orientations found even when moving between individual verses. Medieval poets delivered a sense of religion based in familiar towns and villages, the ecstasy of human eroticism, as well as a discernible emphasis on sensory experiences and physical engagement with the natural environment, one enjoyed by humans and gods alike.

4

Bodily Forms of Devotion

Shiva observes the lovers and his devotees from the fragrant groves in the wilderness, from the highest peaks, and from his home in Chidambaram. However, Shiva's adoring and melting-hearted devotees share little more than their humanity with the lovers and their entourages. *Tirukkovaiyar*'s inherited cast, already established in the classical akam corpus, provides the audience with a number of perspectives on the love story and a number of potential relationships through which to experience Shiva's favor. The poet uses the diversity of characters and relationships to create tensions and sculpt emotional tides over the course of the poem. One site for the push and pull between characters and devotees and the focus of this chapter is along the axis of feminine and masculine experiences, primarily illustrated in the relationship between hero and heroine.[1] These gendered dynamics do not occur only in the characterization of individuals and between male-female pairs. Significant conflict and consolation are also found between men among men and between women among women in their respective social contexts. Previous chapters explored religious experience as it is designed and developed through classical treatises, across literary landscapes, and settled among birds and critters. This chapter focuses on the materiality and iconography of human and divine bodies, their public or domestic spaces, and the aesthetic impact of emotions felt in human and devotional relationships. Rather than find the sweet love shared by mother and child and celebrated by other medieval bhakti poets, we will find in *Tirukkovaiyar* a great deal of dissatisfaction, criticism, and even blame. Shifting from fragrant blossoms and rippling springs to a clamoring battlefield and a sulking wife, this chapter shows the emotional range over which Shiva has command and that these dramatic confrontations and ferocious warriors are part of the sense of religion in *Tirukkovaiyar*.

Before moving deeper into the text, I pause to define my method for reading the human story and gendered relations in a medieval poem, primarily following the strategies of Martha Ann Selby, Sheldon Pollock, and others who have addressed the delicate task of reading literature for representations of human history. Selby's study of early Tamil, Prakrit, and Sanskrit literature negotiates the historical relevance of poetry by reading verses as *aestheticized representations* of romantic and sexual culture indicative of specific attitudes toward the erotic.[2] Set free from notions of a "fixed" interpretation, or the poetry's liminal status between hard history and ahistorical ephemera, Selby embraces the ability of these works to provide us with evidence of social practice manifested in metaphor and idiom.[3]

Like Selby, Pollock shifts the object of study from uncovering an original or authentic voice to grappling with a cultural attitude. In Pollock's words, I aim to make "sense of *a historical form of consciousness*" rather than identifying "*a form of historical consciousness*."[4] I will not read verses of poetry as the direct experience or reality of women or men who lived in ninth-century South India. Instead, I present characters as *real representations*, representations of modes of masculinity and especially femininity that are a testament to the multiplicity of experiences available to poets and audiences of early and medieval Tamil poetry.

Borrowing again from work by Pollock and Dominick LaCapra, I also do not distinguish more or less historical voices within a single composition.[5] Instead, I accept one consistent genre or register of historicity per text and do not distinguish conscious shifts between perceived boundaries between what is real, fake, history, legend, archive, or art. In *Tirukkovaiyar*, I interpret all kings, gods, and people as consciously stylized and, in the case of human characters, anonymous as specified by classical Tamil poetics.[6] I turn now to the heroes of the composition.

Two Heroes

Tirukkovaiyar features two heroes, one human and one divine. These two figures are the focal point of idealized masculinity in this poetic context. The first hero (kilavittalaivan) is the necessary counterpart for the heroine of the akam paradigm. He is a thief, the one who steals the heroine's heart. The second hero is the pattutaittalaivan, or the hero of the composition, and he is usually the historical patron of the poem—frequently a king or landowner, as found in the earliest extant kovai-style poem, *Pantikkovai*. It is the poet's challenge to tell the love story of the first hero and to simultaneously pay tribute to the merits of the second hero in every single verse. Norman Cutler has noted that the appearance of two heroes illustrates the poet's recognition and use of both love and heroic traditions for the praise of Shiva. Cutler concludes and I concur that the primary goal of the kovai is to praise the patron and the hero-lover and the overall "akam framework is an instrument to this end."[7] The poet's acumen is measured by the creativity with which he is able to intermingle and manage the stories of both heroes. By naming Shiva as the patron-hero of *Tirukkovaiyar*, the poet challenged himself to negotiate the stories of a human hero, a divine hero, and their respective idealized worlds.

These two heroes can also be distinguished according to their identities as a hero from the love (akam) poetry tradition and the other as a hero from the heroic (puram) poetry tradition of classical Tamil. Literally meaning "outside," compared to love poetry, puram poetry deals with heroic battles, covert cattle raids, the generosity of victorious kings, and various scenarios from a young warrior's life. The battlefield scenes featured in the heroic-themed anthology *Purananuru* embrace gore, with warrior's corpses piled high and demons tripping through twisted intestines. For example, in *Purananuru* 368, the bard compliments his hero, "You who labor with the plow of your sword so that men are stacked like hay."[8] In *Purananuru* 370 another bard praises his patron with the following lines.

> O greatness! you who are lord of the fearful field
> where a female demon finds and snatches a powerful braceleted arm
> severed by an ax and weeps from exhaustion because her legs are tangled
> in the coils of the ridged guts
> of fearless men, as the vulture and the red-eared eagle wheel in the sky!
> *Purananuru* 370[9]

In addition to the fleshy carnage, the lives of these warriors and bards are punctuated with visceral descriptions of feasts of succulent fatty meats and pungent fermented drinks that do not appear in *Tirukkovaiyar*. In general, one might say that the heroic world is more carnal and confronts the darker realities of human life. Death on the battlefield, mothers mourning their sons, bards begging for the lives of their emaciated families, and ruthless conquest, while incredibly potent topics for the Tamil poet, are not appropriate themes for the amorous landscape of *Tirukkovaiyar*. In fact, compared to the earliest heroic anthologies, both *Pantikkovai* and *Tirukkovaiyar* are noticeably tempered and focus more on victories, territorial claims, and the trappings of a wealthy king rather than the work of a bloodied spear.

The most striking difference between the love-themed hero and heroic-themed hero rests in his identity. While the love-theme heroes fall in love, hunt, serve the king, fight in battles, and travel through treacherous deserts and jungles, the heroic-themed heroes win battles in specific cities and towns, and, especially in the case of historical kings, heroic-themed heroes have names (Figure 15). While the love poetry takes place in an exclusively idealized world, the heroic poetry

Figure 15 Stone heroes, Darasuram.

has an element of historical reference (although this is not to say that heroic poetry does not also use hyperbole and myth to eulogize the albeit historical hero). Thus, the praise of Shiva as patron necessitates some form of historical or geographical specificity. In order to fully appreciate the poet's characterization of the patron Shiva and his deft blending of dynastic and mythological tropes, we turn first to a kovai poem with a royal, human patron named King Netumaran.

Pantikkovai is the earliest extant kovai-style poem, and it survives in fragments that are embedded in a grammatical treatise, *Iraiyanar akapporul.* The date of *Pantikkovai* is tentatively assigned to the seventh century based on the patron praised in verses, who is believed to be the seventh-century Pandya king Netumaran of Madurai.[10] *Pantikkovai* is not only the earliest surviving example of verses in the kovai genre, but also a relatively contemporary case study of a human patron-hero for comparison with the treatment of Shiva as a divine patron-hero in *Tirukkovaiyar*. In the verses that follow, the royal patron is praised for his martial prowess and righteous rule.

> *Asking where it happened*
> Was it on a lotus,
> spreading its aroma,
> and pleasant to those
> who look upon it?
> Or was it on Mount Kolli
> in the West,
> where clouds crawl,
> Mount Kolli of him
>   who conquered and plundered
>   heaps of fine enemy wealth
>   and herds of enemy elephants
>   at Kaṭaiyal?
>   Tell me
>   where this girl,
>   who made your bright
>   garlanded chest slump,
>   resides.
>   *Pantikkovai* 34[11]

The love scene narrated in verse 34 of *Pantikkovai* is spoken between two men. The hero's best friend asks the hero of the love story for details about the heroine. The conversation takes place after the initial meeting of the lovers, and the friend has noticed that the hero's appearance has faded. Suspecting love-sickness, the friend inquires about the girl who has captured the hero's attention. It is this line of inquiry that leads to a transition from the home of the heroine to the territory of the king. The friend suggests two places where she might live. The first place is on a lotus, which is a reference to Lakshmi, the goddess of beauty and good fortune, who is depicted sitting or standing on a red lotus. Although this reference to Lakshmi is subtle, by asking if the heroine lives on a lotus, he compliments the divine beauty of the girl for whom the hero has fallen. The second place that the hero's friend suggests for the home of the beautiful heroine is Mount Kolli. Mount Kolli is not a mythically significant peak like Mount Meru or Kailash, but rather the Kolli Hills are part of the Eastern Ghats central to today's Tamil Nadu. The mountainous area, although a specific place in Tamil country, is also associated with the idealized mountainous region of the kurinji landscape, and thus it corresponds with the sexual union of the lovers. In this verse, the Kolli Hills are possessed as royal territory by the patron-hero, King Netumaran, and thus rendered political capital in addition to its significance as a literary landscape.

Having complimented the geographical reach of his patron, the poet then extols the king's martial prowess, his victory over his enemies in a town called Kataiyal, heaps of booty, and the capture of war elephants. Finally, through the questions of his friend, we get a description of the hero of the love story. He is a man with a bright garlanded chest. In contrast to the garlanded breasts of a female character that are delicate and fragrant adornments, the garlanded chest of the hero indicates that he is a warrior, and its brightness indicates his excellence. When combined with the supernatural beauty of the heroine, the hero is a suitable, if not perfect, counterpart for this amorous union. From this description, the reader can deduce that the patron-hero and love-hero have martial prowess in common, and there is a sense in which the excellence of the love-hero is emphasized in order to elevate the stature of the patron-hero. In this particular verse, we see that both figures of the love story, hero and heroine, are used to direct the audience's attention toward Netumaran.

In the following excerpt from verse 398 of *Pantikkovai*, the poet praises his king by relating the heroine of the love story to a prominent city.

> She who is like
> Kūṭal City in the South,
>   the city of Neṭumāṟaṉ
>   with his elephants
>   like mountains,
>   and his righteous scepter!

Will wedding drums sound all day tomorrow
in our town hall if you don't?
I wonder.
Pantikkovai 398[12]

In the first example (v. 34), the Kolli hills were introduced as a potential home for the heroine, a classical landscape associated with sexual union, and the victorious king's territory. In this verse (398), the featured locale is Kutal, an ancient name for Madurai, known to be the throne of the Pandya dynasty and the cultural center of southern Tamil country. When the heroine is compared to the city, Madurai is the hinge by which the poet pivots from the heroine to the patron-hero's tribute. The poet praises the just rule of the king's righteous scepter but also couples it with praise for Netumaran's martial prowess with reference to his troop of mountain-like elephants. The narrative shifts from panegyric to plans for the heroine's wedding, leaving auditory cues to linger and link the roar of the king's battlefield to the wedding drums about to sound.

From these excerpts, the royal hero emerges as one who is fierce when he conquers, rich in his treasuries, righteous when he rules, and with the stature of a virile garlanded warrior. Grand elephants, flourishing cities, and towering mountains are under his scepter. Kovai is of course not the only literary genre to praise kings. The meykkirtti is a type of panegyric poem commonly used for opening royal inscriptions with significant parallels to attributes considered worthy of praise by kovai poets. They focus on the great deeds of a king and offer blessings for his life and his queen. The grand statement of royal status is typically followed by detailed contracts for land donation, the presentation of gifts, or other such transactions. The following excerpt is a tenth-century definition of a meykkirtti.

> There is a verse for each two metrical lines having four metrical feet, and at the end of narrating all of the famous deeds achieved by the physical prowess of the king, and telling his history, and saying "May you enjoy life with her," and also, after telling his given name, saying "May you prosper for years," capably stating all of this constitutes a meykkirtti. (313)
> They have said that the ending of the
> enduring meykkirtti will end as a prose statement. (314)
> *Panniru pattiyal*

Praise of a king—or by extension, a god—includes the king's physical prowess, his auspicious life history, his given name, and well-wishes for his wife and long life. Taking into account this definition of praiseworthy characteristics combined with the triumphs of King Netumaran we find that the patron-hero's power comes from his physical strength, victories over enemies, wealth, just rule, and the virtue of his queen. Using this rubric for identifying kingship, we turn now to the subject of praise and worship in *Tirukkovaiyar*, lord Shiva.

God-Hero

The patron-hero of *Tirukkovaiyar* is Shiva as he appears in Chidambaram. Much attention has been paid to the places, people, and creatures of *Tirukkovaiyar* in order to demonstrate that the religious sense of the text was developed through an aesthetic and sensory understanding of the material world. Of course, this poetic environment, this kingdom of riches, is home to the supreme deity Shiva. Here we look closely at Shiva as he appears in *Tirukkovaiyar*, keeping in mind the definition of doubt according to which it isn't the heroine but rather the combination of the exquisite heroine encountered in a remarkable environment that causes the hero to waiver. Here too, the poet presents the deity *in combination with* a superior materiality.

The form of Shiva who appears in the Indic pantheon and who is found in the Hindu triad, Shiva, Vishnu, Brahma, is not exactly the god praised in *Tirukkovaiyar*. In fact, the name Civan appears very rarely in the four hundred verses. He is much more likely to be called "The Ancient One" or "He of Ampalam." His romantic chemistry is reserved for his consort Uma. Shiva of *Tirukkovaiyar* is also evoked through praise of the physical appearance of his lotus feet, his warrior anklets, and his matted hair. In fact, the object most lovingly adorned and embellished by the poet is that of Shiva's physical body; the verses of *Tirukkovaiyar* are replete with iconographic vocabulary, a vocabulary commensurate with available paintings and sculptures of this powerful god. He has red matted hair with a crescent moon and the Ganges River resting in it.[13] He has three eyes, which are sometimes described as the planets.[14] From head to toe, he wears konrai flowers, bones, Rudraksha beads, a necklace of skulls, snakes, a tiger pelt, and warrior anklets.[15] His body is smeared with white ash and he is carrying three weapons, a battle-axe, a trident, and a spear stuck with the flesh of a demon.[16] Shiva's bull mount Nandi gallops through many verses and flies high as the insignia on Shiva's flag.[17] In Chidambaram, it is no surprise that Shiva takes the form of the king of dance. Although he is not literally described as the Nataraja, Shiva is named Kuttan in *Tirukkovaiyar*, and he dances with flickering fire in the wilderness, while holding a docile gazelle and surrounded by his devoted servants in the hall.[18]

In addition to his attractive appearance, the poet also constructs an impression of Shiva's strength and superior status. For example, although Shiva of *Tirukkovaiyar* is not the type of king who participates in human battles or retains an army of elephants and horses, he is known for slaying a demon elephant.[19] In fact, Shiva vanquishes many enemies. Shiva destroyed the sun god Pakal by knocking out his teeth.[20] One of the more popular references, given that *Tirukkovaiyar* is a love story, is the god of love Kama's narrow escape from Shiva. Kama, with his lovely flower arrows, agitated Shiva until he opened his third eye and burned Kama to ash. Eventually, Shiva revived Kama, but the god of love returned without his bodily form.[21] Shiva had a similar change of heart after he destroyed the god of death, Yama, and then revived him after insuring the eternal life of a young boy named Markandeya.[22] In addition, Shiva destroyed Daksha's sacrifice, the Lanka king, and the world.[23]

The volatile and destructive nature of Shiva's conquests is tempered by descriptions of those who worship him including rival gods and a Pandya king. Among those who gather at his feet are celestials, demons, the muvar,[24] and Patanjali.[25] According to the verses of *Tirukkovaiyar*, the gracious god grants his faithful followers the destruction of rebirth, the removal of penance, inspiration for the composition of songs, and the melting bones of his devotees.[26] Like a devotee who enters one of Shiva's temples to scatter rows of flowers at his feet, the poet of *Tirukkovaiyar* conducts his own ritual of worship by heaping upon every verse idyllic love trysts, ever-ripening fruits, towering mountaintops, and an overall sense of abundance. In this poem and in the context of singing Shiva's praise, more is more.

A survey of Shiva's activities in *Tirukkovaiyar* shows that four aspects of his character are most prevalent over the course of the love story. The first of these references is Shiva's destruction of the three demon cities. Shiva takes Mount Meru as his bow and shoots a fiery arrow of destruction to level the fortifications in a victory over his enemies.[27] In the second most referenced legend, Shiva heroically imbibes the ocean of poison.[28] While seeking to churn the ocean into nectar, the gods first produced an ocean full of poison that threatens to destroy the world. Shiva drank the poison and kept it in his throat, so as not to be poisoned himself. Both his heroic act and his blue throat are praised many times in *Tirukkovaiyar* for the relief that he brought to his devotees. The third aspect of Shiva's persona emphasized in *Tirukkovaiyar* remains concealed in his superior status. This is because Shiva is praised for his unique quality of being hidden from and unknown by Vishnu, Brahma, and occasionally Indra.[29] Shiva has a special connection with Vishnu, who worships Shiva and then is rewarded with a discus.[30] In one verse Vishnu joins Shiva at the hall in Chidambaram.[31] Finally, the fourth element of Shiva's identity featured in many descriptions is the goddess, a virtuous queen by his side.[32] Shiva shares half of his body with his consort, and she appears in many forms throughout this poem. In all, Shiva of *Tirukkovaiyar* is victorious over his enemies, merciful to his subjects, unmatched by his peers, and united with the perfect feminine counterpart. The identity of Shiva in this poem strongly resonates with the elements found in meykkirtti verses, casting the dominant qualities of the Shiva praised in *Tirukkovaiyar* in a light similar to that of royalty, including the boundaries of a Shiva's realm, his seats of power, his righteous rule, and the people who serve him. Since Shiva is adored by human and divine servants and battles supernatural forces, the bounds of his rule reach far beyond the human world.

Human-Hero

Setting aside for a moment Shiva's peerless qualities, we will analyze the hero's character not in terms of the god-hero but rather as a figure among other human men. Though limited in stature compared to Shiva, the hero of the love story nonetheless makes an equally important contribution to the poet's characterization of a hero-figure. Through the following interactions between the hero and his various conversation partners we learn about his attitude, which, when combined with the emotional dynamics of the love narrative and clues about the lives of devotees, constitutes the mood or sense of *Tirukkovaiyar* and thus the mood or sense cultivated by Tamil religious literature.

In previous chapters, the hero is a strong, adventurous warrior. He is handsome like Murukan. Even the thought of his presence is enough to cause a frenzy. Over the course of *Tirukkovaiyar*, the hero slays dangerous animals, travels great distances, and saves the heroine from drowning in a churning whirlpool. Amid all of these trials and triumphs, a romance between the young man and the heroine develops toward a marriage proposal, at least from the perspective of the women involved. In this reintroduction to the hero, we begin with the words of the heroine's confidante. In the following passages the confidante warns the hero that proposals of marriage are being made to the heroine's family. Although addressing the heroine's situation, these verses also speak volumes to the hero's approach to town gossip and social obligations.

195
Telling a message about the girl
O lord of the ford, decide today!
Decide your intentions for the girl who resembles Chidambaram
    of the supreme lord
    Shiva who wears bones as gems
    who showed compassion to bowing celestials who were bewildered by fear
        of poison.
More and more outsiders[33] intend to adorn her
with lavish amounts of gold.

196
Announcing the adornment of gold
O one of the riverbanks with fragrant flowers
they adorned her with steadfast protection
    with part of her hair woven with flowers
    in Chidambaram of the one ornamented with snakes.
They will adorn her with gold immediately!
Marriage drums rattle and the great conchs sound
    both beautifully arranged standing in front of the house
    where the flag touches the sky and decorations have been strung up.

In the verses leading up to this scene, the heroine's confidante warns the hero that the local people will gossip about her sexual maturity leaving no doubts about the heroine's readiness for marriage when they see the blushing heroine. Her family awaits young men who will offer gold as part of the marriage arrangements. In verses 195 and 196, the confidante cleverly boasts not about the bride's beauty or chastity but rather about the amount of gold that the other men will bring before her family. Although the heroine's confidante (a young woman) is speaking to the hero, her proposition positions him among and creates tension between other men. Through her appeal, we learn that the hero is expected to have a sense of competition with his peers. By threatening the arrival of other young men, the confidante hopes to stir a feeling of jealousy or jilted pride. Eschewing his relationship or duty to the heroine, or taking her excellence for granted, the hero's virtue resides in his superior social status and his ability to attain wealth compared to his male peers.

Despite *Tirukkovaiyar*'s identity as a love poem, its many verses addressing potential marriage proposals or elopement, and the married status of the heroine and hero in the later chapters of the poem, not a word is uttered about their wedding ceremony, feast, ritual, or vows. Thus, some questions remain about the hero's frequent departures, his aloof view of marriage, and the exclusion of the hero and heroine's nuptial details. In the next series of verses, a different dimension of the hero's character is developed through his own words.

8
Speaking about union
Speaking of this moment, "she is nectar, I am its taste."
I am sure
the destiny of my good deeds gave her to me.
Who can understand the beauty of our oneness
her and me
our secret union
    on the stone strewn slopes
    in the Potiyil mountains of the holy one from Chidambaram
having sent away our attendants.

The opening scene of *Tirukkovaiyar* is the amorous union of the hero and heroine. In verse 8, the hero is still basking in the afterglow of their early encounter. High on a rocky mountain possessed by Shiva, the hero and heroine snuck away from their companions to unite in secret. The hero associates their inseparable nature with the impossible task of separating sweetness from honey—she is nectar and he is its taste. In a moment when one might expect the hero to rely on his excellence in character and status for winning such a lovely mate, instead the hero cites his karmic merit. The relationship between karmic destiny and a suitable partner is a trope that is also repeated among the women of the poem. The hero's admiration for the heroine is expressed again in the next sequence.

16
Sending to the play ground
You
    like a creeper spread with bees
    resembling a full moon, white pearls, red fruit, and long splendid bows
Feel free! Go and play!
I will come and reappear there
    hidden on the slope flowing with scattered drops of honey
    on Kailash of the one without compare in Chidambaram
        who is ever expanding
        light without measure.

17

Realizing her rareness

Why did the helpless one with curls ornamented with flower blossoms enter
the garden that surrounds Chidambaram of the ancient one
 who makes his beautiful flower anklets my ornaments of sweet flower petals
 the one who created earth, heaven, and mountain?
If this is her good nature
was it friendship? A dream? Or something else?
I don't know.

In verse 16, the hero calls out to the heroine with a description that would flatter even the goddess Uma. The hero tells the heroine to pay attention to his directions and then to go and join her friends. He plans to meet her later in disguise, hidden in the hills surrounding the girls' meeting place. Often on the lookout for a token blossom or a broken branch as a sign that her lover is near, the heroine is likely relieved to know when and where the hero intends to reappear next. Shiva's role in this verse is primarily one of host, since the meeting will take place on the slopes of Shiva's home, Mount Kailash. The glory of the site and its host is expressed through the exuberant rivers of honey and the god's radiant light. In verse 17, the hero remains stunned at his meeting with the heroine. He wonders how their union occurred. What drew the lovely girl into the garden where he first saw her? The question of the heroine's motivation has echoes of the second verse of *Tirukkovaiyar* in which the hero doubts the earthly origins of his partner. The overall impression of the hero made in these two verses is that the hero is deeply entrenched in his affection for the heroine. In the early days of their romance, he was swept away by the experience of their union and he even humbles himself to meet his lover in secret, hiding from a group of girls, no less. In addition to negotiating or avoiding contact with his lover's playmates, the hero also faces his constant companion, his friend.

The second theme of *Tirukkovaiyar*, known as meeting with his friend, is one of the longest chapters and is dedicated to inquisitive, consoling, and bashful conversations between the young hero and his best friend. The hero shows signs of love-sickness, confesses his affair to his friend, and begins to conspire to meet his lover again. For his part, the friend inquires after the cause of his hero's weakened stature, tests and confirms the splendor of the heroine, and proceeds with full effort to reunite the lovers. In the following verse the friend tries to guess the reason for the hero's anguish.

22
Speaking and admonishing
Is my hero weeping today because the one with a waist like a vine deceived you
with the wide-eyed look of a young fawn in the fertile mango grove
at Kailash of the ancient one in Chidambaram
    who made nectar from poison in his beautiful throat
    who released the celestials
    who saved and enslaved us so that our soul is ever-lasting?

In verse 22, we assume the bruised ego of the hero who has been taken in by the bewitching gaze of the heroine. The slim and swaying girl is likened to ivy, and she is surrounded by the lush botanical environment of a fertile mango grove. Her placement in this particular type of grove elicits a number of sensual and sensory associations. The split mango resembles the eye of the lady. The unripe mango resembles the perky breasts of a young virgin. The actual flesh of a ripe mango is intensely sweet, making monkeys into thieves and bees into drunkards. This is the orchard in which we encounter the heroine. This is also the context in which she is accused of deceiving the hero with her large, gentle, fawn-like eyes. The hero's anxiety aroused by the lovely heroine becomes his embodied state in verse 24.

24
Speaking with grief
O generous patron!
Wind demolished the mountains into piles of rubble
waves of the three-water ocean muddled earth and sky
even then, you were not disturbed.
Why does your mind grieve now
    trembling like those without grace from the one at the small hall
    who is surrounded by a fragrant wreath thick with konrai?

This lover's lament is spoken with concern by the hero's friend. The friend describes the physical impact of the hero's adoration on his body through a stark contrast between the brave, steadfast stature of the hero in the face of natural calamity and the trembling young lover grieved by one soft glance, a dramatic change in the gait of the poem. Although the verses presented here largely emphasize the passion and sensitivity with which the hero approaches his love affair with the heroine, there are also many verses that testify to his valorous qualities more commensurate with the strength and stature exemplified by the patron-hero Shiva. It is only the disruption of his reputation for unwavering clarity and mastery of the world around him that draws the concern of his friend. In these uncomfortable confrontations between the hero and friends, combined with changes in the hero's physical comportment, the poison-filled throat of the god, and the catastrophe of natural disaster, we learn that there is conflict in love and turmoil in devotion. Destruction of bodies and ruined land are indeed contributions to the sense of religion conveyed by the poet. Pausing for a moment in the hero's bold yet delicate pursuit of his beloved, we turn now to the exemplars and challengers in the world of women.

The Heroine

In verses presented in previous chapters, we have met the heroine and learned about the ideal qualities of any heroine found in a Tamil love story. She is defined in commentaries as one who is from a fine family and of excellent social standing. She is chaste and faithful like her mother. She is beautiful. Her tears are like pearls. Her hair is as dark as a thundercloud. She learned Shiva's teachings and she is protected by the council and affection of her confidante (Figure 16). In the final portion of *Tirukkovaiyar*, the poet presents his audience with variations on the theme of separation. In the classical love-themed corpus and in kovai poems, there are a number of reasons why the hero departs from the heroine, sending her into fits of anguish. The departure scenario developed in the final theme is for his visits to his mistress. These verses provide an opportunity to witness the chaste heroine confront her opposition. The exchanges that follow involve the hero, the heroine, a group of public women, the hero's chief mistress, the heroine's confidante, the son of the hero and heroine, and the girl in red. While dialogues between the heroine and her best friend (and to a lesser extent their mothers) are a common feature of the text, voices of the unchaste and publically erotic female figures are unique to this, the final, theme. In brief summary of the theme, the heroine scolds her husband for having affairs with other women. A girl dressed in red, the color of fertility, is sent to pass by the gate of the women's house to let the hero know that the heroine is ready for sexual union with him. The public women then speak and play among themselves, discussing the arrival of the hero and entertaining the chief mistress's boast that she can steal the attention of any man from the other women. The chief mistress directly insults the heroine, and the heroine retorts with equally bitter words. The narrative shifts to the position of the hero standing outside the gate of his house, trying to endear himself to his son and his wife so that he can enter the courtyard. The

Figure 16 Stone heroine with attendants, Darasuram.

confidante and heroine return to speaking among themselves about the hero's behavior and ultimately decide to quietly uphold the status quo of the marital contract. In a closer look at the verses that follow, we will find a remarkably open line of communication between the exemplary heroine and her nemesis; new dimensions of the heroine's personality emerge, and along with them some new conclusions about the roles of femininity in Tamil religious literature.[34] We begin with words spoken by the heroine to the hero, between husband and wife on the topic of his infidelity, betraying the bitterness that has entered their once sweet love.

358
Sulking in bed
O you from Chidambaram
where grace is perfected by Shiva who has release
O father! For what are you blamed today?
We stood here with loathing not having heard of vile behavior.
We with bitter, bad karma did not perform penance.
Don't touch me!
Leave my good sash!
We won't accept new embraces from the jeweled ones.

The heroine confronts her husband, disapproving of his behavior and her fate. First, she sites her own failure to do proper acts of penance that presumably would have earned her a more faithful husband and which yielded positive results for the hero in an earlier verse. She concedes that her bitter karma puts her at a disadvantage to criticize his behavior today. Nonetheless, the heroine issues a second remark of disapproval, this time directed at the hero. The hero may have escaped her scolding, but the heroine will not grant him the pleasure of tugging at her girdle strings. In fact, she refuses to accept his affair (embrace used here as a euphemism for sexual intercourse) with the public women.

The Tamil word that I am translating as "public woman" is "parattai." Suggested translations for this word in the *Tamil Lexicon* include harlot, prostitute, or courtesan, but the lifestyle and value of the parattai's role in early Tamil society is essentially unknown. Furthermore, the verses alone do not employ the term "parattai" to indicate the rival love interests of the hero. It is in the framing subtitles and explanations provided by layers of commentary that ascribe the parattai status to women in the verses. One powerful example of suggestive ambiguity surrounding the parattai's sociocultural and religious roles is found in the very famous wife and "prostitute" duo, Kannaki and Matavi of the revered classical Tamil epic, *Cilappatikaram*. In a comparative study of oral and printed versions of the early epic, Brenda Beck compares portrayals of the relationships between the hero, the heroine Kannaki, and the second female lead who is the hero's mistress Matavi. She discovers that chastity is in fact viewed differently in various versions of the epic. Her thorough examination of the hero's mistress, Matavi, reveals equally diverse characterizations of a woman explicitly living outside of the prescribed role of the good wife. In one account, Kannaki and Matavi "are painted as having opposed characters, one black and the other white, whereas in the oral and in the literary versions both women are moral and deserving in their own right."[35] Put differently, Beck writes, "In the one Madhavi is a true whore, in the other a singularly appropriate mistress."[36] The study concludes that Kannaki was represented on various occasions as magical, with the power of a goddess, without any power at all, or infused with the power of her anklet, her breast, or her body. This specific pairing disrupts any neat system of opposition between the wife and the mistress and tempers our reading of a parattai-like characters' appearance in *Tirukkovaiyar*. Over the course of the four hundred verses, *Tirukkovaiyar* praises the chastity of the heroine very rarely, especially compared to the lines upon lines dedicated to her beauty and her love-sickness, but the chastity of her husband's mistress is not discussed. Moving forward, I translate "parattai" as public women when referring to the general term and as mistress to indicate the specific character of the hero's "second wife" to remind the reader of Matavi's story and the relative flexibility of women's chastity and morality in the literary context.

With this exchange of blame and disapproval between lovers, there is a counter-example that the humans are played against. Shiva has flawless grace and attained release or muttam from the cycles of bad, bitter karma. The home of this blissful god in Chidambaram is also the hometown of the rather sullied hero. On more than one occasion, the voices of the heroine and confidante take on a sarcastic biting tone in these confrontational scenes. We find that while the hero is permitted to occasion the women's house, the heroine likewise is permitted to oppose his habits in word and in action. With this in mind, the opening address is reread not as a nod to the hero's noble origins established by the presence of Shiva's grace, but rather a scoff at how far he has fallen from his previously honorable status. In the end, however, what stands out from the lovers' squabble is the unparalleled excellence of Shiva. Through an exercise in physical and experiential contrast, the poet makes the god's grace to shine brighter by placing him next to the dirtied reputation of the hero and failed penance of the women. Try as she might to keep the hero from leaving again, the heroine fails to tether her lover. In one attempt to call him back to her door, the heroine enlists the help of a uncommon character—the girl in red.

361
Telling by those who are at the gate, having seen the red dress
The fresh red bud tied with silk cloth like red flowers
  with beautiful red sandal on her soft breasts held with leather straps
came and appeared before the sacred house
  to tell the ways of the world to the man from the city
  who wears the beautiful red foot of the one who possesses the sacred small hall
  the gem who has a golden-red body.

The heroine's house sent the girl dressed in red to pass by the women's house as a message to the hero about the heroine's menstruation and her readiness for sexual union. The poet has created a super-saturated sensory experience of red: red flower bud, shining red silk, and red sandal makeup paired with the red foot and glittering ruddy body of Shiva. Red is the messenger, the message of fertility, and red is the perfected god. To the red visual cues of the poetry, the poet adds the scent of the decorative sandal paste and the heat of the red fire that Shiva holds in the verses immediately before and after this scene. The girl dressed in red contributes to the feminine imagery in *Tirukkovaiyar* an example of communication, a feminine agent in her dress and in her message. Narrowly interpreted, the message is between wife and husband. However, the messenger, her method, and attire suggest that the message is announced and received by all the neighbors and townspeople who she passes on her way and by all of the public women who notice the flashy dress of the girl standing at their gate. It is a message to the public from the heroine. The golden-red body of Shiva in verse 361 reignites with glittering heat in verse 370.

370
Stating the happiness at having seen the arrival of the chariot
O you with feet like flowers in the city of Chidambaram
        of the one from the small hall
        who came like fire in his glittering dress.
You embrace the pair of thick shoulders
        of the man from the city with sweet water
        who has come like Murukan.
You did penance for this union long ago.
The tall chariot arrived.

This verse celebrates three strong masculine exemplars. Shiva is seated like royalty in Chidambaram. Shiva also adopts a fatherly persona with the appearance of his son Murukan, a deity often admired for his handsome stature by unmarried girls. To this prestigious duo, the poet initiates the arrival of the hero, who is likened to Murukan, boasts a muscular physique, and displays his status through the height of his chariot. What does this team of super-masculine heroes tell the audience about femininity? The god's brilliant appearance, the hero's wide shoulders, and the image of young, powerful Murukan resonate with the passion and erotic tension of the mistress's interest. Unlike the sulking heroine in verse 358, the mistress reaps the benefits of penance that she performed in her previous lives. All of the characters in this verse, Shiva, the hero, and the mistress, are bold. They are impressive in their actions and in their physical appearances. With some irony then, when the hero's chariot arrives, the mistress is praised for her auspicious behavior and encouraged to enjoy her reward for penance—an affair with the heroine's husband. This sense of the fitness of the mistress for the hero through a combination of merit and karma has echoes of Matavi's story. Essentially granted permission to unite with the hero, it comes as no surprise that the mistress finds herself a bit proud and boastful of her new acquisition.

372

Saying in praise of herself

If I can't draw grace from the sides of those whose smiles spread like lightning
who can fully embrace like those who attained grace from the one of the small hall
who has matted hair spread with fire
who conquered the group of cities with arrows spread with fire
I will be like the flower creeper from the water village
who already separated from the man from the water village.

The hero's mistress speaks for herself, addressing her peers but also standing within earshot of the heroine. She brags that she can attract a man's attention away from the wiles of rival women who offer flashing smiles and the promise of sexual intercourse. If she can't accomplish this task, then she should consider herself as pitiable as the heroine who has already lost her lover. In this verse we find a combination of power, credit, and blame associated with the infidelity of the hero. Significantly, however, the only one not implicated is the hero himself. Rather, the mistress is keeping him from wandering into the arms of other women, demonstrating her prowess over both the hero and the other women. The mistress does not reveal by what methods she maintains the hero's loyalty; however, she does make explicit the erotic tricks of those who smile like lightning. The mistress indicates a sense of competition between these public women in which the hero is a status symbol and an object to be won. Her pride comes not from amorous feelings toward the hero but rather from stealing him from her competitors, a scenario not unlike the hero competing with wealthy suitors for his bride or Shiva conquering his enemy. Her victory over the heroine is expressed as a foregone conclusion. From her perspective the hero and heroine have already split, and she is confident that she has captured the hero from any rivals, married or not.

Where is Shiva and where are the devotees in this verse? What is the sense of religion crafted through these characters and their relationships with one another? When we look at the phrases that present Shiva's tribute, spreading fire abounds! Fire brings with it heat, danger, and destruction, but also something that flickers and tempts the eye. It is a catalyst for change. In this verse, Shiva brings an element of competition and ultimately victory over the conquered demon cities. Shiva's display of prowess over his enemies is paired with his show of mercy to devotees at his side. The poet draws a daring comparison between the public women vying for the hero's grace and the devotee who seeks the grace of Shiva by using the word "arul" in both contexts. The mistress draws the arul of the hero away from the other girls, and devotees draw arul from Shiva. In this model, Shiva is in the position of hero, but the devotees find themselves written into the position of the mistress. In *Tirukkovaiyar*, devotees seek Shiva, travel to see him, and hold the god in their heart. Devotees also lose their way but can be called back to Shiva. The mistress, like the other female characters, has complex relationships with the people around her. She matches the stature of heroes, she competes with the younger women, and she finds favor in the eyes of her master. These positive attributes are in fact honorable qualities for a devotee who is upright and persistent in attaining the favor of Shiva. When the mistress approaches her victory over the heroine, she speaks of a forgone conclusion expressed without defensiveness or difference. Her insults do not go unanswered. In an example of the poet stitching consecutive verses together into a more overt narrative, the heroine responds to her opponent's jabs at her rocky marriage.

373
Telling with laughter
If a younger sister appears, boasting will certainly wane.
Being proud and having boasted
  about the boon of being so close to the city man with strong shoulders
  in Chidambaram of the one of the small hall
  who holds the small deer in the palm of his hand
the breasts fade when the boasting fades, my lord.

The heroine knowingly laughs at the mistress's confidence. She explains to her that her loud boasting will fade when the next younger, prettier woman appears, and the strong man replaces her with a new interest. When that day comes, her voice will fade and so will her beauty. The heroine insults both the mistress's naiveté and her physical body. The saggy breasts of the accused public woman provide a vivid image that is amplified by the presumably perky breasts offered by the younger "sister." We also know from similar imagery in the classical corpus and throughout *Tirukkovaiyar* that the physical body expresses the emotional health or suffering of the character. For example, the hero's shoulders slump when he is prevented from meeting his lover. The heroine's bangles slide up her arms when her limbs wither in her hero's absence. The droop of the breasts mirrors the sinking misery of a woman left behind. The heroine speaks from experience and predicts that the hero's mistress will also fall from favor in the near future. The body is a container and conductor of emotions. The transformation of breasts communicates feelings of betrayal, conflict, tension, and perhaps most importantly desire. Here the aesthetics of the body, the contrast between the waning breasts and the hero's strong shoulders, interlaces emotion, experience, and religious devotion as the entire confession takes place at the throbbing feet of god who balances a soft deer in his hand. In addition, this entire exchange is between women, with no mention of their hero's perspective on their relationships. The hero is passed between women who are in competition with each other. The hero does not choose to leave one woman or go to another. Rather, the hero is taken from one woman by another. In addition to the hero and among the objects manipulated and traded between the women is the heroine's son.

380
Thinking about the nature of the son without getting gate (permission)
He who is rich nectar where beetles stay
the boy with babbling mouth resembles the true one
    who grants a rich place in the sky to those who bow at the small hall
    of the one with konrai flowers where honey bees rest
came but did not embrace me.
Can I reach the breasts where beetles stay by any other path?

The sweet, babbling son of the hero and heroine resides with his mother in the house. His father stands at the gate trying to coax a hug from the child, imagining that his wife's resolve will soften at the sight of their reunion. While in his mother's care, the boy becomes a conduit for a variety of messages and symbolic gestures. In verse 399, he tugs a small toy chariot, foreshadowing both the arrival and departure of his father's chariot, as well as his own likely future as a young warrior. In verse 396, the child has lips stained red from the chewed betel of the mistress's mouth, a symbolic and literal gesture of intimacy. Noticed by his mother, she angrily determines that the mistress must also be courting the little boy. In the example above, their son is viewed by the hero at and as the gateway to re-accessing his wife. The child is viewed as part of the women's world and though mimicking the behaviors of his heroic father, at this point in his life, he is securely positioned within the entourage of the heroine. Imagining that the boy has since tottered off, in the next verse the hero must face the confidante at the gate.

381
Speaking to the confidante, having stood in the gate
Why have those who shine in the good country
    in Chidambaram where clouds rest on grand forts
    where there is the hall of the one who placed the dancing snake beside the great moon
vowed not to relieve the torment of obsession
or withdrawal from the stares of those with eyes like carp?

In verse 381, the hero asks the confidante why the honorable women, referring to his wife, not his mistress, are so prone to suffer at the presence of and stares by the public women with seductive fish-shaped eyes. The hero suggests that the wife's suffering is due to her being intimidated by the sexually and socially emboldened public women. According to him, the heroine also wilts under the passion of her own lusty obsession with the hero. Passionate but conflicted coupling also occurs in Shiva's hair in the form of the snake and the moon. These bitter enemies were placed to live together by Shiva, symbolizing the dichotomy of feminine and masculine power. In this verse, the snake and moon acquire the role of representing the current animosity felt between the two lovers.

389
Reducing her sulking
O you like Chidambaram of Shiva who is without death
  who dances in the jungle with glee
  while a pack of demons leap in fear
when he appeared with the heir on his shoulder
  having embraced him as his helper
  our distress was destroyed.
You are obliged to serve the king.

Verse 389 takes us back to heroic-themed verses with images of demons hopping around the entrails of slain warriors. Demons leap in fear around the master of the cremation grounds. Shiva, who has conquered death and dances victoriously over corpses, is at home in the fiery wilderness. The image of Shiva is one of mastery and triumph. The secondary hero is also described but with considerably less enthusiasm by the confidante. She concedes to the heroine that the hero has reunited with their young boy, suggesting that he shows renewed interest in his wife and child. The confidante follows this underwhelming endorsement with the plain fact that it is the duty of the heroine, whether amiable or distressed, to serve the hero. At the end of this particular verse, the women seem to have relinquished their leverage over the household dynamic. The heroine has been advised by her often outspoken confidante to toe the line. In the near to last verse of *Tirukkovaiyar*, however, the poet gives the women one more chance to retort.

392
Vexing, intending union
O good townsman is this measure of your sacred grace
  enough for us today?

Our house is a house of very small people in beautiful southern Potiyil
of the one of the small hall who wears anklets
who was remembered in his absence by those with a destiny
the one with a bright moon that appears like lightning in his red matted hair.

Are you sure, hero, that your excellence (read: infidelity with local women) won't overpower our humble family (read: of the high ranking, faithful, modest, mother of your son)? The sarcasm is palpable and the women remark at the glaring imbalance of honorable behavior between husband and wife. The hero's exploits are a far cry from his earlier proclamations of devotion to the nearly divine beauty that he met in a mountain grove. In spite of this moment of dissonance, in the examples assembled here there are a number of similar experiences expressed between the men and between the women. Both the hero and heroine speak of passionate devotion to one another but balk at the imposition of social conventions. Both attribute the acquisition of their partners to karmic destiny. Both respond to a sense of competition within their own peer groups. Both hero and heroine express boldness and fragility motivated by erotic desires.

The final portion of this chapter returns to the hero's activities for capturing the heroine's and her family's attention and illustrates one way in which the men's sphere and women's sphere differ. The palm horse ordeal exemplifies the poet's mastery of a well-developed theme in the classical corpus, while also designing a rich aesthetic experience to communicate his sense of religion.

The Palm Horse Ordeal

The hero scrambles up the side of a four-legged beast. It is a horse made from palmyra palms, engineered from tough fronds in order to guarantee a painful ride for its wrangler. The hero's thighs have already begun to chaff as he shifts his weight, but he finds his balance and persists! He reaches down to his group of young friends for an important bit of cloth. His best friend dutifully passes him a canvas, a banner, a portrait of his beloved. Armed with the image of his lover's exquisite beauty, the hero will ride through her village holding her portrait overhead in an ordeal that is certain to force the issue of his relationship with the young heroine. This is his chance to make public the lovers' previously clandestine affair and to extract a response from her family. The tenth love scenario (verses 73–83) explored in *Tirukkovaiyar* is The palm horse ordeal described here.

The palm horse ordeal is a well-developed theme with clear precedent in the classical Tamil corpus.[37] Indeed, the palm horse, its construction, its mount, and the mere threat of the palm horse itinerary occupy the thoughts and dialogues exchanged between the stock characters of Tamil literature: the hero, his friend, the heroine, and her confidante. The young women are primarily concerned with the raucous and the shame that this public display of affection will inevitably bring to their families. In one of the earliest anthologies of Tamil love poetry, *Kuruntokai*, the hero threatens to ride a horse of palmyra stems, wear garlands of yarcum flowers, and then fill the streets with an uproar of shouting.[38] In conversations between the two young men, the hero's friend spends a considerable amount of effort trying to dissuade the hero, citing a variety of excuses and likely hindrances over the course of the ordeal, including the taunts that the hero will face during his ride.[39]

In the opening scene, the hero laments that if the heroine leaves without granting him her favor, his life will wither away. From that moment on, threats and preparations are made in equal measure, including the hero's design of a portrait of his lover. In verse 76, the hero announces his brash plan to paint and then display the features of the heroine, who resembles a female peacock that dances with joy at the start of every monsoon season.

76
After examining (her features)
I will paint her who stands there
  your rainy season peahen and my suffering self on a suitable piece of cloth.
Holding it in my hand I will pass
  through the streets of your small town on a slope
  overflowing with sweet honey at Kailash of the one at the hall
  who destroyed my future births with his feet.

More than an inflammatory prop, the hero takes care to examine the details of the heroine's features before producing her portrait on a deliberately chosen, suitable piece of cloth. The degree to which he studies not only her looks but also her movements is indicated in her nickname—the rainy season peahen—which refers to the habit of peacocks and peahens to strut along riverbanks in celebration of the rains. Before the hero sets out to gather materials for the spectacular event, his friend tries to dissuade the hero from mounting the palm horse by arguing that he does not have a picture of her to carry on display during his procession. Without her image overhead, how can he announce the identity of his beloved? His friend cautions the hero:

78
Preventing due to the difficulty of painting speech and gait
The girl whose soft voice has mastered the notes of the delightful lute—
she resembles Chidambaram of the first one
    who revealed his feet which were unseen by Vishnu or the Vedas
    who took and enslaved me
    who abides in me
    who placed his delightful, big blossoms on my head.
Is there a canvas in your gallery with an image of that girl's goose-like walk?

According to the hero's friend, there is no canvas with this girl's likeness. In subsequent verses, the young men continue to elaborate on the features of the heroine that test the limits of a painting. The full list of the articles to be illustrated correlates directly with classical conventions of beauty: a lute for her voice, pearls for her teeth, a garland of flowers surrounding her long dark hair, a red fruit for her lips, a tender mango split in two for her eyes, the slim wavering vine to match her tiny waist, and her goose-like walk. Furthermore, what great artist could possibly capture the grace of her gait or the melody of her voice on a flat piece of cloth? The warning issued is particularly cruel in its suppression of the hero's plan because of its pronounced counterpoint in the image of Shiva. The characteristics of Shiva praised in this verse, such as his boundlessness, his devotion to his followers in the form of master and caretaker, and his residence in the hearts of devotees, are qualities that would be equally difficult to capture in a painting on canvas.

The entire goal of the palm horse ordeal, the giant mount, and the painted banner is to make love public. Using the poetic vocabulary of the Tamil corpus, we could say that the hero is carrying his akam desires into the puram sphere. The hero's impetus to display and make public is one that is unmatched by the heroine. The heroine primarily communicates via the confidante. Admittedly, the girl in red is an exceptional gesture, visible to neighbors, but the heroine herself does not stroll through town. She does not publically address townspeople, gossips, or bards. She certainly does not announce or materialize her amorous desires on painted signs.

Conclusion

The palm horse ordeal can be read as a microcosm of the work of the poet across the entire *Tirukkovaiyar* poem. The trope is inherited from and makes reference to the classical corpus. The peahen, small town roads, and a gallery of canvases are all elements of the observable material world that point our attention to Shiva's grace, Shiva's home in Chidambaram, and the movements of the heroine's lovely body. The emotional range of this ordeal includes obsession, distress, spiritual release, mastery, and even delight. The heroine is soft, sweet, and melodious. The hero is vexed and determined. Finally, Shiva, the god, surpasses the understanding of other gods and consumes the hearts and bodies of his devotees. This portrait and range of Shaiva devotion is thus expressed through layers of feelings, sensations, and literary reference. Returning again to the basic paradigm of women's spheres and men's spheres within the context of an idealized poetic world designed by the poet in *Tirukkovaiyar*, the lovers express themselves to their peers with similar emotional ranges that indicate both sensitivity and boldness. The hero slays an elephant and frets over a secret meeting. The heroine tells off a mistress, rejects her husband's advances, and then welcomes him back into their home. Similarly, the role of Shiva as patron-hero is characterized as both a fearless conqueror and a generous benefactor. The emotional registers of this poem expand and contract with tensions in love, anger, and competition, all of which are critical contributions to the overall sensory and religious experience of *Tirukkovaiyar*. Drama is passed between the lovers, their friends, and their messengers. The intensity with which interactions occur between and among royalty, men, and women matches the drive with which devotees seek out Shiva and the heat with which Shiva likes to dance. The next chapter leaves the human hero behind to explore connections between the heroine and the patron-hero Shiva, a relationship that is communicated through aesthetics of ornamentation and the beauty of the natural environment.

5

Materiality, Ornaments, and Gifts that Glitter

I stayed in Madurai while visiting the cities farthest from Chidambaram. The temple at Tirupparankundram is just south of Madurai, easy to reach, and famous for containing some of the oldest known inscriptions in South India. I arrived unannounced, hoping to find a manager or temple officer on site to give me permission to enter the interior shrine. To my surprise, it appeared that all of the temple administrators for the entire district were in the temple that morning. They had gathered for a temple ritual that does not take place in the innermost shrine, but rather in the front hall: emptying the untiyals. Although not the reason why I came, I gladly accepted an invitation to observe the great day of counting at the head table of the well-guarded hall.

An untiyal is a donation box. At large temple complexes there are more than one untiyal inside. The largest containers are stainless steel and shaped like a capsule with a slot at the top, but untiyals are also square cubes, made of wood, and come in various sizes (Figure 17). At Tirupparankundram, a group of temple administrators was present to witness the wax seals being broken, multiple keys were brought together to unlock boxes within boxes, and then the contents of each untiyal were poured into trays to be sorted and counted in the main hall by girls from a local school. Representatives from the bank, accountants, and experts in precious stones and metals were also in attendance. The donations were mostly coins and paper money. There were also paper documents, small scraps of metal and paper, balls of wire that were unwound and then weighed for their value as scrap metal, and miniature tridents. There was one more type of donation that I didn't expect to see—jewelry. An occasional ring or pendant was passed to the jeweler for appraisal. One officer explained to me that the larger jewel-encrusted gifts were presented directly to authorities and not usually deposited into the donation boxes. In Tirupparankundram, my research of Tamil literary landscapes encountered the offering of ornaments to Shiva as a living art. Donations of pearl- and gem-encrusted ornaments, crowns, and pedestals

Figure 17 Untiyal at Ekamparanatar temple, Kanchipuram.

are being made in temples today. At this rate of gifting, one might expect temple treasuries to be bursting with gem-studded goodies. While individual temple wealth can be impressive, over time most small ornaments have been sold, melted and repurposed, or stolen.[1] All that remains in some of these cases is an inscription recording the initial donation or a poetic image that intimates the union between devotion, donation, and material ornament.

This chapter is about the enduring role of ornamentation in the religious sense of *Tirukkovaiyar*. Art historian Cynthia Packert provides a vocabulary of ornamentation as active expression.[2] In her analysis of styles and rituals of ornamentation for Krishna and Radha in contemporary North Indian temples, Packert demonstrates that "the continual provision of material abundance for one's chosen deity has positive connotations of providing the best one has to offer for the beauty and enjoyment of one's beloved."[3] She concludes, "Ornamentation, then, is a potent cultural category that has emotionally and spiritually transformative—and not simply descriptive—value."[4] This evaluation of ornaments as transformative and purveyors of enjoyment, a way of interpreting aesthetic design that paints the poet as a curator who works toward an expression of devotion, supports my argument that the material qualities of fragrant blossoms, jingling jewels, and vivid colors give *Tirukkovaiyar* its very life and religious value. In the inscriptions and verses that follow, people, god/desses, and elements of the natural world will be both ornamented or ornaments in their own right. This use of and play with the role of the ornament is the poet's primary method for experimenting with the human experience with the aim of accessing an aesthetic understanding of religious devotion.

Ornaments in Inscriptions

There are literally countless inscriptions covering the landscape of South India and they continue to be rediscovered by farmers, cattle drivers, and others who work, dig, or plow the land today. Inscriptions can be found on stone slabs, pillars, or stretched over the natural contours of a boulder still planted in the ground. They can be found in a variety of scripts, languages, lengths, and hands. The inscriptions considered here are temple inscriptions. The content of Tamil temple inscriptions is dominated by contracts between individuals, groups of donors, merchants, or local political figures and temple assemblies, in which land is given in exchange for money or for a percentage of the crop produced on that land. These documents preserve the boundaries of the land, the terms of payment and taxation, and the identities of the parties involved. Temple inscriptions also record gifts and how they are to be administered. For example, a cow might be donated. This type of gift can be designated for the production of oil for lamps to be lit before a specific deity on temple grounds. Much of this massive corpus remains unstudied or even in the early stages of acquisition. In terms of the material reality of these texts, one of the more perplexing aspects of temple inscriptions is their application to the building itself. Within one temple complex, for example at the Nataraja temple in Chidambaram, visitors can see inscriptions written ceiling to floor on a narrow door frame, in two long lines wrapping along the base trim of the outer hallway and in what appear to be block quotes on shrine walls. Sometimes they run into or over ornamental sculptures, and some are so high or so deep in a niche that they are impossible to see or read without a ladder or a light. Over centuries of building projects and renovations, stones have also been scrambled, replaced upside down, plastered over, repurposed as a paving stone, or carried off to become a pillar in a neighbor's home.

A survey of current inscriptional evidence at each of the sites named in *Tirukkovaiyar* revealed both the presence of poets and the practice of gift giving. For example, in Thiruvenkadu, an allowance was given for a festival that included the procession of the sixty-three poet-saints.[5] In Inkoymalai a land donation was made for various provisions for puja articles, vegetable dishes, and the installment of Campantar, Appar, Cuntarar, and the poet Narkirar.[6] In Madurai, food was distributed for visitors, literally parateci or outsiders, who worship with the *Tiruvempavai* songs attributed to Manikkavacakar on the sacred day in the month of Markali.[7] All of the sites, with the exception of the cave shrines, postdate the poetry and none of the inscriptions surveyed here explicitly named *Tirukkovaiyar*. Nonetheless, something potentially more significant emerged. Like the contents of the untiyals at Tirupparankundram, these stone records represent acts of devotion through acts of adornment. At the sites named in *Tirukkovaiyar*, among the inscriptions, are records of giving gifts of jewelry for the pleasure of the gods. For example, at the Mahalinkasvami temple in Tiruvidaimarudur, a merchant gifted a golden hand set with precious stones that weighed three and a quarter kalancu.[8] The ornamental hand was donated to the image of dancing Shiva.

In Tirukkalukkunram, one inscription located on the south wall of the central shrine of the Bhaktavatsatesvara temple at the base of the hill included how ornaments were procured by donors. A government official named Karanai Vilupparaiyan hired a temple goldsmith from Mutikontacolapuram. He had an ornament made, it was brought to the temple for it to be displayed, and then he graciously put it on the lord of Tirukkalukkunram.[9] The gold ornament presented was in the design of three stripes worn by Shiva and also seen tied to a linga. The remainder of the inscription is incomplete but contains information about weights and measures of gold and silver.

An impressive list of gifts registered on the wall of the Arulmiku Cuvetaranyecuvaracuvami temple in Thiruvenkadu includes donations by queen-mother Parantakan, the queen of Uttama-Cola, Parantakan-Madevi, and several other royal patrons. Gifts include gold and silver pots, lampstands, gold images, ornaments set with gems, and the queen's presentation of a gold flower.[10]

As noted above, many inscriptions speak to the cultivation of land and many are records of gifts. In addition, occasionally gifts and provisions were allocated for a particular festival in which activities and procession routes are also specified. We know from inscriptional evidence that processional bronze figures of deities were taken around towns, to rivers to bathe, and to pause at gardens along their route, all examples of a deity passing through regional landscapes, which connects yet again these inscriptions with the literary world of *Tirukkovaiyar*, as well as the sense of religion with the natural material world.[11]

These gardens were an important part of temple economies due to their yield of local products for trade and because of the need for flowers in daily temple activities. For example, in an inscription issued during the reign of Tribhuvanachakravatti Rajaraja located on the north wall of the first hallway of the Nataraja temple in Chidambaram, a gift of land was designated for two flower gardens and for the provisions for four gardeners. In return for this land, the gardeners were responsible for producing a measure of flowers at the temple everyday.[12] A similar inscription located in the next hallway issued during the reign of Kulottunka III required that each gardener provided one kuruni and four nali measures of flowers daily in exchange for one kuruni and four nali of paddy.[13] The inscriptional evidence records a variety of gift items, practices of giving, ornamenting, and exchange. The materiality of the ornamental objects such as the gold lamps is not unlike the more ephemeral gifts like the flowers or bathing water in that both types of gifts are part of an aesthetic of beauty and of pleasure. Both types of gifts elicit sensory experiences through fragrance, musicality, or visual interest like the flicker of fire dancing across a reflective gold plate.

In a Chola inscription composed in the tenth year of Rajarajakecari, engraved on the northern wall of the central shrine at the Mahalinkasvami temple in Tiruvidaimarudur, a donor by the name of Hrdayacivar from the village of Tirupputtur presented a golden flower made especially for the god. The inscription specified that the flower for the god Shiva weighed six kalancu, and he donated a second flower weighing three kalancu for Pillaiyar, the elephant-faced god also known by the name Ganesh.[14] In this inscription, and others that pledge similar gifts, we find the essence of this chapter manifest at the intersection of ornamentation, material abundance, and beauty derived from the natural environment. Not only do inscriptions describe how to harvest gifts from the land, but they also describe tours through these lovely and often watery landscapes. Among the frequent grants for land designated to produce flowers for temple activities, the occasional golden ornament stands out. In *Tirukkovaiyar*, we have seen natural resources modified for the adornment of beautiful women and a beautiful god. Sandal trees are made into paste, eaglewood burned for its fragrant smoke, precious stones pierced and strung, and jasmine blossoms woven into garlands. The transformation of natural resources into ornamental offerings is the centerpiece of *Tirukkovaiyar*. If we read the symbolic landscapes of the classical love poetry as an inherited interpretation of the natural environment, then the poet of *Tirukkovaiyar* is tasked with deploying these literary tools and tropes to create a suitable ornament for his lord Shiva. Thus, the presentation of a tender flower fashioned out of a precious metal in medieval inscriptions and pendants appraised in the hall at Tirupparankundram are certainly commensurate with the methodology of devotion and beautification practiced by this poet. The poet as the devotee manufactured a gift (of poetry) that references the natural world but also elevated the offering to a unique donation.

Kovai as Ornament

The Tamil word "kovai" means rows or stringing together of beads or flowers. *Tirukkovaiyar* is a sacred garland, like a garland of flowers that is made of love scenes strung together. Like the queen and the donor Hrdayacivar offered a gilded blossom, so too the poet offered a garland of poetry to Shiva. We turn back to the love story of *Tirukkovaiyar* with renewed attention to role of material abundance and the natural environment in acts of adornment and offerings.

150
Standing with a broken heart
Oh heart, languishing
like a lame man who desires honey from the highest mountain peak of Piranmalai
        of the dancer from cool Chidambaram
    who is wild honey
    who crushed the timely one who came saying, "I will not change"
            and made him cry for help
I cannot endure because of your love for that rare woman.

In addition to checking inscriptional records, during site visits, I also sought connections between two bodies of religious art: literature and architecture, the

Tirukkovaiyar and Shiva's temples. Like Inkoymalai and Tirukkalukkunram, Piranmalai has shrines at both the top and the base of the hill that devotees can visit today. At the top of Piranmalai, there is a cluster of tridents at a Shaiva shrine, a small shrine for Ganesh, and a Muslim dargah of Waliullah Sheikh Abdullah Shaheb. The significantly larger and older Shaiva temple is at the base of the hill and is cut into the hill creating a series of tiered cave shrines. At the time of my visit, I was left alone to explore the exterior temple corridor that wrapped around the natural slope of the hill. It turned into a series of organically shaped rooms with edges that bent to accommodate uncut rocks behind thinly applied plaster. Once he arrived for evening services, the remarkably jolly priest guided me up the rocky slopes to the highest tier of the base temple. At the top of the last set of stairs, the priest stopped and turned to face me. He pointed down and gestured for me to watch my step, and with the other hand he pointed up and said, "Look!" I looked up at what appeared to be half of a bicycle tire glued to the ceiling (Figure 18). I felt a triumphant rush when I realized that I was looking at a wild honeycomb poised at the highest point in the whole temple—wild honey in Piranmalai that was sweet, desirable, and unreachable by any lame man or American woman.[15]

Finding honey in Piranmalai redirected my attention to the element of the poetry that turns political territory into a romantic hideaway, namely the value of beauty and sensorial pleasure found in the natural environment of Tamil country. In addition, *Tirukkovaiyar* endorses an enduring relationship between femininity and nature. If we accept the Potiyil hills and the other mountain sites that appear in *Tirukkovaiyar* as purveyors of political and cultural significance, we must also investigate their experiential and sensational contribution to the impact of the natural environment on a poem dedicated to Shiva's praise. The first taste of this sensory technique comes from verse 150 above. The hero stands brokenhearted and empty-handed. He chastises his heart for exhausting him with its desperate desire for the heroine. The hero describes the suffering of his heart by comparing it to the unattainable desire of an anguished, paralyzed man longing for a taste of honey that hangs at the highest mountain peak.

The sweet and indulgent qualities of honey are a natural fit for vocabularies of love, abundance, fertility, and flirtation. Bees swarm around honey like drunkards drawn to toddy and honey is cultivated in flower buds that are tucked into the heroine's thick dark curls. We learn from the classical love-themed anthologies in which natural environment we might expect to find an actual honeycomb:

Figure 18 Honeycombs on the temple hall ceiling, Piranmalai.

> On the good day of the mountain's decoration given by the Vēṅkai, while
> the clouds, going after raining, join the mountains to be kept [there], while
> waterfalls roar on the high mountains hung with honey[-combs].
> *Narrinai* 396[16]

It is not surprising that the place of this intoxicating nectar is in the mountains or kurinji landscape where true love and physical intimacy are initiated. High on a misty peak or overlooking a mighty waterfall, we expect to find hanging a large honeycomb. This honey is not unique to *Tirukkovaiyar*; the desire for reaching the honeycomb also appears in the early anthologies. For example, according to *Kuruntokai* 273, a lover's confusion is "like an ignorant person who mounted without knowing an old bamboo ladder on the mountain, where a great honey[comb] is visible to the eye."[17] The opportunity to merely set eyes on the hero is likened to the sweet treat:

> Sweet to the mind [is] it often to see the lover,
> even if he [is] ungranting, unloving,
> as the great honey [is sweet to] the lame one (muṭavaṉ), seen while sitting
> at the long mountain where the short-trunked Kūṭāḷi sways,
>   who from below forms a little casket with [his] palm,
>   [and] points [upwards and] licks [his lips].
> *Kuruntokai* 60[18]

In *Kuruntokai* 60, the lame man sits at the base of a mountain, gazing up at the oozing, golden honey far beyond his reach. His vivid fantasy causes his mouth to salivate and his appearance is one that communicates desire. More importantly, those who pass by this lame man or hear about him in a verse of poetry notice that he cannot climb the mountain on his immobilized legs. Even if he was carried to the summit, he has no ladder. The lame man is the embodiment of failed longing. This emotional capital was seized by the poet of *Tirukkovaiyar* and redirected in order to praise the place of Shiva. Relevant to our understanding of how classical motifs were adapted and reused for devotional expressive traditions, we find that the lame man of *Kuruntokai* was not recast in terms of desire between humans and gods. Rather the use of an inherited trope preserves the figure and the natural environment in which he was found. The lame man's desire for honey is compared to the hero's heart's desire, enabling this imagery to stay within the akam narrative of *Tirukkovaiyar* while simultaneously contributing to the primary function of the panegyric to praise the god. In the next phrase the mountain peak is modified to include one of Shiva's sacred sites. In addition, the wild honey is extracted from the akam honeycomb and then used in a devotional context as a name for Shiva, Wild Honey. The emotional narrative of this verse also runs parallel between the lame man, the hero, and the conflict between Shiva and Kalan via a story of longing taken from Shiva's own biography. Shiva claims victory over Kalan the timely one. In this story, Kalan, the god of death, came to take the life of a young devotee Markandeya. Shiva killed Kalan and then revived him under the condition that Markandeya remain untouched by the timely hand of death. The last desperate cry of Kalan let out as he was crushed by Shiva parallels the same desperate reach for something *or someone*, just beyond the grasping hand. These classical motifs, which draw from environmental cues, are used here to mirror, to enhance, but not to be synthesized with the equally impassioned story of the patron lord Shiva. The heart, the paralyzed man, and the god of death all experience crushing failure, while Shiva emerges as the triumphant and wild, sweet honey. This incredibly powerful, dominant portrait of Shiva illustrates again that the poet's method of layering the love story, the myths, and these poignant details from the natural world delivers a huge sensorial impact from each individual vignette or verse and ultimately culminates in the aesthetic and religious value of the whole *Tirukkovaiyar*. Furthermore, it is by the same hand that the most delicate and subtle moments also emerge.

Ornaments for the Heroine

The following verse is a poignant portrait of the heroine in *Tirukkovaiyar* that unites nature and beauty. Keeping with the poet's strategic use of inherited texts, this is also among the most powerful images the poet could have chosen to anchor his heroine in the Tamil literary corpus. This verse is followed by just one excerpted example from the classical anthologies that confirms the intertextual resonances of this particular image, namely the comparison of the heroine to an unworn flower kept hidden in a box.[19]

374
Speaking with exaggeration having seen shyness
She who is like an unworn flower kept alone in a closed little box
she who is like the small hall of the one who dances with fire
  feeling shy
  thinking that a scandal would be unfitting for the townsman of
    Chidambaram

like that, she keeps a secret today.
She is my eye.
She has a good nature; her chastity has the nature of our mother.

Like a flower kept alone in a vessel famed for its clasp,
unworn, her body is emaciated.
Ashamed among us she plays hiding
the faithlessness of the man from the cool ghat.
Kuruntokai 9[20]

In the verse taken from *Tirukkovaiyar* (v. 374), the heroine is described in four ways. She is like Shiva's hall where he dances. She has the eye of her confidante, since they are like sisters. She is chaste. The combination of the heroine's chastity and loyalty to her maid with none other than the site of Shiva's cosmic dance, made explicit by his description as the fire dancer, certifies her virtues and ideal nature. In addition to these qualities, the heroine is compared to a beautiful, fragrant, and fresh flower that is intended to be worn as a desirable ornament taken from nature. However, this flower is locked in a dark, airless box. The hidden flower calls to mind the heroine's secrets that are hidden in her heart and the heroine's heart itself, which is locked away from strangers and suitors because of her chaste nature. When we put this characterization of the heroine in conversation with its predecessor in *Kuruntokai*, the cumulative effect of this inherited image influences both the heroine and *Tirukkovaiyar* as a whole. In spite of the quintessential anonymity of akam lovers, there is a way in which the unworn, boxed flower is an epithet for a recognizable heroine who has starred in a number of Tamil compositions. She is familiar to the audience, a cultural icon that is made of the cumulative figures of the akam heroines who have come before her. By virtue of her predecessors, the heroine of *Tirukkovaiyar* is already known to her audience. More than that, the unique heroine of *Tirukkovaiyar* is thus inducted as a new member into the rich ancestry of akam heroines. The panegyric to Shiva plays on a sense of dual citizenship between the realms of classical and devotional literary contexts. By identifying his heroine with this classical lineage of femininity, the poet of *Tirukkovaiyar* finds yet another way to simultaneously claim the prestige of his newly conceived composition and initiate the composition into the ranks of classical love poetry.

In addition to its literary referents, the natural environment is another shared point of comparison for the verses' southern audience. Knowledge of animal behavior, the nature of a green parrot, or the color and shape of an insect—or at least the accepted tropes associated with these creatures—is an essential part of composing and appreciating *Tirukkovaiyar*. In the following verse, we find such a botanical wonder rival the heroine's beauty.

184
Interrogating the goose
O goose on the wide lotus in the paddy fields in Chidambaram
  of the one who destroyed Pakan by extinguishing his lotus eye!
The punnai tree
  adorned with pearls and superior gold
  leaf-like earrings swinging from its face
  and with beetles like sapphires
refuses to answer
if the one who left will halt his return to our wide river banks
or not.

In this verse the heroine asks a goose why the nearby tree will not provide her with information about her absent hero. According to the heroine, the punnai tree stubbornly withholds details that it might have witnessed from its location at the river's edge. In addition to the heroine inquiring after the hero, the verse is populated with a significant number of nonhuman characters. Shiva of Chidambaram and the defeated sun god, Pakan, add a divine element to the cast. The goose is interrogated by the heroine, who has previously sought answers from the sea and other trees. Her inanimate object of frustration, however, is the silent punnai tree. In addition to its role as tormentor, the punnai tree brings to life an exchange of ornaments between humans and nature. Verse after verse, the heroine is compared to a flower, a vine, a pearl, and other elements that reflect her refinement and beauty. In addition, she wears flower garlands, perfumes her hair with fragrant smoke, and smears her body with pastes and powders to highlight her appearance through acts of adornment. In this verse a tree wears the jewels of such a woman and with stunning effect. It wears strings of pearls, dangling earrings, and sparkling sapphires in the forms of buds, branches, leaves, and beetles. The transformation of the punnai tree into a well-adorned woman is a testament to the intimate relationship between methods and materials used to adorn beautiful creatures, natural and human. Ornaments for women and trees are interchangeable, can be mistaken one for another, and are all derived from the natural world.

So far, the sensuality and beauty of *Tirukkovaiyar* has been articulated in terms of the heroine and the natural environment, both of which are deeply influenced by motifs developed in the classical anthologies and shared between medieval poets. The third beautifying technique of *Tirukkovaiyar* considered in this chapter is the poet's play with color. The following verse (35) is a description of the heroine that was observed and reported to the hero by his friend. Here we find the poet's three-branch method for beautification: feminine beauty augmented by an abundance of appealing natural elements and color dynamics (Figure 19).

35
Declaring her appearance
O hero of the hills!
On the blossomed lotus there are carp, aren't there?
Behind the ripe red coral there are even rows of pearls, aren't there?
There are a pair of caskets with the nature of Shiva's hall, aren't there?
There are tumbling rain clouds on our fresh creeper
    swaying, dark, and surrounded by flowers, aren't there?

The heroine has the essential qualities of a beautiful woman. She has large, dark eyes on a bright face. She has a white smile and full lips. She has large, round breasts. She is slim and youthful. She has long bouncing curls of hair. However, among the features of this lady the friend never utters the words "teeth," "lips," or "hair." In fact, with exception of her casket-like breasts, all of the anatomical features have been replaced with the finest material of the natural world. The blossoming lotus is home to Lakshmi, the goddess of beauty and wealth. Coral and pearls are the jewels of the sea. The final description of her body combines fresh greenery in the form of the creeper and decorative flowers with the ultimate symbol of fertile life-giving power in the form of dark clouds carrying monsoon rains. When we combine the visual effects of the heroine's features, three bold colors stand out; the white of her teeth, the red of her lips, and the black of her hair. These three colors are used to punctuate the marks of the heroine's beauty and, as we will see in the following verses, are also used to accentuate relationships between actions and iconography throughout *Tirukkovaiyar*.[21]

170
Urging marriage, telling about her sorrow
O king!
When you reach Chidambaram of the first one
    who wears a crown of long, thick matted hair
    whose flowery hand holds a battle-axe, a fawn, and a serpent with a mouth
        and hood

at that moment raise the black horn to your red lips
or a long string of pearls will pour out
from the long, dark water lilies
the huge flower-like eyes of the tiny lady.

Verse 170 is composed of three powerful visual portraits of the three main characters in *Tirukkovaiyar*: the heroine, the hero, and Shiva. This verse opens with the iconography of Shiva in Chidambaram that emphasizes his victory over the triple demon cities, wielding a battle-axe and carrying the fawn. In addition to these particular references to legends about Shiva's life, the foundation of his iconography is the embodied color combination in his red matted hair, black or dark blue throat, and the white ash applied to his body. We find that the other two figures in this verse are completely intertwined through visual cues. More specifically, the poet has used the color scheme black, white, and red, to create balance between the hero's action and the heroine's reaction.[22] The heroine's confidante warns the hero that he should announce his return to Tillai as soon as he enters the city by trumpeting a black horn with his red lips. Meanwhile, the heroine awaits on the brink of tears—threatening to cry steady streams that will resemble strands upon strands of white pearls. There is a suggestion of

Figure 19 Detail of hair and ornaments in red, white, and black, Pondicherry.

fragility and timidity in the relative sizes of the heroine's features. The reader's attention is drawn to the dark, deep pools of her huge, sad eyes that overwhelm her otherwise tiny figure. Although not explicit in this verse, the heroine's kohl-rimmed eyes are often the sites of these three powerful colors when they redden before her pearl-like tears pour forth.[23]

More tears flow in the next sequence from the story of departure told in the sixteenth theme. In the verses that follow we witness her coming of age, when the heroine trades her childhood for her lover. Not only is this a representation of affection between hero and heroine, but also a sensitive portrayal of love felt between the girl and her best friend the confidante.

199
Speaking, knowing his weariness
The golden bangle with loins like the hood of a glittering snake,
  noticing the glittering black waves of the sea,
  noticing the beautiful marshy grove of fragrant kaitai trees with flowers
    opening their petals,
embraced all the women with slender waists that appear illusive
in Chidambaram of our throated lord.

200
Speaking about her intention
Today my golden bangled maiden gave her koel bird to me.
She gave me her beautiful golden ball.
Hugging me, she gave her doll.
She also granted me her green parakeet.
I don't know the intentions of her with black eyes
  whose red lips rule over rich kovai fruits
in fertile Chidambaram of he who shares his side with her
  whose soft gaze rules over fawns.

Each of the verses uses sets of items to establish and then to reiterate the emotional impact of the heroine's narrative. Verse 199 describes the heroine among her girlfriends. Throughout *Tirukkovaiyar*, these girls join together to frolic in mountain springs, collect flowers, play catch with bundles of flowers, play echo games in the valley, and build mud castles. These girls are the lovely and innocent playmates of the heroine, but today in Chidambaram the heroine embraced their small waists to say goodbye. Memories of the idyllic pastimes made with these childhood friends stand in stark contrast to the imagery of sexual awakening that dominates the verse. The heroine's loins have unfurled like the flared hood of a snake. The sense of openness and the waving hood are represented in the motion of ocean waves. The blossoming petals of the kaitai tree buds also symbolize the moment of sexual awakening by a young woman, frequently compared to a flower coming into bloom. Although the hero is absent in this scene, his anticipation of the heroine's readiness for union encroaches at the edges of the verse.

In the second verse (200) of this sequence the audience draws one step closer to answers about the lovers' eventual union. After leaving behind her playmates, the heroine finally turns to her best friend and confidante. For her part, the confidante notices the heroine's unusual behavior and senses that she is about to announce an uncharacteristic decision. The audience stands close by as the heroine gives away her most prized possessions, the playthings of a young girl, to her life-long companion. Her gifts include a koel bird, a golden ball, her doll, and her green parakeet.[24] In the description of the young girl, the boldness of red and black appears in the contrast of her lips and eyes.

Verse 200 also illustrates the seamless description of feminine beauty across human and divine figures in the transition from the heroine in Chidambaram to the soft gaze of the goddess. The goddess Uma is described in one short phrase that captures both her gentleness and power. The audience witnessed the emotional separation of the heroine from her friends and was enticed by the growing desire of the lovers for each other. The poet described the sexual awakening of the lively heroine. Yet with one soft look, the moment of climax is stolen away by the power of the divine feminine. This shift of attention and status within the verse illustrates that even ideal human love and the emotional bonds shared between childhood friends ultimately defer to the perfected beauty of the divine pair, and this is where the poet's grand act of praise culminates. Two girls exchanging trinkets are the charming diversion while the goddess rules over the cosmos with perfected divine stature. The beauty of the goddess and the heroine intersects in a slightly different way in verse 194.

194

Saying the appropriate stage

O generous hero!

If our people see the flushed, swollen breasts in this condition—

    scattered with golden pollen

    spread with smooth yellow spots

full of nectar
smeared with perfume paste
of her with a shining forehead from Chidambaram
of the one who shines and has two beauties in one body
won't they start to wonder?

Verse 194 unites the heroine with an iconic form of Shiva. In this verse, the heroine's confidante warns the hero that the local people will gossip when they see the blushing heroine, and at the sight of her sexual maturity they will wonder about her prospects for marriage. The poet communicates this message with obsessive attention to the heroine's breasts. It is in the heroine's breasts, which have been idealized in fullness, fleshiness, ornamentation, and fragrance, that the short epithet for Shiva comes to life. The full-breasted heroine is from Chidambaram, and Chidambaram is possessed by brilliant Shiva. Shiva has one body, which is occupied by two beauties. We know very well the beauty of Shiva's body, which is ruddy in color and glistens with cool white ash. The second beauty is his consort, a goddess of unparalleled beauty who has been praised by the poet for her invisible waist, perfect breasts, and bewitching eyes. For an audience that has followed the discourse of praise in the nearly two hundred preceding verses, the description of the heroine's breasts embraces the ambiguity of shared abundance and beauty expressed by the human heroine and the goddess who is the counterpart of the divine hero of the poem. The relationship between human and divine femininity is a significant aspect of the poetry in its own right, and as will be demonstrated in the conclusion of this chapter, the blending of the human and divine "heroines" in this verse fuels the relationship between Shiva's and the heroine's narratives.

Ornaments for Shiva

The remaining pages of this chapter focus on the marriage of provision for ornamentation and praise for the patron-hero Shiva. As seen previously, the poet purposefully names the towns possessed by Shiva so that the god is localized in the South Indian context. Shiva abides on cool mountaintops and by fertile fields, which are places of beauty and abundance. Similarly, the love story of the hero and heroine acts as a landscape in its own right, and the context in which the most beautiful and most gracious love, that of Shiva and his consort, is to be displayed. To be clear, Shiva and Uma are not parallel or maximized versions of the human lovers; rather the human love story in its sophisticated environments and drama is the setting in which the deities are placed as divine jewels. The verses below illustrate the poet's program for worshipping Shiva through ornamental landscapes, powerful feminine sources, and acts of servitude and adornment.

There are many emotions, actions, sensations, and environmental cues in the love story that serve as parallel examples for devotional elements directed at the patron of the composition. Sometimes the heroine feels loss like the loss of devotees who fail to draw near to Shiva. Other times, the hero's martial strength is exerted in the same verse in which Shiva crushes one of his opponents. Although explicit similes are not made in many of these verses, relationships between Shiva and the love story appear throughout the composition. In the following example, the aesthetics of devotion in *Tirukkovaiyar* are conveyed through elements of the natural landscape.

248
Speaking about the nature of the world
Sandal desired by bees, pearls scooped out of the sea, and white conches
all of these go to those who desire them
and become ornaments worn on their bodies.
To those who are perceptive, she with soft speech like sugar cane
as sweet as the small hall of lord Shiva
who wears the great flood called the vast Ganges as his crown
she is of that same nature.

23
Refuting the opposing reproach
You haven't yet seen her soft shoulders, sweet as sugar cane.
You wouldn't scold me, if you'd seen the portrait of tender shoots made of gold
my life
her swelling breasts where ornaments rest
or the peacock from great Kailash in the north
whose lord is the dancer
like a gem at the small hall in Chidambaram
where golden mansions can be seen from a distance.

The poet opens with the most fragrant, most brilliant, and most prized of luxuries. Sandal, pearls, and conchs are the natural ornaments of Tamil country, as well as suitable gifts for the pleasure of beautiful women, kings, and gods. The poet indicates that the most salient qualities shared by these precious decorations including the heroine are that they are desired, sought after, and acquired for display on the bodies of their admirers. The heroine is like the pearl scooped from the ocean; she is a precious jewel. Set in the midst of these literal and symbolic ornaments is the ultimate centerpiece in any garland or crown; it is Shiva in the small hall wearing the Ganges as a king wears his crown. The relationship between the god, the heroine, precious metals, and gems is reinterpreted in the second example.

In the second scene, the hero scolds his friend and lists the qualities of the heroine that have driven him into his pitiable state. She is like a beautiful peacock strutting through the shady hills of Shiva's Kailash. She has full breasts covered in ornaments that rise and fall with her breath. She is the hero's *āvi*, his breath, his soul, and she is an *ōvi*, a picture. Her limbs are like a picture or portrait of tender branches made of gold. The concept of a portrait is used to emphasize specific attributes of the heroine's beauty while maintaining that the full measure of her virtues cannot be captured on canvas. We also find here the proposal to cast a tender green shoot in gold, a gesture found realized in the golden flowers donated at Thiruvenkadu. The counterpoint to the portrait of the precious, fertile, and graceful heroine is the equally stunning impression made by the master of Mount Kailash.

Verse 23 is representative of the agenda of *Tirukkovaiyar* as a whole: the praise of dancing Shiva in Chidambaram. In a few brief phrases, the poet does just that: Shiva dances. Shiva is a precious jewel, the centerpiece of the hall where he dances. The cityscape of Chidambaram glitters on the horizon and thus reflects and emanates the grandeur of its master through its golden mansions. The ornamental cues in this verse connect the golden limbs of the heroine, the jewelry around her neck and chest, the golden palaces of Chidambaram, and the jewel that is Dancing Shiva. In both verses, the heroine and Shiva are connected.

The position of Shiva as the focal point of *Tirukkovaiyar* is established most generally and exhaustively by virtue of his title of patron-hero. The point made by verses 248 and 23 is that the poet stayed true to the mission of praising and elevating the stature of the patron in every verse. In particular, these examples illustrate the divine patron's grandeur through elements of kingship and precious gems. Beyond praise through flattering metaphor or opulent landscapes, the poet teaches the audience how to conduct our own acts of worship—this time by mirroring the behavior of the people who inhabit not the temple grounds but rather the love story.

125
The confidante comes and meets (the heroine)
O gentle fawn,

don't pluck the soft buds
grieving your soft fingers like those who do not acquire grace
from the one who is like lightning
with thick matted hair full of angry snakes
the one who is like gold in Chidambaram.
I brought these fragrant flowers perfect for your sweet-smelling swaying curls.

63
Standing in distress
Should I launch a boat into the sea?
Or catch fish in the tossing waves?
Or dive for many conches?
Or sell bangles in front of the god in Chidambaram?
Or do petty errands for your elders?
Or string fresh ornamental flowers for your curly hair?
You command it!

Verse 125 is a demonstration of devotion between friends. The confidante spares the heroine the trouble of picking fresh flowers, not because the heroine is incapable, but because the confidante is offering to labor on her behalf. In verse 63, the hero pledges to carry out any order commanded by the heroine, including the varied jobs of coastal people. Like the confidante, the hero is willing to run petty errands for the heroine and her kin. In both cases, the heroine is the object of affection and desire. Her "devotees" seek to relieve her of tasks—to impress her with their acts of service. These acts of devotion have two phases. The first is service or volunteered labor. The second act of devotion in both examples is that of offering ornaments. Both devotees, one a kindred confidante and the other an eager warrior-hero, string flower garlands for the adornment of the heroine's hair. The garlands are fresh, fragrant, and made of a natural resource that is at once both abundant in the Tamil landscape and yet constitute a very special, ephemeral, and handmade offering. Based on these interpersonal expressions of human devotion, the poet has indicated his expectations for acts of devotion directed at a divine figure or icon, namely service and adornment. The poet follows his own prescription for devotion as he conducts his acts of service to Shiva and ultimately offers a special garland, or *kovai*, to his master. The first act of service and adornment is to establish a beautiful setting for lord Shiva.

217
Removing weariness

Having just crossed this miserable wilderness
which is approached by lowly people of evil deeds
who did not consider the grace of the ancient one in previous births,
today we will reach Chidambaram in the south
full of beautiful, golden mansions covered in jewels
and see the small hall of the lord who dances and rules those who praise him
saying, "O lord of the South!"

Verse 217 is an example of the terrible beauty of Shiva. Characteristic of Shiva by many accounts, the master's dance is beautiful, awesome, and wields incredible destructive powers. In this verse, the poet unleashes the wild side of Shiva and situates his dance alongside the miserable wilderness through which the lovers have suffered. There is a marked contrast between the miserable wasteland of the sinners and the golden palaces that fill the town of Shiva. Although Shiva is located in the beautiful, favorable side of the dichotomy, the audience is acquainted with a Shiva of the wilderness, who lives as an ascetic, communes with animals, and dances in cremation grounds. In the combination of the wilderness and the flourishing town, the association of two distinctive sensory experiences, we find the two homes of Shiva. Significantly, both of these types of homes for Shiva are located in the south, and he is hailed "lord of the South." The deliberate planting of Shiva and his abodes in the south will come into focus with the addition of the following verse.

222
Pointing out the city
O modest girl!
Just as we enter the good, grand city
geese with a gait like yours appear before us
and a mansion with tridents
adorned with the crescent moon like the king of flourishing Chidambaram
that boasts golden walls resembling the northern mountain
and flags like lightning that unfurl in the sky like waves in the sea.

Many verses analyzed in Chapter 2 achieved a synthesis of divine and human landscapes by comparing Shiva's cities to the heroine of the love story. In verse 222 the city is compared to the head of Shiva where the crescent moon rests and to the trident that he wields. In addition, the city of Chidambaram is compared to Shiva's primary residence, Mount Kailash. Chidambaram is thereby transformed into a paradise on earth and aquires the mountaintop culture of Kailash and Potiyil discussed in Chapter 3. The combination of verses 217 and 222 is representative of the trend traced throughout the second chapter of this book, namely Shiva has found his home on earth and it is in the varied landscapes of Tamil country. He resides by the waterfalls in Kutralam, on the coast in Sirkali, atop Inkoymalai, and even in the fiery jungles in the uncultivated, uncivilized wilderness. In part because of the lands' virtues and fertility, and also through the enhanced prestige contributed by their divine inhabitant, the rural and urban landscapes of Tamil country are elevated to a supernatural-like status. Conceived of in this way, the poet asserts that the places and spaces of *Tirukkovaiyar* are exceptional and have caught the favor of Shiva. Shiva has claimed the geography of the south for himself—a shady grove claimed as an ornament for his pleasure.

In addition to the development of cityscapes and natural landscapes as gifts for Shiva, not unlike the gardens and farming fields donated to medieval South Indian temples, there is another style of dedicated praise performed throughout the narrative. The poem emphasizes the position of humility or servitude adopted by divine figures in response to Shiva's excellence, a relationship that also correlates with some of Shiva's royal traits.

86
Speaking deceptive words
Vishnu laid down for a boon at the front of the hall in Chidambaram saying,
"having shown one foot of the one that gave me two hands for his two feet,
show me that other one there too"
and begging,
"O mother, pity me who did not understand
even after I entered and dug into the earth
seeking the feet of the one who destroyed cities."

The two greatest compliments to Shiva's excellence from the divine realm are his rival, Vishnu, and his consort, Uma. In verse 86 above, Vishnu throws himself down in the courtyard of Shiva's temple and begs him like a child begs a parent. Vishnu identifies himself again as the boar that tunneled into the earth in search of Shiva's feet. Ultimately, both he and Brahma were defeated by Shiva's limitlessness, and Vishnu was left unsatisfied by his lack of understanding. In this verse, Vishnu continues to humble himself before Shiva, practicing submission like a devotee who desires Shiva's grace. Vishnu says that he has two hands to worship Shiva's feet with and thus he wants the opportunity to praise both of Shiva's dancing feet in Chidambaram. The servitude of those who seek Shiva in his temples and the desire for Shiva's favor do not belong to Vishnu alone. As we know from anthologies of medieval Vaishnava hymns and institutional evidence of temples, the poet of *Tirukkovaiyar* and the community from which he came had a counterpart in the Vaishnava tradition. By placing Vishnu in Shaiva territory and begging like a child for Shiva's foot, the poet places members of the Vaishnava sect in a subservient position to lord Shiva and, by proxy, under his devotees. The social hierarchies of the human world became ordered through the mythological rivalry of these two gods. Having praised Shiva for his dominance over rivals, we turn to a verse that praises him through the excellence of his equal.

71
Harmonizing minds
Joy and affliction come equally to the exalted one and to the peahen
    on the mountain of the lord over the hall in the great grove
        who is the unique lord
        who is one with the manifestation of all things.
Like the single pupil that appears in the two eyes of a crow
I believe there is one life between their two bodies today.

One of the most beautiful verses devoted to the unity of lovers, verse 71 describes the relationship sought by the heroine when she traded her childhood in pursuit of the hero. For all of the erotic imagery woven between bodies and the fertility of the natural landscape, the poet has not forgotten to align his hero and heroine in terms of their emotional constitution. The exalted hero feels his joy and sorrow in sync with his sweet peahen. The unity of their minds is emphasized by a simile that plays on a popular sentiment that a crow has only one eye. This charming characterization of the crow aims to explain why the bird looks with a tilted head—to roll its single eye into the preferred socket. In addition to this playful image of the crow, the poet also speaks to another unified pair. While the human lovers live in two separate bodies with a single mind, Shiva and his consort share one body, not only as king and queen, but in an actualized form of union between god and goddess. It is impossible for the hero and heroine to attain this physical realization of unity achieved by the divine figures and the crow. Nonetheless, their shared life is the truest human union celebrated by akam poetry, and this lesson in love is appropriately located in the sensual kurinji landscape. The god and goddess find themselves in an equally cool, fertile garden, a natural landscape designed by the poet and located in the south for Shiva's delight. The great heroes of *Tirukkovaiyar* are paired with and matched by their equals in beauty and in stature. In verse 71, Shiva is the unique

Lord, suggesting that he is indeed without a peer; however, there is one who is worthy of his companionship. Uma is one with Shiva and she is no less than the manifestation of all things, making her a suitable match. The final verses presented in this chapter illustrate the sensory impact of this poet's style of praise.

Union of Devotion and Material Aesthetics

246
Carefully explaining union
Mother!
On the path between the hills we saw a pair with the qualities that you described.
What a blessing!
With similar minds, we considered bowing to worship their beauty
thinking that they were the lord of Chidambaram joined with her who possesses all things
being one, his white clothes and her red silks glowed
his heroic anklets and her tinkling anklets cast off clusters of lightning.

Verse 246 is spoken by a group of people. The heroine's mother and foster mother are seeking information about their daughter after she escapes into the wilderness with her lover. We might imagine that the frantic women are searching along the paths leading out of the village and questioning travelers in case the young couple had been spotted. Fortunately, some observant neighbors saw the hero and heroine in question and the encounter is described as an overwhelmingly sensual experience. First, the colors of their clothing—red and white—provide visually striking counterpoints to each other, intimating the heat and cooling rays of the sun and moon, goddess and god. The audience can imagine the soft, smooth feel of the heroine's glowing red silk running through their fingers. The otherwise silent movement of the lovers is embellished with the bright jingling sound of her anklets. The hero is also properly adorned with the thundering anklets of a young warrior. To the rippling red silk and pulsing music of their tinkling anklets, the poet adds blinding flashes of light generated from the girl's feet. Such an encounter confused its witnesses and stirred in their hearts a desire to worship the dazzling duo. This incredible image of complimentary masculine and feminine beauty and the textures and musicality of their presence in the wilderness calls to the minds of the travelers and the minds of the audience the ultimate combination of sensuality, power, and elegance—namely, Shiva with his consort.

The identity of Shiva is not complete without a closer look at the role of the heroine in establishing the characteristics of the god praised in *Tirukkovaiyar*. In Chapter 2, the heroine and Shiva were linked by virtue of significant sites. They also suffered parallel losses and separation from her hero and his devotees. In Chapter 4, the heroine faces threats of loss: first, in the form of a hero stalling his marriage proposal. The heroine is left to entertain offers of gold from a number of suitors all while fearing that her true match with the countenance of Murukan will not show her the same fidelity that she has shown to him. Second, the heroine must face off with bold mistresses, threatened again by the infidelity of her husband and the resultant harm done to their virtuous reputations. Taking into consideration this theme of infidelity and the need for a virtuous patron, we look back at verse 217 of *Tirukkovaiyar* presented above.

The hero and heroine have travelled through the wilderness, usually characterized by unbearable heat, drought, and thorny vegetation to arrive in Shiva's capital city Chidambaram. As they leave the wilderness behind and enter a city that sparkles and shines, there is an impression of culmination, by moving from darkness to light and moving from the wilderness to Shiva's throne. Once united with those who praise him in the south, Shiva performs his cosmic dance and embraces his role of master over his followers. Based on this selective reading of verse 217, Shiva appears to have it all—a palatial home, adoring devotees, and free reign to dance and rule his kingdom. Although we cannot deny that Shiva is the victor by the end of this verse, there is nonetheless a point of tension met with in the wilderness. Another characteristic of this treacherous terrain is that it is the land of people who have karmic debt from previous lives. According to this and other verses, there is one evil deed in particular that leads people to wander in the wilderness, namely, the failure to recognize Shiva's ageless grace. This transgression might serve as an admonishment to the audience to seek Shiva's favor. Nevertheless, another more precarious conclusion can be drawn from this example. Shiva faces the possibility of rejection in the same way that the heroine is portrayed quietly suffering from her unrequited hope for marriage to her hero. The lingering fear of an unfulfilled promise or unrequited love tempers the confident portrayal of Shiva, as it has certainly vexed the heroine and her confidante verse after verse. That kernel of doubt, one that echoes intermittently over the course of the poem, is revealed through the presence of the lowest people in the first two lines of verse 217. Ultimately, it seems that the people who fail to recognize Shiva's splendor are duly punished in this and future lives, but what about Shiva? Does he worry that people will not accept his invitation to worship him at the hall in Chidambaram? We learn from the appearance of wayward sinners in the wilderness that some people will refuse Shiva's favor. There is a dependence of Shiva on devotees in the same way that the heroine is dependent on the hero to marry her after their secret liaison. Both Shiva and the heroine are sought after with gifts and offerings—and yet both are affected by the uncertainty of rejection. The emotional vulnerability of Shiva is indeed a counterpoint to the warrior who smashed the sun god, burned the god of love, and destroyed death. The poet of *Tirukkovaiyar* succeeded in creating a complex portrait of Shiva that emphasizes the unflagging feminine desire that we know to be essential to the classical love drama and contributes a manifestation of Shiva that is not widely known but is deeply rooted in Tamil country and the Tamil literary corpus by the verses of *Tirukkovaiyar*.

Conclusion

The verse presented below is a final exemplar of the aesthetics of devotion mastered and promoted by the poet of *Tirukkovaiyar* to honor a complex, divine patron.

54
Enquiring about a way
Oh you two ornamented with anklets
tell me the way leading to your small town at cloudy Kailash
    of the one who abides in the hall and wears snakes as ornaments
    the one who granted me as a servant to a group of his excellent slaves
        the one who has as his side
        small red feet
        adorned with anklets.

This verse demonstrates the way in which the strategies used to compliment the aesthetics of the female figure in the love story are redirected to portray the divine excellence of Shiva. The scene opens with the hero sheepishly approaching the heroine and her companion to ask directions to their hometown. Those familiar with this classical love theme know very well that the hero is not lost but rather is searching for an excuse to speak with the intoxicating heroine. The two girls stand there, poised with anklets that jingle when they move about the field, but the focus of the verse quickly turns away from the ornamented young ladies. The remaining lines of this verse represent the architecture of the poet's devotional aesthetics. We find Shiva's hometown in Kailash, a great cosmic mountain paired with the localizing effect of a small southern village. We find Shiva's residence in the hall at Chidambaram where devotees go to see his dance and where Vishnu begs to see his foot. Shiva is adorned with live snakes as his ornaments and jewelry—snakes that wriggle and glitter around his neck. We find the poet himself enters the verse and claims his place among the ranks of Shiva's devotees, like he claimed a place for *Tirukkovaiyar* among the ranks of Tamil literary giants, and he pledges his own acts of service to Shiva. Finally, we close with a look at the most beautiful and powerful ornament that adorns Shiva's body, namely, his lovely consort Uma. The poet has provided his audience with a lord who has a regal presence and superior features. His compliment is the goddess in the form of a beautiful young woman who is not unlike the idealized heroine and her friend. She has the petite features of a lady and she is appropriately adorned with her playful, tinkling anklets. Although the initial inquiry of the hero is a half-hearted question about the way to the girls' village, the poet has transformed the direction of the verse to guide the audience on their way to Shiva. The body of this verse tells us where to find Shiva and how to recognize his signature dress and his salvific countenance. Once Shiva has been reached, the poet intimates that one should behave with an attitude of servanthood like his own. By the design of the devotee-poet, at the hall in Chidambaram, Shiva is adored and adorned by his snakes, his servants, and the delicate body of his goddess.

By attending to the bodies, animals, land, and ornaments, the poet delivers a sense of religion that is present in and intrinsic to the material world. Each of these things carries with them physical qualities observed in the human world, as well as literary and historical references. The multivalent objects and creatures are the cumulative context in which devotion is encountered and enacted. Verse 54, a study of anklets, draws our attention to the foot, a site of great humility but also of delicately hued beauty. The anklets, whether draped serpent or hollowed metal hoop, offer us a focal point, one with both visual and auditory features. The well-dressed body is a strong iconographic representation of both the human and divine figures. Each of these components, along with regional and literary landscapes, is a dazzling facet full of information for our interpretation of the total devotional composition dedicated to Shiva and the goddess. When considered together as a sensory corpus, like the hero sighting the heroine *in combination with* her surroundings in a lush grove, we are struck if not silenced by the excellence of Shiva.

Conclusion

Can a honeycomb, a pearl, or the wriggle of a snake be a site for religious devotion? If the test for identifying religious literature, art, and architecture is simply the appearance of a god, then scholarship suffers the loss of entire worlds of implicit, suggestive, and inspired works. *Tirukkovaiyar* is an occasion to rethink ways of defining and reading literature by prioritizing the material as a central, formative element of devotion.

I adopted Prohl's description of religious aesthetics, which deliberately combines textual analysis with materiality, and used it as a model for my approach to the South Indian verses dedicated to Shiva. My concept of a sensory corpus is designed to further expand upon the sources that are considered if not required in the development of a sensory-centered reading of a devotional text. This concept enabled me to address the rich history and affect of a poem such as *Tirukkovaiyar*, which puts so much emphasis *through words* on sensory experiences of religion. The result of my study is a portrait of a deity that is located in and emanates from a very super-sensory world: four hundred verses collectively illustrate the ever-expanding grace of Shiva. The god is at once grand and vulnerable, present in the southern landscape, and realized in fire, light, water, gold, and other pulses of sensation.

In addition, this study of material religion further demonstrates that the flowers, ornaments, and natural landscapes of *Tirukkovaiyar* are critical components of devotion as expressed in medieval Tamil culture. Again, the concept of a sensory corpus (the text, the literary and historical references, and the sensations cultivated in the poetic world) encourages interpretative work that emphasizes the powerful visual, auditory, and olfactory impact of the verses as critical components of the deeply intertextual composition.

Proximity to Desire

This final cluster of verses joins the central themes of this book, including materiality, special places, proximity, ornamentation, and transformation. The verses invite us to consider new impacts and shimmers generated by the humor, activity, and profound emotion of the lovers captured in the presentations of leaves, bees, and a sparkling stone.

60
Doubting
Who is he
  who inquires about the elephant and stag
  without luster like those who do not praise the one in Chidambaram
      who conquered Pakal leaving him toothless
  without a bow
  with nakam leaves in hand
  celebrating his hunt?
He is without a word of truth. Oh how he speaks!
He will not leave this field by mountain springs.

62
Inquiring about her sadness
Having sported and bathed in the mountain spring
  mixed with sacred water from the tall peaks of Kailash
  where roams he who is always dancing at the small hall
  and who has a unique eye in his forehead
having called out into the hills
becoming weary
isn't this why she like a soft natured liana wilted?

64
Perceiving his intention
The master, deserving sympathy, has one true thought.
When the lady who resembles Chidambaram of the lord goes a short way and then stops
  to drive off the parrots that remain
  amorous bees mount her brilliant hair,
or if she just sits without any significance
like the light of a nearby object settles on a crystal
his lustrous face having appeared one way, then dims another way.

The hero stands by the field guarded by the heroine. He starts a conversation with the young women by pretending to be on a hunt for stags or elephants although his only "weapon" is a bouquet of leaves. The confidante and heroine seem both shocked and pleased by all of the tales the hero has told as excuses to linger. They don't dare accept his offered gift, assigning a great deal of value to a plant that grows nearby. The women have an equally circuitous way of confessing their affections. The heroine bathes in sacred waters and plays an echo game by yelling into the valley. The confidante knowingly blames the heroine's emotionally derived bodily exhaustion on the enchanting activities of her day rather than on the absence of her hero. In the third passage, our attention remains on the heroine, but through the admiring eyes of her lover. The hero's face brightens or fades like a crystal according to the light cast by his beloved. Whether chasing parrots from the field or casually posed, the heroine is the sole focus of the hero, his very light. He studies and reflects her movements and proximity. While the hero admires the heroine from some distance, the poet simultaneously allows intoxicated bees to actually touch her, resting on her still or tussled hair. The poet invites us to savor the very slow, gentle movements, the calm spiraling, and the low drunk hum of a bee enjoying pollen-laden blossoms, interrupted in a moment by the tight flick of the fleeing parrot's wing. These are the movements of material devotion. Incomparable Shiva also resides in each verse. He is the master of Chidambaram, he is the conqueror of Pakal whose countenance he transformed with a swift blow, and he is the dancer. Although separate from the lovers' narrative, Shiva is nonetheless present, peacefully roaming alongside the mountain spring in which the waning heroine bathes. His third eye shines like an ornament placed in the center of his arched forehead.

Lovers, Locality, Audience

The constitutive elements of *Tirukkovaiyar* and of what becomes known as the characteristics of the kovai genre rely on an extended engagement with and initiation into the canon of classical Tamil love poetry. Within the narrow bounds of early medieval devotional literature produced by Shaiva and Vaishnava saints, *Tirukkovaiyar* and its contemporaries did not shy away from the emotional landscapes or the physicality of human or divine erotic love inherited from their predecessors. However, unlike other devotional hymns composed in that period, our poet does not take the voice of the heroine, nor does Shiva inhabit the position of the classical literary hero. Instead, in *Tirukkovaiyar*, the akam drama unfolds as supplement, support, sometimes counterpoint to the activity of Shiva and his identity as the supreme dancer. For example, in the verse above, Shiva is powerful conqueror but also roams the same mountain slopes as the gentle heroine and her confidante. The young women are anonymous and idealized characters seemingly unaware of the nearby god. The heroine and her confidante scramble to preserve the heroine's chastity and the secret of their romantic meetings by day and by night. The heroine's position eventually transforms from ethereal muse to respectable but unsatisfied mother of a son. Her husband, the hero, seeks reunion with his nearly divine lover, competes for wealth, and proves his loyalty to the king. With very, very few exceptions, the heroine and hero do not interact with Shiva or seek his divine blessings explicitly or implicitly. Again, the humans reside in the same special places and seasons as Shiva and Uma, while their experiences and concerns in the akam narrative remain separate from the deities' activity. Shiva does not speak with the hero. The heroine does not encounter Uma in her family's courtyard.

In spite of their similar but separate plains of residence, the heroine and Shiva do have similar emotional and aesthetic tides. Both figures occupy roles that thrive on being adorned and adored. By reading the emotions of the heroine as the same tension felt by Shiva, we have a portrait of the mighty god that is colored by his desire to unite with his devotees.

If we turn from the classical cast of lovers and kin to the devotees of Shiva described in the poetry, this group of lustrous people bring another type of experiences to the sensory corpus. Shiva's devotees have melting bones and hearts and sometimes turn off the path that leads to Chidambaram and his brilliant dance. The devotees' experimentation with the conduct and completion of their journey to Shiva's gracious feet also displays the consequences of their devotional failures and successes. In addition to the lovers and devotees, people such as you and I also contribute to the poetry's audience of humans who observe, enjoy, study, and wonder about the various figures that move through the kovai.

In search of intersections between the poetic figures, devotees, the god and goddess, and the external audience of the poetry, Chidambaram or one of the other places named lures all types of human and divine audiences to special sensory locales. The twenty-one towns, Shiva's playground, enhance cultural and social prestige through reference to physical locations, historical figures, and legendary encounters. And these cities and landmarks also wield the ability to unite the heroine who resembles them, to the god who possesses them, to the audience and poet who might live in or visit them.

Alongside the temples towns, *Tirukkovaiyar* provides occasions for encountering a god and goddess in a forest grove or while standing on the shore or riverbank. Over and again, the text plants religion in the regional landscapes of southeast India. Similarly, *Tirukkovaiyar* places the god in a lit flame, in a tumultuous whirlpool, and in the sway of a flower garland, creating vast and diverse possibilities, intersections, gatherings for religious sensations to occur in the material. There, in proximity to sensations, sounds, pleasant aromas, and other deftly combined ethereal and real sensations, we are close to and are invited to find the deity. The continuous, rolling even tumbling accumulation of materialities moves from verse to verse, but also outward into new genres, new poets, new gardens, and through temple halls. From this vantage point, the mountain slopes and cool streams enjoyed by the human cast of the poetry are a generative devotional context even before (but also after) Shiva enters the landscape.

Transformation

Upon his eventual arrival, Shiva's presence in and proximity to the physical world is a more significant pairing when the complexity and amplification of that material world has also received developed analytical consideration. In the case of *Tirukkovaiyar* and its lush landscapes, the environment immediately and already belongs to Shiva. He is the true host of the lovers and he wanders freely throughout the stylized world. In addition to naming and inhabiting South Indian sites, the deity's arrival transforms the poetic landscape. I return to Ahmed's model in which affect changes through contact or proximity to objects, to find that the presence of Shiva like the droning hum or single tic influences and contributes to the mood of the scene and thus to the entire love-themed composition. So too, the human lovers' story endorses Shiva's excellence, either as its compliment or counterpoint.

The Vaigai becomes the Ganges River. The Potiyil Mountains are the Himalayas. Chidambaram is Shiva's home on Mount Kailash. Among the human characters, the heroine takes on the identity and lineage of the classical heroines through her resemblance to the boxed flower. The palm horse ordeal and the unreachable wild honey connect and influence our reception of a single verse because of its proximity to other genres, phrases, or observable natural events. Within individual verses, we also encountered sensations of sweetness, despair, or awe that were enhanced by our knowledge of a previous verse or by the image of Shiva in that same verse; the hero's sharp failure to capture the heart of the heroine cuts deeper with the reminder of Shiva's perfect union with the goddess. The impact of every comparison of the heroine's appearance to a vine, flower, bamboo, coconut, fish, or storm cloud relies on the sensory perception of organic forms. The aesthetic vision communicated by the poet also relies on the audiences' willingness to experience and experiment with known behaviors of the human and animal worlds and to engage with a variety of commentaries and styles of interpretation.

Feelings are dynamic, creative, and subtle. They shift. Love, loss, union, and despair react and mingle. *Tirukkovaiyar* requires extended peripheral vision of its audiences because we must watch and weave together the stories told by the god, the people, the creatures, and even the natural and architectural cues presented over the course of the poem. Each facet of these verses is an invention, and each scene a test or twist on the limits of the human experience. The webs of emotion that connect the hero, the heroine, their kin, and the creatures that surround them speak to both the lush, ripened feelings that they call forth and the weariness and wilt caused by some of the lover's games. And it is precisely through literary tropes, rhyme, and wordplay that the audience synthesizes the people, natural landscapes, and emotive cues into a sense of religion.

Material Religion: A Kingdom of Riches

He arrives at the edge of the field. He brings leaves and anticipation. She bathes in water that flows from the chilled heights of god's home. The god delivers that cool, clean air to Chidambaram when he comes to dance. The dance creates excitement. The devotee sits in the hall, observing the dance, quietly studying the movements. With the shifts of the god-dance-crystal, the devotee's heart dims and then glows. By the god's presence, the temple town becomes a sacred place, as does the mountain where the hero and heroine first united.

In this sacred and affectionate moment, and in this curated poetic world, what is religion? What is Tamil religion? Where is Tamil religion?

Religion is in this world, here, the human world known as the Tamil south. It is a shaded hill, a nearby paddy field, and a rippling stream of bathing water.

Religion is ornament. It glitters and curls. It is a gift, contest, contract.

Religion is attraction. It desires, loves, and makes curious. It drives contact, even if fleeting or failed.

Figure 20 Dancing Shiva woven with red and yellow fabric, Thiruvadavur.

The natural world, precious ornaments, and the desire for proximity to god or to each other constitute the sense of religion. Each of these elements is achieved in the poetry through a series of four hundred encounters with sensations, stylized aesthetics of the Tamil love story and a heroic god (Figure 20). In the end, the poet of *Tirukkovaiyar* has presented to the world in literary form a unique glimpse into the welcoming and nervous heart of Shiva. As a result, this profoundly expressive material opened our understanding of what constitutes devotion, devotional literature, and devotional arts in medieval South India. In addition to its impact as a closed corpus of verses, *Tirukkovaiyar* has also been showcased as a cultivator of religious experience. When a particular sequence or encounter caught your attention or your mind drifted into a realm of counterexamples from another pool of religious studies, the poetic landscape inhaled a life breath. The ninth-century aesthetic is alive, impactful, and continues to make people curious about how to steal a glimpse of beauty, special things, a smooth palm leaf, and moving light, both in the past and today.

As the field of material South Asian religion begins to emerge and compete with the materialities of other types of religions, some trajectories of expression tested in *Tirukkovaiyar* will grow branches. Some might be cut off. What inarguably survives is the ripple, the proposal, ideas, and the transformation of her eyes from black to red and from red to streaming white pearls. The poet, the scholar, and the heroine all anticipate a response to the colorful emotion and ornaments poured forth in so many gestures and pages.

The final verse of *Tirukkovaiyar* is a presentation of treasure. The Karpakam tree glitters in heaven. It can fulfill any wish, and so can the wish-fulfilling Cintamani gem. The Cankaniti is the treasure of conch shells protected by Kubera, god of wealth. Trees, jewels, and shells all appear as ornaments or ornamented throughout the poem. This final flourish of treasure is a tribute and culmination of the poet's devotional vision. The poet collected the most sought-after and quite literally supernatural ornaments imaginable and added his kovai alongside them. The combination of these gifts, the impression that they make, communicates a sense of religion, a sense of the supernatural, a sense of material devotion, a sense of Shiva.

For the finale, the hero of *Tirukkovaiyar* offers himself as a string of cool soft flowers, a garland, a kovai, at the feet of his god and the poet offers his verses to Shiva, *Tirukkovaiyar*—an intoxicating love story and a kingdom of riches.

400
Ending the quarrel by praising his benefits
The Karpakam tree adorned with clouds
    the good companion to the learned ones, kin to the bards
    the Cintamani gem adorned with excellence
    he who is the konrai garland for the feet of Shiva in beautiful Chidambaram
    the Cankaniti to the worthy ones—
to those who approach the drinking water according to the rule, and to anybody else
the man of the village is of value.

Glossary

Aintinai five stylized landscapes that correspond with five stages of love
Aiyam doubt, an opening scene of a kovai poem
Akam interior, category for Tamil poetry with love themes; counter-category is puram
Akapporul love themed, refers to literary styles
Alvar group of twelve medieval Tamil poet-saints dedicated to Vishnu
Ananku force or power often attributed to goddesses
Anpu affection, love
Arul grace or favor
Bhakti devotion, love
Bhumi goddess of the earth
Brahma god of creation
Calantaran demon born from Shiva's third eye and then decapitated
Cankaniti conch shell treasure
Chidambaram city in South India, site of dancing Shiva's temple, alias Tillai, Puliyur (literally tiger town)
Cintamani wish-fulfilling gem
Cirrilakkiyam minor genres of Tamil literature, alias pirapantam
Darshan seeing a deity and being seen by a deity in a Hindu devotional context
Ganges River major river in north India, flows from Shiva's crown
Indra king of the gods
Kailash, Mount Kailash Shiva's home on a silver mountain peak, alias Kayilai
Kalan the timely one, god of death, alias Yama
Kalancu form of measurement (used for metal ornaments for example)
Kama god of love
Kamam desire, love
Karpakam tree wish-fulfilling tree
Karu, karuporul environmental elements and objects
Katci sighting, the first scene of a kovai poem
Kattalai kalitturai literary meter used in kovai poems
Kaveri River major river near Chidambaram, alias Ponni, Kaviri
Kilavittalaivan hero of the love story in a kovai poem

Konrai flower preferred by Shiva
Kovai literally garland, genre of poetry with four hundred love-themed verses
Kurinji plant referring mountain landscape, indicates union
Kuruni a measure of grain or flowers, for example
Kuttan dancer, Tamil name for Nataraja
Lakshmi goddess of beauty and prosperity
Manikkavacakar poet of *Tirukkovaiyar* and *Tiruvacakam*, alias Tiruvatavurar
Markali month in the Tamil calendar, mid-December to mid-January
Markandeya a boy who escaped death with the help of Shiva
Marutam plant referring to agricultural landscape, indicates sulking
Matam monastery
Meykkirtti panegyric verses used to open royal inscriptions
Mullai plant (jasmine) referring to forest landscape, indicates waiting
Murukan South Indian heroic god, son of Shiva
Mutal, mutalporul regional and temporal setting
Muvar three saints of Tamil Shaivism named Appar Cuntaram, and Campantar; attributed authors of *Tevaram*
Nagas supernatural cobras that live in the underworld called Nagaloka
Nali a small measure of grain or flowers, for example
Nalvar four saints of Tamil Shaivism named Appar, Cuntaram, Campantar, and Manikkavacakar
Nandi a bull, vehicle for Shiva
Nataraja lord of dance, name for Shiva in his dancing form at Chidambaram
Nayanmar group of sixty-three medieval Tamil poet-saints dedicated to Shiva
Neytal plant (waterlily) referring to seashore landscape, indicates lament
Pakal sun god who has his teeth smashed by Shiva, alias Pakan
Palai plant referring to desert landscape, indicates separation
Parattai public woman
Patikam poem in praise of a deity, usually ten stanzas
Pattiyal index of literary genres
Pattutaittalaivan the hero of the kovai composition as a whole, often the patron of the poem
Pillaittamil minor Tamil literary genre which praises a deity or patron as a child
Pillaiyar name for Hindu god Ganesh, the remover of obstacles
Potiyil hills Western Ghats, hills praised by the Pandyas, alias Potiyam, Malayam, Potiyay Malayam
Puram exterior, category for Tamil poetry with heroic themes, counter-category is akam

Sangam literature body of extant early classical Tamil literature, categorized by love and heroic themes
Shakti divine feminine power
Shiva Hindu god praised by *Tirukkovaiyar*, alias Aran, Aravan, Arurar, Civan
Talaivan hero of a Tamil poem
Talaivi heroine of a Tamil poem
Tevaram an anthology of early medieval hymns to Shiva
Tirukkovaiyar love-themed poem dedicated to Shiva, alias *Tiruccirrampalakkovai*; attributed to Manikkavacakar
Tirumal Tamil name for Vishnu, see Vishnu
Tirumurai twelve volumes that constitute the Tamil Shaiva canon
Tiruvacakam anthology of hymns dedicated to Shiva, including *Tiruvempavai*; attributed to Manikkavacakar
Uma goddess and consort of Shiva, alias Parvati
Untiyal vessel for collecting temple donations
Uri, uripporul scenes or themes of human behavior
Vaigai River major river that flows near Madurai, alias Vaiyai, Vaikai
Varaguna ninth-century Pandya king named in *Tirukkovaiyar*
Varaivu attached love, wedded love, a theme from Tamil love poetry
Vishnu Hindu god, alias Tirumal, Mal, Mayavan, father of Ayanar
Yama god of death, alias Kalan, Yaman

Notes

Introduction

1 Chidester (2005: 1).
2 For a history of how material cultures have been incorporated into or excluded from religious studies, see Fleming and Mann (2014: 3–7).
3 Plate (2015: 4).
4 Hardy (1983) and Prentiss (1999).
5 Champakalakshmi (2011).
6 Flood (2009: 9).
7 Plate (2015: 4).
8 Prohl (2015: 14).
9 Stewart (2010: 339).
10 See Emmrich (2011) and Subbiah (1991) for two perspectives on the periodization of Tamil literature and its various sociocultural repercussions.
11 See Hardy (1983), Cutler (1987: 1), Peterson (1989: 4), and Monius (2004: 194). See Novetzke (2007) for an addendum to this definition, which argues that bhakti is a devotional expression that takes an audience or public.
12 Peterson 1989. I return to this point in Chapter 3.
13 The technical qualities of this stylized love poetry will be explored at length in Chapter 1.
14 The best summary of the evidence used to date Manikkavacakar is in Yocum (1982: 45–54). For additional arguments for the ninth-century date for Manikkavacakar, see Narayana Ayyar (1936), Zvelebil (1973), and Cutler (1987). For arguments for the fifth century, see Vedachalam (1965). In addition to *Tirukkovaiyar* verses, the texts used by scholars for dating evidence span 700 years: *Tiruttontattokai* was composed in the eighth century by Cuntarar, *Tiruppavai* was composed in the ninth century by Antal, *Tiruvacakam* was composed in the ninth century by Manikkavacakar, *Tiruvilaiyatal puranam* was composed in the thirteenth century by Parancoti, and *Tiruvatavurar puranam* was composed in the fifteenth century. For an entirely different method for determining relative dates for the Tamil literary corpus, see Tieken (2001).
15 Nilakanta Sastri (1955).
16 The text in square brackets is written in Tamil script.
17 We also learn that Pope believed the text was composed in the twelfth century, a three hundred year discrepancy from the current consensus on the poetry's age.

18 Pope (1879: 205).

19 The title of this hagiography is derived from Manikkavacakar's alias Tiruvatavurar, after his hometown Thiruvadavur. For more details from this hagiography, see Shulman (2002: 135–137).

20 *Tiruvilaiyatal puranam* is the sthalapurana of the Meenakshi-Sundareshwara temple in Madurai. It contains sixty-four stories about Shiva's mischievous adventures, four of which are about Manikkavacakar. Episodes from this text can be seen in panels painted on a wall facing the central tank in the Meenakshi temple complex.

21 This particular episode is corroborated by a Sinhalese chronicle, *Nikayasangrahaya*, which reports that Sinhalese King Sena I, who ruled from 833 to 853 CE, was converted to Shaivism and his daughter was cured by an ascetic who was dressed as a priest in Chidambaram.

22 For descriptions of Manikkavacakar's role in this festival, see Younger (1995: 54–58). For a theological reading of the festivals at Chidambaram, see Davis (2010). For another example of the use of Manikkavacakar's *Tiruvempavai* during a Chidambaram festival, see Wenta (2014). For festivities associated with Manikkavacakar's date of liberation, see Loud (2004: 127–139).

23 Younger (2002: 157).

24 For studies of Manikkavacakar's influence on Shaiva Siddhanta thought, see Dhavamony (1971), Mowry (1974), Schomerus (1912), and Navaratnam (1963). For an overview of Shaiva Siddhanta thought, see Davis (1991). See also Arunachalam 1981 for a study of Shaiva philosophy with twenty-one translated verses from *Tirukkovaiyar*.

Chapter 1

1 Plate (2015: 4).

2 The role of puram themes will be explored in Chapter 4.

3 For a table that includes many more details for each landscape, see Ramanujan (1967: 107).

4 Translated by Selby (2011: 112).

5 Ramanujan (1967). In his "Afterword" to this book, Ramanujan provides an eighteen-page overview of classical Tamil poetry and offers a tidy table of "Some Features of the Five Landscapes," where he notes, "This is not an exhaustive list" (Ramanujan 1967: 107).

6 Arguments for and against the occurrence of sexual union (in contrast to emotional union) of the hero and heroine in akam poetics are articulated in *Iraiyanar akapporul*. In this case, commentator Nakkiranar argues that physical intimacy is required (Buck and Paramasivam 1997: 33–34).

7 The three volumes of this grammar are divided thematically into letters, words, and subject matter. Scholars agree that *Tolkappiyam* is a cumulative composition

with its earliest chapters dated to the first three centuries CE and its later chapters, including those addressing akapporul, dateable to the fourth through sixth centuries CE. The commentaries that interpret Tolkappiyar's sutras were composed much later by Ilampuranar (twelfth century), Peraciriyar (thirteenth century), and Naccinarkkiniyar (fourteenth century). See Zvelebil (1995: 705–709) and Takahashi (1995: 116–119).

8 The *Tolkappiyam* treatment of akam themes is arranged by speaker rather than by theme. Within such a category the themes are arranged in serial order, comparable to the style of *Iraiyanar akapporul*. For a more detailed discussion, see Takahashi (1995: 221).

9 For a full translation, see David C. Buck's book, *The Study of Stolen Love*. For more information about the date of *Pantikkovai*, see Zvelebil (1995: 462–463, 518–519). The author of *Pantikkovai* is unknown.

10 Other kovai verses sited include excerpts from *Tirukkovaiyar*.

11 Takahashi (1995: 220).

12 Takahashi (1995). For another foundational study of literary conventions of early Tamil love poetry, see Zvelebil (1986).

13 Takahashi (1995: 11).

14 The most famous ethnographic study of the complexities and hidden nature of anpu in Tamil culture is Trawick (1990). See also Trawick (1988).

15 I thank Jean-Luc Chevillard for his notes on time and seasons in *Tolkappiyam*.

16 *Tolkappiyam* (Porulatikaram) verses 6–12.

17 *Tolkappiyam* (Porulatikaram) 6 || kāru mālaiyu mullai ||.

18 Many examples of disagreements among commentators can be found in the copious notes made in P. S. Subrahmanya Sastri's translation and English commentary of *Tolkappiyam* (Porulatikaram) (1999).

19 Sections 1–4, 9, 13–18, and 20–255 of the *Tirukkovaiyar* all have themes that correspond with those listed in *Akapporul vilakkam*.

20 For theorization of pattiyal including the kovai genre, see Clare (2011: especially 64–67), in which she describes various ways that medieval poets blended and reused akam poetics to praise kings and other named patrons, a task classically assigned to the poets of the puram anthologies.

21 The intermediate stage of love, known as varaivu, is not included in *Tirukkovaiyar*. V. S. Rajam has raised an objection to reading varaivu as marriage. She recommends that varaivu be read as attachment, a designation or mark specifying that the woman belongs to the man, though not necessarily formalized through marriage (Personal communication, May 2011).

22 For more on Tamil prosody, see Niklas (1993). See also Zvelebil (1989).

23 For those versed in Tamil metrics, kattalai kalitturai "is composed of four neṭilaṭi (i.e. a line having five cīr). The first four cīr of each line should preferably be iyaṟcīr, and they must be connected in the veṇṭaḷai manner. The fifth cīr of each line must be

kūviḷaṅkāy or karuviḷaṅkāy. A kaṭṭaḷai-kalitturai should have as its last letter an –ē" (Niklas 1988: 189).

24 For the most exhaustive study in English to date of kalavu, karpu, and varaivu themes, see chapter six in Takahashi (1995).

25 Navalar (1955).

26 There are copious lists of extant kovai-themed poems in various Tamil sources; however, the titles I've provided here are exclusively from texts that I have personally verified. For a comparative study of *Tirukkovaiyar* and *Makkakkovai* see Comeau (2016).

27 Since *Iraiyanar akapporul* has been presented in its entirety in Buck (1997), I've limited my analysis to *Maranakapporul* and *Akapporul vilakkam*.

28 The Shaiva Siddhanta commentators have also contributed a reading of the lotus as her face, blue nelumbo as her eyes, kumil as her nose, the petals of the red glory lily as the fingers of her hands, and the konku flower as her chest.

29 Tancai is an old name for the town Tancakkur near Madurai (Takahashi 1995: 34).

30 Nilakanta Sastri (1955: 387). See also Zvelebil (1995: 12) and Takahashi (1995: 34).

31 Nampi's excursus on sighting (katci) is located in the second section of his treatise.

32 *Ciramalaikkovai* 1937: viii.

33 Morgan (2010: 8).

34 Morgan (2010: 8).

35 Ahmed (2010: 33).

36 1 crore = 10 million.

37 See Rajam (1986) and Hart (1973).

38 Zvelebil (1995: 384).

39 For key verses, see Gopal Iyer (2005: (Intro) xxxvii–xxxviii).

40 See Gopal Iyer (2005: (Intro) xxx). The varaiviyal theme is found in chapter twenty-two of *Tiruppatikkovai.*

41 Alternative translations for "lord and lady" are god and goddess, husband and mistress, or king and queen.

42 Although I have not yet encountered an aiyam verse in which someone other than the hero is the doubter, women express doubts in other sections of *Tirukkovaiyar*, including verse 60.

43 For more on Nammalvar, see Dehejia (1988: 108–116).

44 *Akapporul vilakkam*, part 2, verse 2.

Chapter 2

1 Kim (2013: 146–147).

2 Kim (2013: 90).

3 Kim (2013: 90).

4 Bronner (2007: 119).
5 Bronner (2007: 123).
6 Bronner (2007: 120).
7 For example, in *Ainkurunuru* the heroine is described as "this woman who is like Tēṉūr in the good lands of the Pāṇṭiya king" (v. 54), "this girl who resembles Tēṉūr, that city of the king who is rich in chariots" (v. 55), and "the girl resembles Āmūr, that town of Cōḻa conquerors" (v. 56) (Selby 2011: 39).
8 *Purananuru* 347 (Hart and Heifetz 1999: 198). Kutal is also named in akam poem *Narrinai*, verse 298.
9 Cutler (2008: 44).
10 Cutler (2008: 51).
11 The Tamil line reads, "Her breasts have not been crushed."
12 Tiruperunthurai is not mentioned in the devotional anthology *Tevaram*, but it is one of the prominent places included in the hymns of *Tiruvacakam*.
13 My translation is based on the edition Cōmacuntarak Kavirāyar (1943).
14 For a study of temple aesthetics and iconography at Tirukkalukkunram, see Comeau (2019b).
15 The poet filled this verse with climbing imagery, some of which has been lost in translation. I have preserved some of the wordplay with the use of mount, raise, and ascend. The confidante is speaking about the hero in this verse. When she says that he destroyed the mountain, according to the commentary she refers to the elephant that the hero drove away to protect the women.
16 Selby (2011: 56).
17 There are several forms of golden gifts to be made for a marriage: gold worn by a cow or bull, gold for cows and bulls presented by in-laws, and gold given to the heroine by her family.
18 For another example of Tirumal worshipping Shiva, see verse 86.
19 The word I've translated as love is "anpu," the ideal affectionate desire.
20 Translated by Wilden (2008: 341).
21 Translated by Hart and Heifetz (1999: 226).
22 For variations of this spiraling emotional and visual practice, see Venkatesan (2010: 198).
23 Literally, the text says, "go and see the manner where it (the waist) is not diminishing." The implied criticism is that the heroine's waist continues to fade in her lover's absence.
24 The verb "pukuntu" means both arrived and entered and is repeated for front rhyming in this stanza. The four entrances are viti (+utaiyar): the one with wealth, pati: the one with a town, kati: the one with a path, and mati: the one with knowledge. The references are to the priest, Yama, one above all, and the son or boy.
25 The meaning of viti includes destiny, good karma, or wealth. I've translated it here as "good fortune."

26 See *Tiruvacakam*, Hymn 2, verses 74–80.
27 Translated by Wilden (2008: 153). See also *Narrinai* verses 273 and 288.
28 Translated by Wilden (2010: 605). See also *Kuruntokai* verses 53, 111, 360, 362, 366.

Chapter 3

1 See Hardy (1983), especially Part Three for more analysis of deities and religious themes as they appear in classical literature.
2 For a study of Karaikkal Ammaiyar's life and works see Pechilis (2012 and 2006).
3 See Peterson (1989, 1983, and 1982).
4 For a study of Antal's life and works, see Venkatesan (2010) and Venkatesan and Branfoot (2015).
5 For a translation and analysis of Nammalvar's poetry, see Venkatesan (2014).
6 Although the individual texts were composed over a long period of time, it is believed that these canonical volumes were compiled toward the end of the reign of Chola king Kulottunka III (1178–1218 CE).
7 For the etymology of *Tevaram*, see Gros (1984: xxxix-xl). Like the term "patikam," the use of the term "tevaram" can be found in inscriptions as early as the tenth and eleventh centuries but without specific reference to the muvar (see S.I.I. VIII, 260). It is not until the sixteenth or seventeenth century that *Tevaram* becomes the general name for the three saints' poems, nearly a millennium after their composition (Zvelebil 1995: 263). Even today, *Tevaram* can be found organized under two different principles: one classifies the hymns by the sites to which they refer, and the other system classifies the hymns by musical mode.
8 According to fourteenth-century *Tirumuraikanta Puranam*, by Shaiva philosopher Umapati Civacariyar, the *Tevaram* hymns as we know them today are not complete. He gives the poets credit as follows: 16,000 patikam by Campantar, 49,000 by Appar, and 38,000 by Cuntarar. Although the story of his work appeared more than three hundred years after the poems were composed, Nampiyantar Nampi is credited with rediscovering and anthologizing the remaining lost hymns. See Gros (1984: lxi–lxii) for a review of evidence for the current verse count.
9 For a translation of Cuntarar's hymns, see Shulman (1990).
10 Evidence for hymn-singing in temple inscriptions is present as early as the ninth century; however, the term used for hymns is "patikam" or "patiyam," without reference to the *Tevaram* anthology. See Zvelebil (1995: 266).
11 See Spencer (1970: 232–244) and Peterson (1989: 12–13).
12 There are four primary meters used in these hymns. For the verses mentioned above, see Hymn 19 and Hymn 39, verse 3.
13 The first English translation of *Tiruvacakam* was composed by G. U. Pope and was published in 1900. Pope included extensive notes with his translation, including the

legends of Manikkavacakar, the legends of Shiva from local and puranic sources, legends of Chidambaram, theological terms and themes from Shaiva Siddhanta thought, and metrical systems.

14 Ramachandran (2001: xii).

15 Tirukkalukkunram receives most of its attention in the refrain of Hymn 30.

16 In her study of *Tevaram*, Indira Peterson collated the occurrences of various sites throughout the seven volumes, listing sites that receive mention five or more times by the muvar saints.

17 Madurai is called Alavay in *Tevaram* and Kutal in *Tirukkovaiyar*.

18 Orr (2014: 214).

19 Orr (2014: 215).

20 According to the *Tevaram* saints, the eight feats of Shiva are as follows: the decapitation of Brahma in Tirukkantiyur, the impaling of Andhaka at Kovalur, the burning of the triple cities at Tiruvatikai, the destruction of Daksha's sacrifice at Pariyalur, the war with Jalandhara at Virkuti, the skinning of the elephant at Valuvur, the burning of Kama at Kurukkai, and the slaying of Yama at Tirukkatavur (Shulman 1990: xlix–l). According to Gros, the two most celebrated stories are the legend of Lingodbhavamurti and of Ravana (1984: lv). The details of these legends can be found in Peterson (1989: 343–348).

21 Translated by Hart and Heifetz (1999: 4).

22 Mention of Potiyay Malayam is primarily concentrated in themes twelve, fourteen, and twenty-five.

23 All translations of *Tevaram* verses are my own unless otherwise noted. I use the numbering system and text from the edition by T. V. Gopal Iyer (1984).

24 Hardy (1983: 10–11). See Hardy (1983: 141) for further discussion on the union of sensuality and emotionalism in Hardy's characterization of bhakti literature. Again, this is distinct from the sensory (which can include sensuality) characteristics that I argue are essential to the religious sense of *Tirukkovaiyar*.

25 Ali (2000: 176–177).

26 See Orr (2014: 208) for *Tiruvempavai* in inscriptions. See Cutler (1979) for a comparative study of *Tiruvempavai* and Antal's *Tiruppavai*.

27 Translations are mine. Text cited according to Māṇikka-vācakar [No date]. *Tiruvempāvai*. Ceṉṉai: Tirunelvēli teṉṉintiya caivacittānta nūṟpatippuk kaḻakam lit.

28 See Steven Hopkins' masterful work on messengers, most recently Hopkins 2016.

29 Translated by Archana Venkatesan (2014: 40).

30 For the most recent scholarship on and complete translation of *Tiruviruttam*, see Venkatesan (2014).

31 Translated by Hart and Heifetz (1999: 88).

32 Translated by Selby (2011: 117).

33 For Selby's developed explanation of these zoomorphic relationships in early Tamil love poetry, see Selby (2011: 14–20).

34 Hart and Heifetz (1999: 80).
35 Ramanujan 1981: Introduction.
36 Translated by Ramanujan (1981: 84).
37 See also Champakalakshmi 2004 and Gurukkal 1995 on the social and political roles of bhakti poets.
38 See Venkatesan (2014, especially pages 110–124) for a comparison of *Tirukkovaiyar* and *Tiruviruttam.*
39 Pope notes in his commentary that this tear-filled mad woman is Manikkavacakar's reference to Karaikkal Ammaiyar, the nayanar and poetess who preceded the muvar (1900: 111–113).
40 The Tamil compares her words to the sound of a flute.
41 For examples of pillaittamil poetry see Richman (1997).
42 The story of Cekkilar's life comes to us in a short poem composed in the fourteenth century by Umapati entitled *Cekkilar Puranam.*
43 For more on the relationship between text, hagiography, and devotional interpretation in these sources, see Cutler (1984).
44 Commissioning *Periyapuranam* seems in part to have also been a defensive move against rival literary production. Although Cekkilar insisted that his inspiration for the sixty-three saints was Cuntarar's work, there was a Jain work in Sanskrit known as *Mahapurana* that narrated the lives of sixty-three great Jain figures, Trishashti shalakapurusha. In Umapati's account of Cekkilar's life, *Periyapuranam* was written to replace the king's fascination with a different Jain classic, *Civakacintamani,* which was scorned by Cekkilar for its erotic content. There was also a growing body of literature cultivated by Vaishnava poets. Around the time of Nampi's collection of the Shaiva hymns, Nathamuni collected the work of the twelve alvars into the Vaishnava canon called *Nalayirativyaprabantam* or *The Four Thousand Holy Hymns.* See Gros (1984: xlviii–xlix), Ryan (1998), and Peterson (1994).
45 Monius (2004: 168).
46 Monius (2004: 186).

Chapter 4

1 I accept to Judith Butler's claim that gender is performative. Behaviors or qualities that are evaluated as feminine or masculine are culturally determined, change over time, and are not determined by or reliant on a person's biological sex. See Butler (1990).
2 Selby (2000: 100–101).
3 Selby (2000: 101).
4 Pollock (2007: 379).

5 LaCapra writes, "It should be obvious that a significant text does not simply fall within or illustrate a genre but in part rewrites the genre by testing its limits and at times by transgressing them" (2013: 28).
6 Pollock (2007: 381).
7 Cutler (1987: 83).
8 Hart and Heifetz (1999: 210).
9 Translated by Hart and Heifetz (1999: 212).
10 Buck and Paramasivam 1997: xi. Other scholars have suggested that the poet is praising a composite representation of the entire Pandya dynasty (Zvelebil 1995: 519).
11 Translated by Buck and Paramasivam (1997: 63).
12 Translated by Buck and Paramasivam (1997: 178).
13 See verses *TKV* 56, and 123.
14 See verses *TKV* 13.
15 See verses *TKV* 24, 187, 68, 309, 11, 75, and 267, respectively.
16 See verses *TKV* 164, 315, and 283.
17 See verses *TKV* 326.
18 See verses *TKV* 52, 348, 399, and 302.
19 See verses *TKV* 15.
20 See verses *TKV* 60.
21 See verses *TKV* 61.
22 See verses *TKV* 150.
23 See verses *TKV* 92, 59, and 160.
24 We have seen above that muvar usually refers to the three poets of the *Tevaram*; however, the three referred to here are the gods Indra, Vishnu, and Brahma.
25 See verses *TKV* 368, 355, 337, and 171.
26 See verses *TKV* 76, 108, 140, and 185.
27 Although this story is referenced frequently in *Tirukkovaiyar*, it is not associated with a specific city in Tamil country, unlike *Tevaram*, which places it in Tiruvatikai.
28 See verses *TKV* 22.
29 See verses *TKV* 300.
30 See verses *TKV* 180.
31 See verses *TKV* 86.
32 See verses *TKV* 254.
33 Literally, the Tamil reads, "many outsiders increasingly intend."
34 See Comeau (2019a).
35 Beck (1972: 25).
36 Beck (1972: 27).
37 For one example, scenes from the palm horse ordeal can be found in the Tamil anthology *Narrinai*, verses 146 and 152. See Zvelebil (1986: 22–28) for a detailed description of mounting the palm horse as it occurs specifically in the classical akam corpus.

38 The promise of their shouts can be found in *Kuruntokai* 17.

39 The ridicule that the hero faces is mentioned in *Kuruntokai* 182.

Chapter 5

1 I speak here only of ornaments and gifts made from fine metals. Temple wealth has also historically come from land holdings.

2 Packert (2010: 202).

3 Packert (2010: 203).

4 Packert (2010: 205).

5 This inscription is recorded in ARE (1918: 511). My reading of the inscription is based on a handwritten copy consulted at the Archaeological Survey of India (ASI) office in Mysore.

6 This inscription is recorded in ARE (1965–66: 332B). My reading of the inscription is based on a handwritten copy consulted in Mysore.

7 This inscription is recorded in ARE (1943–44: 192). My reading of the inscription is based on a handwritten copy consulted in Mysore.

8 The inscription was engraved on the north wall of the central shrine of the temple, and it is published in SII XIX, 90 (ARE 1907: 198).

9 This inscription is recorded in ARE (1932–33: 122). The inscription is dated to the twelfth century based on the style of writing. My reading and translation of the inscription is based on a handwritten copy of the inscription consulted at ASI in Mysore.

10 See SII XIII, 144 (ARE 1918: 444).

11 For one example of a procession that visited gardens, see ARE (1934–35: 104), published in SII XII, 245.

12 This inscription is published in SII XXVIII, 130.

13 The inscription is published in SII XXVIII, 155. More examples of garden donations recorded at Chidambaram can be found in SII XXVIII, numbers 113, 118, 120, and 121. See SII XXVIII, 125 for an example of a garden designated for mangoes, jackfruits, and plantains, rather than flowers.

14 This inscription is recorded in ARE (1907: 197). The inscription has not been published in any volumes of *South Indian Inscriptions*. My reading and translation of the inscription is based on a handwritten copy of the inscription consulted in Mysore.

15 I later learned that there was an extra-long ladder on the temple grounds, which was used to occasionally reach and harvest the honeycomb.

16 Translated by Wilden (2008: 851).

17 Translated by Wilden (2010: 625).

18 Translated by Wilden (2010: 198–199).

19 In his notes on this verse, Ramachandran also cites parallel imagery in several early Tamil verses, including *Narrinai* 11, *Manimekalai* 4, 6, and 65, and *Kalittokai* 68:15. For relevant passages see Ramachandran (1989: 400).

20 Translated by Wilden (2010: 96–97). The relevant phrase as follows: "maṭaimāṉ ceppiṟ ṟamiya vaikiya peyyāp pūviṉ."

21 In a fascinating study of color in South Indian rituals, Brenda Beck explains the ritual transformation of the color white to red and back to white. Red, or the heat of a fire, serves as a point of transition between two states of cool white (see especially Beck 1969: 557–558).

22 This color combination of red and white is most commonly seen today in temple painting schemes to symbolize tension between feminine and masculine divine power, also conceptualized as hot and cold forces.

23 For examples of the heroine's eyes shifting from black to red when her toys are destroyed, see *Ainkurunuru* 69 and 135. For an example of this color scheme applied to the animal world, see *Ainkurunuru* 92 in which the reddened eyes of a mother buffalo play off of the color of her black horns and flowing white milk.

24 For another list of the possessions distributed by the departing heroine, see *Ainkurunuru* 375 and 377, in which she leaves behind her doll, green parrot, ball, and molucca beans. In the *Narrinai* anthology, the young heroine can be found playing with a ball and doll and flashing her sharp quill-like teeth (see verse 179).

Bibliography

Primary Sources

Annual Report on Indian Epigraphy (ARE). Vols 1–43 (1887–1996), Delhi: Archaeological Survey of India.

Āṇṭāḷ. (n.d.), *Tiruppāvai*, Ceṉṉai: Tirunelvēli teṉṉintiya caivacittānta nūṟpatippuk kaḻakam lit.

Ceṭṭiyār, P. Cu. P. (1978), *Cēlam kōvai*, Irācipuram: Muttu Piras.

Cōmacuntarak Kavirāyar. (1943), *Tirukkaḻukkuṉṟak kōvai*, Ceṉṉai: Kapīr Accukkūṭam.

Comacuntaranar, Po. Ve., ed. (1970), *Tirukkovaiyar, palaiya uraiyum putiya vilakkamum*, Cennai: Kalakam.

Cuppiramaniya Pillai, Ka., ed. (1972), *Manikkavacaka cuvamikal arulicceyta Tirukkovaiyar. Peraciriyar uraiyum, palaiyavuraiyum*, Tiruppanantal: Sri Kachimatam.

Cuppiramaṇiyaṉ, M. C. Ve., ed. (2007), "*Pirapantam tīpam*," in *Tamiḻ ilakkaṇa nūlkaḷ*, Ceṉṉai: Maṇivācakar āpceṭ piriṇṭars.

Cuppiramaṇiyaṉ, M. C. Ve., ed. (2007), "*Paṉṉiru pāṭṭiyal*," in *Tamiḻ ilakkaṇa nūlkaḷ*, Ceṉṉai: Maṇivācakar āpceṭ piriṇṭars.

Gopal Iyer, T. V., ed. (2005), *Māṟaṉ Akapporuḷ and the Tiruppatikkōvai of Tirukkurukaipperumal Kavirayar: A Treatise of Tamil Poetics Illustrated with a Narrative Poem*, Pondicherry: French Institute of Pondicherry and École française d'Extrême-Orient.

Gopal Iyer, T. V., ed. (1984), *Tēvāram: Hymnes Śivaites du pays tamoul*, Pondicherry: Institut francais d'indologie.

Innaci, Mu. Cu. (2001), *Kirittavat tamizkkotai*, tokuti 1, Citamparam: Meyyappan Tamizaylakam.

Iṟaiyaṉār. (1964), *Kaḷaviyal eṉṟa Iṟaiyaṉār akapporuḷ Nakkīraṉār aruḷiya uraiyuṭaṉ*, Tirunelvēli: Teṉṉintiya Caivacittānta Nūṟpatippuk kaḻakam.

Kaṇṇaṉ, R. (2002), *Ciṟṟilakkiya Ārāycci*, Ceṉṉai: Appar Patippakam.

Māṇikkavācaka-suvāmikaḷ (1950, reprint 1972), *Tirukkōvaiyār (pērāciriyaraiyum paḻaiyavuraiyum)*, Shrivaikuṇṭam: Shri kumarakuruparaṉ caṅkam.

Māṇikka-vācakar. (n.d.), *Tiruvempāvai*, Ceṉṉai: Tirunelvēli teṉṉintiya caivacittānta nūṟpatippuk kaḻakam lit.

Mutaliyār, Tiru Kā. Rā. Kō., ed. (1992), *Naṟkavirācar nampi iyaṟṟiya akapporuḷ viḷakkam paḻaiya uraiyuṭaṉ*, Tinnevelly: The South India Śaiva Siddhanta Works Publishing Society.

Mutaliyār, A. S. M., ed. (1949), *Kuṟṟālak kōvai (Kuttalak kovai with notes and comments)*, Travancore: University of Travancore.

Navalar, V. (1955), *Ānandaraṅkan kōvai* (with commentary by Mr. N. Balarama Iyer), ed. V. N. Subrahmanian, Madras: Government Oriental Manuscript Library.

Nāvalaravarkaḷ, C. E. (n.d), *Tiruvārūr kōvai*, ed. Es. Pi. Kē. Lāl Avarkaḷ, Ceṉṉai: Saṉ Āp Intiyā Piras.

Piḷḷai, A. (1937), *Cirāmalaikkōvai*, ed. U. Vē. Cāminātaiyarvarkaḷ, Maturai: The Madura Tamil Sangam.

Sastri, P. S. S., ed. (1999), *Tolkāppiyam: Poruḷatikāram*, Chennai: Kuppuswami Sastri Research Institute.

South Indian Inscriptions (SII). Vols 1–27 (1890–2001), Madras: Archaeological Survey of India.

Tamil Lexicon and Supplements (1982), Madras: University of Madras.

Secondary Sources

Ahmed, S. (2010), "Happy Objects," in M. Gregg and G. J. Seigworth (eds), *The Affect Theory Reader*, 29–51, Durham: Duke University Press.

Ali, D. (2004), *Courtly Culture and Political Life in Early Medieval India*, Cambridge: Cambridge University Press.

Ali, D. (2000), "From Nāyikā to Bhakta: A Genealogy of Female Subjectivity in Early Medieval India," in J. Leslie and M. McGee (eds), *Invented Identities: The Interplay of Gender, Religion and Politics in India*, 157–180, Oxford: Oxford University Press.

Arunachalam, P. (1981), *Studies and Translations, Philosophical and Religious*, Columbo, Sri Lanka: Department of Hindu Affairs, Ministry of Regional Development.

Beck, B. (1972), "The Story of a Tamil Epic: Several Versions of *Silappadikaram* Compared," *Journal of Tamil Studies*, 1 (September): 23–38.

Beck, B. (1969), "Color and Heat in South Indian Ritual," *Man*, 4: 553–572.

Bronner, Y. (2007), "Singing to God, Educating the People: Appayya Dīkṣita and the Function of Stotras," *Journal of the American Oriental Society*, 127: 113–130.

Buck, D. C., and K. Paramasivam, trans. (1997), *The Study of Stolen Love: A Translation of Kaḷaviyal eṉṟa Iṟaiyaṉār Akapporuḷ with Commentary by Nakkīraṉār*, Atlanta: Scholars Press.

Butler, J. (1990), *Gender Trouble: Feminism and the Subversion of Identity*, New York: Routledge.

Champakalakshmi, R. (2011), "The Making of a Religious Tradition: Perspectives from Pre-colonial South India," in R. Champakalakshmi (eds), *Religion, Tradition, and Ideology, Pre-colonial South India*, 1–50, Oxford: Oxford University Press.

Champakalakshmi, R. (2004), "From Devotion and Dissent to Dominance: The Bhakti of the Tamil Ālvārs and Nāyanārs," in D. Lorenzen (ed.), *Religious Movements in South* Asia *600–1800*, 47–80, Oxford: Oxford University Press.

Chellappan, K., and P. Parameswaran, trans. (1997), *Poetic Petals in the Interior Landscape: Uttaṇṭaṉ kōvai*, Chennai: Institute of Asian Studies.

Chidester, D. (2005), *Authentic Fakes: Religion and American Popular Culture*, Berkeley: University of California Press.
Clare, J. (2011), "Canons, Conventions and Creativity: Defining Literary Tradition in Premodern Tamil South India," PhD diss., University of California, Berkeley, Berkeley.
Comeau, L. E. (2019a), "Representations of Women and Divinity in Medieval Tamil Literature," *Journal of Feminist Studies in Religion*, 35 (1): 51–66.
Comeau, L. E. (2019b), "Saturated Space, Signs of Devotion in South Indian Temples," *South Asian Studies*, 35 (2): 181–192.
Comeau, L. E. (2016), "Islamic Devotion, Tamil Aesthetic: A Study of the *Makkākkōvai*," *Journal of Hindu Studies*, 9: 168–185.
Cort, J. E., ed. (1998), *Open Boundaries: Jain Communities and Cultures in Indian History*, Albany: State University of New York Press.
Cutler, N. (2008), "Four Spatial Realms in *Tirukkōvaiyār*," in M. A. Selby and I. V. Peterson (eds), *Tamil Geographies: Cultural Constructions of Space and Place in South India*, 43–57, Albany: State University of New York Press.
Cutler, N. (1987), *Songs of Experience: The Poetics of Tamil Devotion*, Bloomington: Indiana University Press.
Cutler, N. (1984), "The Devotees Experience of the Sacred Tamil Hymns," *History of Religions*, 24 (2): 91–112.
Cutler, N. (1979), *Consider Our Vow: Translation of Tiruppāvai and Tiruvempāvai into English*, Madurai: Muttu Patippakam.
Davis, R. H. (2010), *A Priest's Guide for the Great Festival: Aghorasiva's Mahotsavavidhi*, Oxford: Oxford University Press.
Davis, R. (1991), *Ritual in an Oscillating Universe: Worshiping Śiva in Medieval India*, Princeton: Princeton University Press.
Dehejia, V. (1988), *Slaves of the Lord: The Path of the Tamil Saints*, New Delhi: Munshiram Manoharlal.
Dhavamony, M. (1971), *Love of God According to Śaiva Siddhānta: A Study in the Mysticism and Theology of Śaivism*, Oxford: Oxford University Press.
Eck, D. (1985), *Darśan: Seeing the Divine Image in India*, 2nd edn, Chambersburg: Anima Books.
Emmrich, C. (2011), "The Ins and Outs of the Jains in Tamil Literary Histories," *Journal of Indian Philosophy*, 39: 599–646.
Fleming, B. J., and R. D. Mann. (2014), "Introduction: Material Culture and Religious Studies," in B. J. Fleming and R. D. Mann (eds), *Material Culture and Asian Religions: Text, Image, Object*, 1–20, New York: Routledge.
Flood, F. (2009), *Objects of Translation: Material Culture and Medieval "Hindu-Muslim" Encounter*, Princeton: Princeton University Press.
Gros, F. (1984), "Introduction," in T. V. Gopal Iyer (ed.), *Tēvāram: Hymnes Śivaites du pays tamoul*, v–lxviii, Pondicherry: Institut francais d'indologie.

Gurukkal, R. (1995), "The Beginnings of the Historic Period: the Tamil South (Up to the End of the Fifth Century A.D.)," in R. Thapar (ed.), *Recent Perspectives of Early Indian History*, 246–274, New Delhi: Book Review Trust.

Hardy, F. (1983), *Viraha-bhakti: The Early History of Krisna Devotion in South India*, Delhi: Oxford University Press.

Hart, G., and H. Heifetz, trans. (1999), *The Four Hundred Songs of War and Wisdom: An Anthology of Poems from Classical Tamil: The Puṟanāṉūṟu*, New York: Columbia University Press.

Hart, G. L. (1973), "Woman and the Sacred in Ancient Tamilnad," *The Journal of Asian Studies*, 32 (2): 233–250.

Hopkins, S. P. (2016), *The Flight of Love: A Messenger Poem of Medieval South India by Venkatanatha*, New York: Oxford University Press.

Kim, J. (2013), *Receptacle of the Sacred: Illustrated Manuscripts and the Buddhist Book Cult in South Asia*, Berkeley: University of California Press.

LaCapra, D. (2013), *History, Literature, Critical Theory*, Ithaca: Cornell University Press.

Loud, J. A. (2004), *The Rituals of Chidambaram*, Chennai: Institute of Asian Studies.

Manuel, I. (1997), *Literary Theories in Tamil (with Special Reference to Tolkappiyam)*, Pondicherry: Pondicherry Institute of Linguistics and Culture (PILC).

Monius, A. (2004), "Siva as Heroic Father: Theology and Hagiography in Medieval South India," *Harvard Theological Review*, 97 (2): 165–197.

Morgan, D. (2010), "Introduction: The Matter of Belief," in D. Morgan (ed.), *Religion and Material Culture: The Matter of Belief*, 1–17, New York: Routledge.

Mowry, M. L. (1974), "The Structure of Love in Māṇikkavācakar's *Tiruvācakam*," in H. M. Buck and G. E. Yocum (eds), *Structural Approaches to South India Studies*, 207–224, Chambersburg: Wilson Books.

Narayana Ayyar, C. V. (1936), *Origin and Early History of Saivism in South India*, Madras: University of Madras.

Natarajan, D. (1964), "Studies in Tirukkōvaiyār," Thesis for M.LITT. degree, Madras University, Chennai.

Navaratnam, R. (1963), *Tiruvachakam: The Hindu Testament of Love*, Bombay: Bharatiya Vidya Bhavan.

Niklas, U. (1993), *The Verses on the Precious Jewel Prosody Composed by Amitacakarar Tamil Text on Prosody with English Translation*, Pondichéry: Institut Francais de Pondichéry.

Niklas, U. (1988), "Introduction to Tamil Prosody," *Bulletin de l'École française d'Extrême-Orient*, 77, Paris: École française d'Extrême-Orient.

Nilakanta Sastri, K. A. (1955), *A History of South India from Prehistoric Times to the Fall of Vijayanagar*, Madras: Indian Branch, Oxford University Press.

Novetzke, C. L. (2007), "Bhakti and Its Public," *International Journal of Hindu Studies*, 11 (3): 255–272.

Orr, L. (2014), "The Sacred Landscape of Tamil Saivism: Plotting Place in the Realm of Devotion," in V. Gillet (ed.), *Mapping the Chronology of Bhakti: Milestones, Stepping*

Stones, and Stumbling Stones—Proceedings of a Workshop Held in Honour of Pandit R. Varada Desikan, 189–219, Pondichéry: Institut Français de Pondichéry/Ecole française d'Extrême-Orient.

Packert, C. (2010), *The Art of Loving Krishna: Ornamentation and Devotion*, Bloomington: Indiana University Press.

Pechilis, K. (2012), *Interpreting Devotion: The Poetry and Legacy of a Female Bhakti Saint of India*, New York: Routledge.

Pechilis, K. (2006), "The Story of the Classical Tamil Woman Saint, Kāraikkāl Ammaiyār: A Translation of Her Story from Cēkkiḻār's Periya Purāṇam," *International Journal of Hindu Studies*, 10 (2): 171–184.

Peterson, I. V. (1994), "Tamil Śaiva Hagiography: The Narrative of the Holy Saints (of Śiva) and the Hagiographical Project in Tamil Śaivism," W. M. Callewaert and R. Snell (eds), *According to Tradition: Hagiographical Writing in India*, 191–228, Wiesbaden: Harrassowitz Verlag.

Peterson, I. V. (1989), *Poems to Siva: The Hymns of the Tamil Saints*, Princeton: Princeton University Press.

Peterson, I. V. (1983), "Lives of the Wandering Singers: Pilgrimage and Poetry in Tamil Śaivite Hagiography," *History of Religions*, 22 (4): 338–360.

Peterson, I. V. (1982), "Singing of a Place: Pilgrimage as Metaphor and Motif in the Tevaram Songs of the Tamil Saivite Saints," *Journal of the American Oriental Society*, 102 (1): 69–90.

Plate, S. B., ed. (2015), *Key Terms in Material Religion*, London: Bloomsbury Academic.

Pollock, S. (2007), "Pretextures of Time," *History and Theory*, 46 (3): 366–383.

Pope, G. U. (1900), *The Tiruvācagam or "Sacred Utterances" of the Tamil Poet, Saint, and Sage Māṇikka-vācagar*, Oxford: Clarendon Press.

Pope, G. U., trans. (1879), *A Description of the Character, Manners, and Customs of the People of India; and of Their Institutions, Religious and Civil, by the Abbe J. A. Dubois*, 3rd edn, Madras: Higginbotham and Co.

Prentiss, K. P. (1999), *The Embodiment of Bhakti*, New York: Oxford University Press.

Prohl, I. (2015), "Aesthetics," in S. B. Plate (ed.), *Key Terms in Material Religion*, 9–16, London: Bloomsbury Academic.

Rajam, V. S. (1986), "Aṇaṅku: A Notion Semantically Reduced to Signify Female Sacred Power," *Journal of the American Oriental Society*, 106 (2): 257–272.

Ramachandran, T. N. (2001), *Tiruvachakam: Tamil Text and English Translation*, Chennai: International Institute of Tamil Studies.

Ramachandran, T. N. (1997), "Tirukkōvaiyār-Ārāycciyurai," in *Māṇikkavācakar Tirukkōvaiyār eṭṭām tirumuṟai-2*. Mayilāṭutuṟai: Ñāṉacampantam patippakam, Tarumai Ātīṉam.

Ramachandran, T. N., trans. (1989), *Tirukkovaiyar*, Thanjavur: Tamil University Offset Press.

Ramanujan, A. K., trans. (1981), *Hymns for the Drowning: Poems for Viṣṇu by Nammāḻvār*, Princeton: Princeton University Press.

Ramanujan, A. K. (1967), *The Interior Landscape, Love Poems from a Classical Tamil Anthology*, Bloomington: Indiana University Press.

Ramanujan A. K., and N. Cutler (2000), "From Classicism to Bhakti," in V. Dharwadker (ed.), *The Collected Essays of A.K. Ramanujan*, 232–259, Oxford: Oxford University Press.

Richman, P. (1997), *Extraordinary Child: Poems from a South Indian Devotional Genre*, Honolulu: University of Hawai'i Press.

Ryan, J. (1998), "Erotic Excess and Sexual Danger in the *Cīvakacintāmaṇi*," in J. E. Cort (ed.), *Open Boundaries: Jain Communities and Cultures in Indian History*, 67–84, Albany: State University of New York Press.

Schomerus, H. W. (1912), *Der Çaiva-Siddhānta: eine mystik Indiens*, Leipzig: J. C. Hinrichs'sche Buchhandlung.

Selby, M. A. (2011), *Tamil Love Poetry: The Five Hundred Short Poems of the Aiṅkuṟunūṟu, an Early Third Century Anthology*, New York: Columbia University Press.

Selby, M. A. (2000), *Grow Long, Blessed Night: Poems from Classical India*, Oxford: Oxford University Press.

Selby, M. A., and I. V. Peterson, eds (2008), *Tamil Geographies: Cultural Constructions of Space and Place in South India*, Albany: State University of New York Press.

Shulman, D. (2002), "Tirukkovaiyar: Downstream into God," in D. Shulman and G. G. Stroumsa (eds), *Self and Self-transformation in the History of Religions*, 131–149, Oxford: Oxford University Press.

Shulman, D. D., trans. (1990), *Songs of the Harsh Devotee: The Tēvāram of Cuntaramūrttināyaṉār*, Philadelphia: Department of South Asia Regional Studies, University of Pennsylvania.

Shulman, D. D. (1980), *Tamil Temple Myths: Sacrifice and Divine Marriage in the South Indian Śaiva Tradition*, Princeton: Princeton University Press.

Sivaraman, K. (1987), "The Spirituality of Love in the Śaiva Hindu Tradition: The Esoteric Implications of *Tirukkōvaiyār*," *Journal of the International Institute of Śaiva Siddhanta Research*, 3 (5).

Sivathamby, K. (1974), "Early South Indian Society and Economy: The Tinai Concept," *Social Scientist*, 3 (5): 20–37.

Spencer, G. W. (1970), "The Sacred Geography of the Tamil Shaivite Hymns," *Numen*, 17 (3): 232–244.

Stewart, K. (2010), "Afterword: Worlding Refrains," in M. Gregg and G. J. Seigworth (eds), *The Affect Theory Reader*, 339–353, Durham: Duke University Press.

Subbarayulu, Y. (2002), *Glossary of Tamil Inscriptions*, Vols 1–2, Chennai: Santi Sadhana.

Subbiah, G. (1991), *Roots of Tamil Religious Thought*, Pondicherry: Pondicherry Institute of Linguistics and Culture.

Takahashi, T. (1995), *Tamil Love Poetry and Poetics*, New York: E.J. Brill.

Tieken, H. (2001), *Kāvya in South India: Old Tamil Caṅkam Poetry*, Groningen: Egbert Forsten.

Trawick, M. (1990), *Notes on Love in a Tamil Family*, Berkeley: University of California Press.

Trawick, M. (1988), "Ambiguity in the Oral Exegesis of a Sacred Text: Tirukkovaiyar (or, the Guru in the Garden, Being an Account of a Tamil Informant's Responses to Homesteading in Central New York State)," *Cultural Anthropology*, 3 (3): 316–351.

Vedachalam, S. (alias Maraimalai Adigal) (1965), *The Saiva Siddhanta as a Philosophy of Practical Knowledge*, Tirunelveli: The South Indian Saiva Siddanta Works.

Veluthat, K. (1993), *The Political Structure of Early Medieval South India*, Hyderabad, AP: Orient Longman.

Venkatesan, A. (2014), *A Hundred Measures of Time: Tiruviruttam*, New York: Penguin.

Venkatesan, A. (2010), *The Secret Garland: Āṇṭāḷ's Tiruppāvai and Nācciyār Tirumoḻi*, New York: Oxford University Press.

Venkatesan, A. and C. Branfoot (2015), *In Andal's Garden*, Mumbai: Marg Foundation.

Wenta, A. (2014), "The Great Ārdrā Darśanam Festival: Performing Śaiva Ritual Texts in Contemporary Chidambaram," *International Journal of Hindu Studies*, 17: 371–398.

Wilden, E. (2010), *Kuṟuntokai: A Critical Edition and an Annotated Translation of the Kuṟuntokai*, Pondicherry: École française d'Extrême-Orient.

Wilden, E. (2008), *Naṟṟiṇai: A Critical Edition and an Annotated Translation of the Naṟṟiṇai*, Pondicherry: École française d'Extrême-Orient.

Wilden, E. (2006), *Literary Techniques in Old Tamil Cankam Poetry: The Kuruntokai*, Wiesbaden: Harrassowitz.

Yocum, G. E. (1982), *Hymns to the Dancing Śiva: A Study of Maṇikkavācakar's Tiruvācakam*, New Delhi: Heritage Publishers.

Younger, P. (2002), *Playing Host to Deity: Festival Religion in the South Indian Tradition*, Oxford: Oxford University Press.

Younger, P. (1995), *The Home of Dancing Śivaṉ: The Traditions of the Hindu Temple in Citamparam*, New York: Oxford University Press.

Zvelebil, K. V. (1995), *Lexicon of Tamil Literature*, Leiden: E.J. Brill.

Zvelebil, K. (1989), *Classical Tamil Prosody, and Introduction*, Madras: New Era Publications.

Zvelebil, K. V. (1986), *Literary Conventions in Akam Poetry*, Madras: Institute of Asian Studies.

Zvelebil, K. (1973), *The Smile of Murugan on Tamil Literature of South India*, Leiden: Brill.

Index

accumulation 5, 57, 61, 173
aestheticized representation 114
affect 5, 50, 169, 173
Agastya 70, 93
Ahmed, S. 50, 173, 183 n.35
Ainkurunuru
  animals 31, 103–4
  color 190 n.23
  hero 71, 104
  heroine 184 n.7, 190 n.24
  human behavior 33
aintinai 24, 32. *See also* five landscapes
aiyam 43, 183 n.42. *See also* doubt
Akananuru 33
akapporul kovai 29
Akapporul vilakkam
  doubt 49, 53–4, 183 n.44
  grammar for five landscapes 32–7, 41, 57, 183 n.27
  relation to kovai 43, 182 n.19
  sighting 47
Alavay 186 n.17. *See also* Madurai
Ali, D. 96, 186 n.25
alvar 106, 187 n.44
Ampal 22, 74–5
ampalam 72, 91–2, 120
ananku, force 51–2
Ananta Rankan 42
Anantarankan kovai 42–3
animal behavior 103, 151
animals
  in *Ainkurunuru* 31–3, 190 n.23
  behavior 75, 103, 151, 174
  in five landscapes 36, 85, 88, 167
  with Shiva 161
  in *Tirukkovaiyar* 100
  in wilderness 72, 86, 122
anpu 35, 40, 64, 67, 182 n.14, 184 n.19
Antal 7, 87, 180 n.14, 185 n.4, 186 n.26
Appar 18, 88, 95–6, 144, 185 n.8
Appayya Dikshita 60
architecture
  cityscape 159, 162, 165
  in poetry 86, 94, 174
  as religious expression 15, 27, 146, 169
Aricil river 75
arul 132
Arunachalam, P. 181 n.24
Aruntati 104
Arurar 42
ash
  on bodies 108
  Kama burned 46, 121
  worn by Shiva 19, 120, 154, 157

Bahour 103 (Figure 14)
Beck, B. 129, 188 nn.35–6, 190 n.21
beetle 134, 152
Bhairava 107
bhakti
  classicism to 106
  defined 6–7, 180 n.11
  eroticism 95–6, 105–6, 186 n.24
  hymns 25, 67, 87–8, 107, 111
  saints 15, 18, 54, 113, 187 n.37
Bhumi 52
bird
  behavior 75, 100–1, 104, 163
  in five landscapes 28, 32, 35, 56, 113
  form of Brahma 69
  kept by heroine 154–6
  messenger 101
  at Tirukkalukkunram 22, 68
Bodleian Library 10, 12
boundaries
  aesthetic 40
  disciplinary 25, 114
  literary 45
  narrative 46
  religious 4
  spatial 45, 53–4, 60–1, 86, 91, 94, 122, 143

Brahma
in bird form 69
in relation to Shiva 72, 107, 110, 122, 162, 186 n.20
supreme deity 53–4, 100
in triad 120, 188 n.24
Bronner, Y. 60, 62, 184 nn.4–6
Buck and Paramasivam 33, 181 n.6, 182 n.9, 183 n.27, 188 nn.10–12
Buddhism 17, 59–60, 93
buffalo 31, 190 n.23
bulls
as gift 184 n.17
as hero 47
Nandi 69, 70, 85, 97, 120
trainer 36
Butler, J. 187 n.1

Calantaran 76–7
Campantar
background 18
hometown 84, 90, 108
hymns 88, 97–8, 185 n.8
inscription 144
Cankaniti 176
carp 9–10, 48, 95, 134, 153. *See also* fish
cave shrine 20, 144, 147
Cekkilar 109, 187 n.42, 187 n.44
Cekkilar puranam 187 n.42
celestials 71–2, 76, 107, 121, 123, 126
Champakalakshmi, R. 5, 180 n.5, 187 n.37
chariot 75, 82, 131, 134, 184 n.7
chastity
of heroine 37, 53–4, 64, 76, 104, 123, 172
of mistress 129, 151
Chera dynasty 9, 16, 54
Chevillard, J. L. 182 n.15
Chidester, D. 3, 180 n.1
children
child of lovers 38, 134–5
deities 162
essay contests 16
heroine as child 65–6, 155–6, 163
and parents 87, 113
pillaittamil 108
Chola dynasty
cities, territory 10, 54, 90, 94, 184 n.7
inscription 145
kings 10, 109, 185 n.6
queens 144–5
Cilappatikaram 49, 129
Cintamani gem 176
Ciramalai 49
Ciramalaikkovai 48–9, 183 n.32
Civakacintamani 52, 93, 187 n.44
Civanakar 77
Clare, J. 182 n.20
colors red, white, black 27, 153–5, 164, 190 nn.21–3
Comeau 183 n.26, 184 n.14, 188 n.34
commentary
and classical grammars 18, 33, 36, 43, 55, 182 n.7
by G. U. Pope 187 n.39
on *Tirukkovaiyar* 6, 24, 32, 59–60, 65, 82, 109, 127, 129, 182 n.18, 184 n.15
Vaishnava 60
conch
iconography of Vishnu 106–7
ornaments 36, 158
rare 83, 176
in sea 160
sound 123
courtyard 94, 127, 162
cow 11, 143, 184 n.17
crane 83, 85
cremation ground 87, 135, 161
crow 163
crown
of gold 141
of Shiva 9, 19–20, 98, 153, 158, 159
of Vishnu 60
Cuntarar
hymns 88, 185 nn.8–9
inscription 144
nalvar 18
Tiruttontattokai 109, 180 n.14, 187 n.44
Cutler, N.
analysis of kovai 63, 114, 180 n.14, 184 nn.9–10, 187 n.43, 188 n.7
bhakti 25, 180 n.11
classicism to bhakti 106
Tiruvempavai 186 n.26

Daksha 121, 186 n.20
Dancing Shiva
in Chidambaram 14, 90, 92, 159 (*see also* Kuttan; Nataraja)

iconography 83
in temple 21–4, 144, 175 (Figure 20)
union with 27, 84
Darasuram 116 (Figure 15), 128 (Figure 16)
Davis, R. 181 n.22, 181 n.24
death
in battle 115
conquered 135, 150, 166
Yama 46, 73, 81, 121
deer 49, 133–4
Dehejia, V. 183 n.43
demon
Calantaran 77
dancing 115, 135
destroyed by Shiva 120–1, 132, 154
possession 81
separation 102
Dhavamony, M. 181 n.24
digital copy 12, 14
digital devotion 16
donation
gold 144–5, 159
inscription 143–4, 189 n.13
manuscript 12
natural resources 119, 146, 162, 189 n.13
at temple 1, 20, 141–6
doubt
background 43 (*see also* aiyam)
defined 49–50, 52
example 51–5
in *Tirukkovaiyar* 45–6, 120, 165, 170, 183 n.42
Dubois, Abbe J. A. 11

Eastern Ghats 118
Ekampam 91
elephant
behavior 100, 104, 111
compared to hero 32
destroyed by hero 139, 184 n.15
destroyed by Shiva 71, 110, 121, 186 n.20
Ganesh 145
as gift 51
hunted 66, 68, 171
of a king 9, 82, 119
literary motif 29, 38, 85, 170–1
temple 20
in warfare 117–18
elopement 37–8, 40, 76–7, 123
Emmrich, C. 180 n.10
experiment 3, 28, 40, 143, 174

Facebook 16
fawn 93, 126, 153–5, 159
fidelity
hero 82, 104, 128, 132, 136, 165
heroine 76, 104, 165
fire
arrows of Shiva 32, 132
dance of Shiva 21, 65–6, 82, 105, 120, 131, 145, 150–1, 169
red color 130, 190 n.21
three fires 93
fish
body of woman 135, 174
fertility 96, 111
kentai 95, 96
in sea 74, 160 (*see also* carp)
five landscapes
Akapporul vilakkam 34–7
defined 24, 29, 32, 181 n.5 (*see also* aintinai)
inherited forms 56
in kovai 40–2
Flemming and Mann 180 n.2
Flood, F. 5, 180 n.6
fortress 32, 134

Ganesh 145, 147
Ganges River
goddess 52, 84, 98
in Shiva's hair 9, 17, 84, 102, 120, 158–9
transformed 173
gates
house-yard 32, 127, 130–1, 134
temple 1, 13, 18, 21, 94
gender 113, 187 n.1
gift of nakam leaves
hero's gift 38, 64, 85, 170–1, 174
rejected 38
verse analysis 65, 68–9
girl in red 127, 130, 138
gold flower 145, 159
gold hand 144

Golden hall 18, 92
goose
  behavior 83–5, 100–1
  messenger 75, 152
  walk 1, 44–5, 138
Gopal Iyer, T. V. 183 nn.39–40, 186 n.23
Gros, F. 185 nn.7–8, 186 n.20, 187 n.44
Gurukkal, R. 187 n.37

hagiography
  interpretation 6, 187 n.43
  Manikkavacakar 16, 18, 67, 90, 94, 181 n.19
  Periyapuranam 87–8, 109–10
Hardy, F. 25, 96, 180 n.3, 180 n.11, 185 n.1, 186 n.24
Hart, G. 183 n.37
Hart and Heifetz 184 n.8, 184 n.21, 186 n.21, 186 n.31, 187 n.34, 188 nn.8–9
heron 101
Himalaya Mountains 10, 52, 83, 92–3, 98, 173
Hopkins, S. 186 n.28
horse 16–18, 121
human behavior, uri 34–6, 42–3

ibis 101–2
iconography
  Buddhism 59
  Manikkavacakar 18
  saints 109
  Shiva 72, 83, 85, 97, 110, 113, 120, 153–4, 167, 184 n.14
  Vishnu 107
Ilampuranar 182 n.7
imagination
  audience 94, 96–7, 164
  poetic 10, 35, 57
imagined journey 86
imagined pilgrimage 60
Indra 46, 53–4, 122, 188 n.24
Inkoymalai
  background 70, 92–3, 147
  image 70 (Figure 10)
  inscription 144
  verse analysis 69–70, 76, 162
inscription
  donation 189 nn.5–14
  memorial 27
  ornament, ornamental 141–6
  patikam 185 n.7, 185 n.10
  royal praise 10, 119
  temple source 6, 15–16, 23, 91, 111
  Tiruvempavai 186 n.26
insect 12, 99, 151. *See also* beetle
Iraiyanar akapporul
  background 33–4, 54–5, 117
  love themes 37, 182 n.8, 183 n.27
  union 181 n.6

Jainism 33, 52, 55, 93, 187 n.44
jewelry 25, 99, 141, 144, 159, 167

Kailash
  mountainous 57, 118, 170
  Shiva's home 46, 83, 92, 124–6, 137, 158–9, 161, 166–7, 173
  substitution 49, 81, 92
Kalan 78, 81, 150. *See also* Yama
Kalittokai 190 n.19
Kama 1, 44, 46, 110, 121, 186 n.20
kamam 35, 40, 64, 67
Kanchipuram
  images 51 (Figure 8), 79 (Figure 11), 142 (Figure 17)
  temple city 15, 20, 91
  verse analysis 78–9, 94
Kannaki 49, 129
Karaikkal Ammaiyar 87, 185 n.2, 187 n.39
karma 124, 128–31, 136, 165, 184 n.25
Karpakam tree 48, 176
Kataiyal 117–18
Katavul mamunivar 16
katci. *See* sighting
kattalai kalitturai 41–2
Kaveri delta 91
Kaveri River 53, 75, 88, 90
Kavivira Rakava Mutaliyar 68
Ketilam River 95
kilavittalaivan 114
Kim, J. 59–60, 64, 183 nn.1–3
koel bird 155–6. *See also* bird
Kolli Hills 117–19
Korkai 53–4
Kotunkunram 72. *See also* Piranmalai
kovai genre
  defined 29, 41–2, 55, 171
  love theme 33

Pantikkovai 117
places named 8
Krishna 96
Krishna and Radha 142
Kubera 176
Kulottunka II 109
Kulottunka III 145, 185 n.6
kurinji
five landscapes 29, 35, 163
flower 31
mountaintop 48–9, 95, 105, 118, 149
Kurukai 54, 56
Kuruntokai
background 33
flower in box 151
frenzied priest 80, 189 n.38
honeycomb 149
palm horse ordeal 137, 185 n.28, 189 n.39
Kutal 63, 118–19, 184 n.8, 186 n.17. *See also* Madurai
Kutralam
image 30 (Figure 6)
mountaintop 92, 94
temple 22
verse analysis 65–6, 69, 71–2, 162
Kuttan 120. *See also* Dancing Shiva; Nataraja

LaCapra, D. 114, 188 n.5
Lakshmi 46, 52, 118, 153
linga 21, 144
Lingodbhavamurti 186 n.20
lion 32, 65–6, 68, 82, 85–6
Loud, J. A. 181 n.22

Madurai
Cilappatikaram 49
inscription 144
Manikkavacakar 13, 16–17, 19
names (*see* Alavay; Kutal)
Pandya dynasty 61, 63, 91–2, 94, 117, 119
regional cities 79, 81–2, 92, 111, 141, 183 n.29
temple 20–1, 181 n.20
verse analysis 62, 64, 83, 92, 186 n.17
Mahapurana 187 n.44
Makkakkovai 43, 183 n.26
Malayam 93. *See also* Potiyil hills
Manikkavacakar
attributed work 43, 89, 99, 144
contemporaries 87, 187 n.39
date 180 n.14
festival 23, 100, 181 n.22
hagiography 10, 16, 18, 67–8, 90, 105, 109, 181 nn.19–20
images 2 (Figure 1), 17 (Figure 3), 19 (Figure 4), 67 (Figure 9), 89 (Figure 12)
inscription 23
poetic techniques 7, 63
sculptures and figures 13, 15, 18, 20–2
social media 16
special places 1
theology 24, 181 n.24, 186 n.13
Manimekalai 93, 190 n.19
mansion 61, 158–9, 161
map 46, 60, 85, 88–95, 111
Maranakapporul 43, 52–5, 183 n.27
Maravarman Kulacekara I 47
Markali 23, 99–100, 144
Markandeya 81, 121, 150
matam 16
Matavi 129, 131
Mecca 43
Melakadambur 76, 78
mental journey 60, 63–4, 75
mental picture 60
messenger 46, 100, 130–1, 139, 186 n.28
meter 41–2, 89, 119, 185 n.12
meykkirtti 119, 122
monastery 14, 16
Monius, A. 109, 180 n.11, 187 nn.45–6
monkey 31–2, 126
Moovalur 18, 82, 100
Morgan, D. 50, 183 nn.33–4
Mount Kailash. *See* Kailash
Mount Kolli. *See* Kolli Hills
Mount Meru 118, 121
Mowry, M. L. 181 n.24
Muhammad, Prophet 43
mural 13, 17 (Figure 3), 18
Murukan 52, 73, 80–1, 122, 131, 165
muvar
hymns 110, 186 n.16, 187 n.39
inscriptions 185 n.7
worship of Shiva 121, 188 n.24

Naccinarkkiniyar 182 n.7
Nakkiranar 181 n.6
Nalayirativyaprabantam 187 n.44
nalvar 18, 89 (Figure 12)
Nammalvar 54, 87, 101, 106, 183 n.43, 185 n.5
Nampiyakapporul 33
Nampiyantar Nampi 109, 185 n.8, 187 n.44
Nandi 70, 120
Narayana Ayyar, C. V. 180 n.14
Narkaviraca Nampi 33, 47–9, 52, 183 n.31
Narkirar 144
Narrinai
  anthology 33
  cities named 75, 184 n.8
  flower in a box 190 n.19
  heroine's behavior 80, 185 n.27, 190 n.24
  honeycombs 149
  palm horse ordeal 188 n.37
Nataraja 9 (Figure 2), 21, 92, 120, 143–5. *See also* Dancing Shiva; Kuttan
Nathamuni 187 n.44
Navalar, V. 183 n.25
Navaratnam, R. 181 n.24
nayanmar 15, 18, 109, 187 n.39
Netumaran 117–20
Nikayasangrahaya 181 n.21
Niklas, U. 182 n.22, 183 n.23
Nilakanta 69, 121, 126–7, 154–5
Nilakanta Sastri, K. A. 10, 180 n.15, 183 n.30
North Star. *See* Aruntati
Novetzke, C. 180 n.11

Orr, L. 91, 111, 186 nn.18–19, 186 n.26
Oxford 10, 12–14

Packert, C. 142–3, 189 nn.2–4
Pakal, Pakan 61–2, 121, 152, 170–1
Palani Mountain 81
Pallava 91
palm horse ordeal 39, 69, 85, 136–8, 173, 188 n.37
palm leaf 10–15, 18, 20–1, 24, 42, 176
Panaiya urai 24
Pandya dynasty
  flag 53
  kings 8–10, 47, 82, 94, 117, 121, 188 n.10
  Manikkavacakar 13, 16–17
  territory 54, 61, 63, 91–2, 119, 184 n.7
Panniru pattiyal 41, 119
Pantikkovai 28, 33, 114–15, 117–19, 182 n.9
parakeet 31, 102, 155–6
Parancoti 180 n.14
Paripatal 87
parrot 8, 89, 102–3, 151, 170–1, 190 n.24
Patanjali 13, 121
pattutaittalaivan 8, 114
peacock 31, 46, 137, 158–9
peahen 36, 137–8, 163
pearl
  gem 74, 141, 152, 158–9, 169
  tears 74, 127, 154–5, 176
  teeth 124, 138, 153
Pechilis, K. 185 n.2
Peraciriyar 24
Periyapuranam 18, 87–8, 91, 109–10, 187 n.44
Peterson, I.
  bhakti hymns 180 n.11, 187 n.44
  Tevaram 180 n.12, 185 n.3, 185 n.11, 186 n.16, 186 n.20
pilgrimage 7, 14–15, 85, 88, 91, 111
pillaittamil 108, 187 n.41
Pillaiyar. *See* Ganesh
Piranmalai 22 (Figure 5), 72, 85, 92, 146–7, 148 (Figure 18)
Pirapanta tipam 41–2
Plate, S. B. 4–5, 35, 180 n.3, 180 n.7, 181 n.1
Pollock, S. 113–14, 187 n.4, 188 n.6
Pondicherry 10, 12–14, 42, 154 (Figure 19)
Pope 11–12, 180 n.17, 181 n.18, 185 n.13, 187 n.39
Potiyil hills
  comparison 161, 173
  significance 92–5, 147
  in verse 124, 136, 186 n.22
Poyyamolippulavar 47–8
Prentiss, K. 25, 180 n.4
Prohl, I. 5, 169, 180 n.8
proximity
  between lovers 170–1

to deity 14, 46, 173, 175
as religion 4, 6
public women
in *Cilappatikaram* 129
competition 127, 129, 132–3, 135
finding favor 83
messenger 131
separation theme 34, 38, 40, 86
Pukar 53–4
Purananuru
animal behavior 102
battlefield 115
cities named 63, 75, 184 n.8
praise of heroine 104
praise of king 93

rain 48, 80, 137, 149, 153
Rajam, V. S. 182 n.21, 183 n.37
Rajarajakecari 145
Ramachandran, T. N. 89, 186 n.14, 190 n.19
Ramanujan, A. K.
bhakti poetry 25, 106, 187 nn.35–6
classicism to bhakti 106
five landscapes 32, 181 n.3, 181 n.5
Ravana 186 n.20
reception history 10, 36, 109, 173
rejection
between lovers 59, 68–9, 85, 139
of devotees 70, 165–6
of gifts 38, 64–5
religious sensations 3, 50, 74, 173
religious sense 120, 142, 186 n.24
renovation 144
Richman, P. 187 n.41
Ryan, J. 187 n.44

sandal
in nature 68, 85–6, 158
paste on body 1, 13, 20, 22, 130, 146
Schomerus, H. 181 n.24
Selby, M. A.
aestheticized representation 113–14, 187 nn.2–3
Ainkurunuru 181 n.4, 184 n.7, 184 n.16, 186 n.32
animal behavior 103, 186 n.33
sensory corpus 7, 167, 169, 172
sensory experience
in color 130
in gifts 145
in landscape 94, 111, 161
in literary world 25, 59
Prohl 5
in religion 169
Shaiva Siddhanta 24, 38, 89, 181 n.24, 183 n.28, 186 n.13
Shakti 24
Shamcuttacin kovai 43
shimmers 5–6, 170
Shulman, D. 181 n.19, 185 n.9, 186 n.20
sighting
combined with surroundings 167
defined 37, 43, 47, 52, 183 n.31
example 48, 53, 69
verse analysis 1, 44
Sirkali
location 54, 162
relation to Campantar 90, 108
temple statues 18
in *Tevaram* 97–8
verse analysis 84
Sivapuram 76–7
snake
body of heroine 108, 155–6, 169
inhabiting landscapes 85
Naga 46
Patanjali 13
rivalry with moon 134–5
worn by Shiva 73, 120, 123, 160, 166–7
social media 16
Spencer, G. 185 n.11
Sri Lanka 17, 23
Srivanchiyam 18, 78–9
stag 38, 170–1
Stewart, K. 5, 180 n.9
stotra 62
Subbiah, G. 180 n.10
Subrahmanya Sastri, P. S. 182 n.18

Takahashi, T.
general 183 nn.29–30
love themes 183 n.24
order of love themes 182 n.8, 182 nn.11–13
survey of grammars 33, 182 n.7
Tamil lexicon 49, 129
Tancaivanankovai 33, 47–8, 51

Tevaram
background 7, 185 nn.7–8, 185 n.10
cities named 87–93, 111, 184 n.12, 186 nn.16–17, 188 n.27
saints 18, 84, 109, 188 n.24
Shiva 105, 109–10, 186 n.20
verse analysis 95–7, 186 n.23
Thiruvadavur 21, 175 (Figure 20), 181 n.19
Thiruvannamalai 45 (Figure 7)
Thiruvenkadu 21, 78, 81, 90, 144, 159
Tieken, H. 180 n.14
Tiru Makkakkovai. See Makkakkovai
Tiruchuli 18, 83–4
Tiruccirrampalakkovai 8, 12, 56
Tirukkalukkunra puranam 68
Tirukkalukkunrak kovai 69
Tirukkalukkunram
iconography 184 n.14
images 89 (Figure 12), 98 (Figure 13)
inscription 144
Manikkavacakar visits 17
mountaintop 92, 147
temple bronze 22
in *Tiruvacakam* 89, 186 n.15
verse analysis 68–9
Tirukkovaiyar unmai vilakkam 24
Tirukkovaiyar unmai 24
Tirukkural 52
Tirukkurukaipperumal kavirayar 52–3
Tirumal 46, 184 n.18. *See also* Vishnu
Tirumurai 12, 21, 22 (Figure 5), 88
Tirumuraikanta puranam 185 n.8
Tirumurukarruppatai 87
Tiruperunthurai 10, 13–16, 17 (Figure 3), 18, 19 (Figure 4), 20, 23, 65–6, 67 (Figure 9), 89, 184 n.12
Tiruppalanam 61–2, 90
Tiruppanaiyur 71–2
Tirupparankundram
significance 66, 81, 92
temple 20, 141, 144, 146
verse analysis 65, 73, 79, 102
Tiruppatikkovai 52–4, 183 n.40
Tiruppavai 180 n.14, 186 n.26
Tirupputtur 145
Tiruppuvanam 82, 104
Tiruttontar tiruvantati 109
Tiruttontattokai 109, 180 n.14, 187 n.44
Tiruvacakam
background 23, 89, 99, 110, 180 n.14, 185 n.13
cities named 80–1, 90, 184 n.12, 185 n.26
golden hall 92
literary motifs 48, 94
theology, mysticism 24, 109
Tiruvempavai excerpted 99–100, 105
Tiruvarur 109
Tiruvarurkovai 42
Tiruvatavur. *See* Thiruvadavur
Tiruvatavurar puranam 16, 180 n.14
Tiruvatavurar 181 n.19
Tiruvavatuturaikkovai 48–9
Tiruvaymoli 106
Tiruvempavai
auditory cues 105
compared to *Tiruppavai* 186 n.26
general 109–10
inscription 186 n.26
performed 23, 99, 144, 181 n.22
translated verses 99, 105, 107, 109, 186 n.27
watery details 107
Tiruvidaimarudur 2 (Figure 1), 78–9, 90, 144–5
Tiruvilaiyatal puranam 16, 180 n.14, 181 n.20
Tiruviruttam 101, 106, 186 n.30, 187 n.38
Tiyakar 49
Tolkappiyam
background 30, 33
commentary 182 n.8, 182 n.18
composition 181 n.7
time cycles 36, 182 n.15
verses cited 182 nn.16–17
Tolkappiyar 33, 182 n.7
toys 134, 190 n.23
trajectories 6–7, 28, 43, 57, 61, 176
transformation
bodies 3, 133, 152, 171
color 176, 190 n.21
heroine 172
literary motif 106, 167
nature 77, 146, 152, 170
ornamentation 143
places 46, 59, 76–8, 86, 161, 173

Trawick, M. 182 n.14
tree
 canpakam 69
 environmental element 35, 56, 75
 jaumoon-plum 100
 kaitai 155
 Karpakam 48, 176
 on landscape 1, 68, 102
 Manikkavacakar seated under 13
 nakam 32
 pinti 65
 plaintain 65
 punnai 75, 152
 sandal 146
Tribhuvanachakravatti Rajaraja 145
trysting
 by day 72, 93
 love theme 34, 40, 86, 121
 at night 31–5, 71–2, 84
Twitter 16

Uma
 beauty 96, 125, 157
 consort 77, 97, 110, 120, 162
 half of Shiva 8, 65–6, 72, 122, 163, 167
 from Himalayas 52, 98
 image 51 (Figure 8)
 in landscape 68, 172
 power 156, 164–5
Umapati Civacariyar 185 n.8, 187 n.42, 187 n.44
untiyal 21, 141, 142 (Figure 17), 144
Uttantan kovai 43
Uttarakocamankai 17, 90

Vaigai River 17, 51–2, 173
Varaguna 8–10, 82, 94
Vedachalam, S. 180 n.14
Vedas 21, 54, 93, 138
Venkatesan, A. 184 n.22, 185 nn.4–5, 186 nn.29–30, 187 n.38
Venkatesan and Branfoot 185 n.4
Virattan 95–6
Vishnu
 in boar form 69
 extended meditation 60
 praised in poetry 87, 106–7
 relation to Shiva 122, 138, 162–3, 167
 supreme deity 46, 52–4
 in triad 72, 99–100, 110, 120, 188 n.24
Viyakirapata 13

Waliullah Sheikh Abdullah Shaheb 147
wedding 52, 83, 119, 124
Wenta, A. 181 n.22
Western Ghats 92
Wilden, E.
 Kuruntokai 189 n.17, 190 n.18, 190 n.20
 Narrinai 184 n.20, 185 nn.27–8, 189 n.16

Yama 46, 73, 110, 121, 184 n.24, 186 n.20. *See also* Kalan
Yocum, G. 180 n.14
Younger, P. 23, 181 nn.22–3
YouTube 16

Zvelebil, K.
 classical love poetry 182 n.7, 182 n.12, 183 n.30, 183 n.38
 dating literature 180 n.14, 182 n.9, 188 n.10
 meter 182 n.22
 palm horse ordeal 188 n.37
 Tevaram 185 n.7, 185 n.10

www.ingramcontent.com/pod-product-compliance
Lightning Source LLC
Chambersburg PA
CBHW052039300426
44117CB00012B/1897
9781350283183